UNITED BY FAITH

UNITED BY FAITH

THE MULTIRACIAL CONGREGATION
AS AN ANSWER TO THE PROBLEM OF RACE

CURTISS PAUL DeYOUNG
MICHAEL O. EMERSON
GEORGE YANCEY
KAREN CHAI KIM

OXFORD
UNIVERSITY PRESS
2003

OXFORD
UNIVERSITY PRESS

Oxford   New York
Auckland   Bangkok   Buenos Aires   Cape Town   Chennai
Dar es Salaam   Delhi   Hong Kong   Istanbul   Karachi   Kolkata
Kuala Lumpur   Madrid   Melbourne   Mexico City   Mumbai   Nairobi
São Paulo   Shanghai   Taipei   Tokyo   Toronto

Copyright © 2003 by Oxford University Press, Inc.

Published by Oxford University Press, Inc.
198 Madison Avenue, New York, New York 10016

www.oup.com

The Scripture quotations contained herein are from the New Revised
Standard Version of the Bible, copyright © 1989 by the Division of Christian
Education of the National Council of the Churches of Christ in the United
States of America. Used by permission. All rights reserved.

Scripture quotations indicated NIV are from HOLY BIBLE, NEW
INTERNATIONAL VERSION®. Copyright © 1973, 1978, 1984 by
International Bible Society. Used by permission of Zondervan Bible
Publishers. All rights reserved. The "NIV" and "New International Version"
trademarks are registered in the United States Patent and Trademark Office
by International Bible Society. Use of either trademark requires the
permission of the International Bible Society.

Scripture quotations indicated KJV are from
The Holy Bible, King James Version.

Library of Congress Cataloging-in-Publication Data
United by faith : the multiracial congregation as an answer
to the problem of race / Curtiss Paul DeYoung ... [et al.].
p. cm.
Includes bibliographical references and index.
ISBN 0-19-515215-8
Race relations—Religious aspects—Christianity.
I. DeYoung, Curtiss Paul.
BT734.2 U55   2003   261.8'348—dc21
2002013709

1 3 5 7 9 8 6 4 2
Printed in the United States of America
on acid-free paper

To the pioneers of multiracial congregations—past and present

CONTENTS

PREFACE

This book is the collaborative effort of four authors who have set aside their need for individual credit and attempted to synthesize their words and thoughts into the sound of one voice. We believe that our endeavor to blend our personal styles and preferences into the singular written expression found in this book is a small example of what needs to occur in congregations all across the United States, and the world for that matter.

The designations used for identifying groups of people by culture and race are fluid. This book employs terms that reflect accepted usage at the time of writing. Of course, each classification includes a broad range of cultural expressions. For example, "Asian American" includes people from places like Korea, India, and Cambodia. The terms "Latino" and "Hispanic" are used interchangeably in the book, since both are currently in use and neither has emerged as a singularly representative term. The same is true for the designations "African American" and "black." We use gender inclusive language. The word "Latino," which in Spanish is masculine, is considered an inclusive term. Perhaps, in the future, this will change, as in the case of English words once considered to be inclusive such as "mankind" (now humankind). We also rarely use the word "America" for the United

States and "American" to identify a citizen of the United States. America includes people from North, South, and Central America. In the case of "African American," "Asian American," and "Native American" we make an exception because these terms are used by members of these groups. However, we do not employ "Hispanic American" to denote a citizen of the United States who speaks Spanish. Most "Hispanics" were citizens of the Americas before arriving in the United States. Therefore to call them Hispanic or Latino Americans is redundant. We also do not use the word "slave" to identify a person. Identifiers carry power, and no person's identity should be that of a slave. So we use the term "enslaved African" to note individuals from the continent of Africa who were kidnapped and sold into slavery. The primary exceptions to all the above are found when quoting sources—we do not change the words of others.

ACKNOWLEDGMENTS

As we begin this endeavor at acknowledging the many people who made this book possible we must first thank Cynthia Read and the staff at Oxford University Press for their enthusiasm in embracing this project. It is an honor to have our work associated with this long tradition of excellence.

We would like to express our appreciation to the many pastors and church members who opened their homes and lives to us to make the Multiracial Congregations Project possible. This project could not have been possible without the enthusiastic support of Chris Coble and the Lilly Endowment. They provided the funding, direction, and encouragement to conduct the research and to write this book. Rice University was a perfect home for this project, and we extend our gratitude to the university, Bob Stein, and the members of the sociology department for their support. We extend our appreciation to our project advisers Nancy Ammerman, Wade Clark Roof, Johan David Sikkink, and Christian Smith. We would also like to thank R. Stephen Warner for his help in bringing together our project team.

There are many individuals whose efforts contributed in significant ways to the completion of this project. We would like to offer a word of thanks to the students who did phone calling, addressing, mailing, and data entry: Sharon Bzostek, Mayra Cuello, Bob Groux, Uri McMillan, Mike Nepali, Bill Prescott, Sarai Sanchez, and Rachel Tolbert. We also express our gratitude to Sally Faubel, who was invaluable to our project as we embarked on our fieldwork. Although the coinvestigators conducted the bulk of the personal interviews, we were greatly aided by some excellent interviewers and research assistants: Esther Chang, Bob Groux, Pedro Moyo, Judy Rodriguez, and Sarai Sanchez. A special thank you for the excellent work and important contributions made by Rachel Tolbert and Mayra Cuello, who served as the head research assistants. They helped the project succeed. Thank you to Patsy Garcia, whose administrative skill and efficiency kept the project going, and whose patience helped us negotiate the red tape of modern bureaucracy. Thanks to Cindy Farrar, who designed our project logo, and Todd Welbes and Michael Leggett, who designed the congregations.info Web site. We are grateful to Michelle Friesen, Tracy Xu, and Sarah Mueller, who typed portions of the manuscript.

We would like to especially note our appreciation to the persons who read and commented on the book manuscript: Thomas Baima, Jim Bundy, John Canary, Karen DeYoung, James Earl Massey, Aldean Miles, and Rodney Woo. Their encouragement and critique strengthened this book.

A special thank you to Scottye Holloway, Marc Erickson, Rodney Woo, and James Earl Massey, who spent years patiently acquiring, teaching, and imparting their knowledge of and passion for multiracial congregations. They are role models and inspirations for many.

Other people who were a special encouragement to us in the process of writing this book and whom we must mention are Chris Coble, Terry Coffee, Tyrone Cushman, Anita Edwards, Cain Hope Felder, Paul Freitag, Darrell Geddes, Mark Horst, William Huff, Robert Hulteen, Claudia May, Chris McNair, Brad McNaught, Sean Moodley, Robert Odom, Mercy Olson Ward, Cheryl Sanders, Kou Seying, Alroy Trout, and Cecilia Williams.

We express our gratitude for the support of the organizations for which we worked during the writing of this book: Bethel College, City Gate Project, Rice University, Twin Cities Urban Reconciliation Network (TURN), University of Houston, and the University of North Texas.

And our biggest thank-you goes to our families: Karen, Rachel, and Jonathan DeYoung; Gioni, Antonio, Giosia, Lia, and Sofia Emerson; Sherelyn Yancey, Rose Taylor, and Ann Ashley; and Matthew Jino Kim, Stanley Kim, Soo Hyuk Chai, and Chae Hyun Chai.

Finally we give all praise and honor to God. This book ultimately is a testament to our faith in Jesus Christ who came to reconcile us to God and to build a house of prayer for all the nations.

UNITED BY FAITH

INTRODUCTION

DIVIDED *or* UNITED BY FAITH?

The nation's racial landscape is vividly changing. In 1960, less than 15 percent of the population of the United States was not of European origin, with the vast majority of that percentage being African American. According to the 2000 Census, people of color as a percentage of the United States population have *more than doubled* to 31 percent since 1960, and the growth of non-Europeans is expected to continue at an accelerated rate. In just the last twenty years (1980 to 2000), while the non-Hispanic white population grew about 8 percent, the growth rate of other groups is far larger. During the same period (1980 to 2000), the African American population grew by nearly 30 percent, the Native American population by 75 percent, the Latino population by 142 percent, and Asian American population by 185 percent. In absolute numbers, the United States has well over 35 million *more* people of color in 2000 than it did in 1980.[1] This is more people than lived in the entire United States during the Civil War period of the early 1860s.[2]

Race, as it always has, plays a significant part in the lives of people living in the United States. It shapes where people live and whom they live with, where people send their children to school, with whom they can most easily become friends, their likelihood of having access to wealth and health, whom they marry, how they think about themselves, and their cultural tastes. Race also shapes how people value others, how much they trust others, provides quick stereotypes by which to classify people, and shapes fears of crime.[3] As Cornel West succinctly puts it, "Race Matters."[4]

For many of these reasons, race matters in where one worships. The nation's religious congregations have long been highly racially segregated. If we define a racially mixed congregation as one in which no one racial group is 80 percent or more of the congregation, just 7.5 percent of the over 300,000 religious congregations in the United States are racially mixed. For Christian congregations, which form over 90 percent of congregations in the United States, the percentage that are racially mixed drops to five and a half.[5] Of this small percentage, approximately half of the congregations are mixed only temporarily, during the time they are in transition from one group to another.

The explosion of racial and ethnic diversity in the United States has introduced dramatic tensions within faith communities. How should they respond to a pluralistic society? What should congregations look like racially? Does considering the racial composition of congregations sidetrack faith communities from more important religious matters? Given the current and historical racial context of the United States, are certain racial and ethnic communities best served by having their own congregations?

This book sets out to make a bold, clear, controversial argument: *Christian congregations, when possible, should be multiracial.* It may be stunning or even offensive to some that we state our argument so imperatively. But before deciding whether we go too far, we hope the reader will carefully examine the evidence and follow the reasoning presented in our chapters. This work is not polemic. We take our task seriously and spend a significant amount of time considering alternative viewpoints. In fact, we devote two entire chapters to assessing the arguments that call for *uniracial* or *uniethnic* congregations, writing from viewpoints found within each major racial group in the United States. In the end, we nevertheless conclude that congregations, when possible, should be multiracial. Given how far we are from this reality, this book issues a call for the emergence of a movement toward more multiracial congregations. The twenty-first century must be *the century of multiracial congregations.*

This conclusion rests in part on the premise that multiracial congregations can play an important role in reducing racial division and inequality and that this should be a goal of Christian people. On its release in 2000, *Divided by Faith: Evangelical Religion and the Problem of Race in America,* written by our co-author Michael Emerson (and Christian Smith), caused quite a splash in the Christian community. The book made the cover of the Billy Graham–founded magazine *Christianity Today* and was the topic of discussion in churches, in para-church organizations, and among religious leaders around the nation.

The book showed how theology, history, and the very structure of religious organizations combine in powerful ways to divide Christians in the United States along racial lines—in their perceptions and racial attitudes, concentrating them in separate congregations. *Divided by Faith* also outlined how separate congregations have a number of negative consequences for racial division and inequality. If this is so, might multiracial congregations have the opposite effect?

Even before *Divided by Faith* was published, Michael Emerson realized that it was not enough to document and announce the problem. In one of the closing chapters of the book, the authors pondered whether multiracial congregations might be a strategy for making progress on the racial reconciliation so needed in the United States. To find out, Emerson invited two other sociologists to join him in a research project funded by the Lilly Endowment and called "Multiracial Congregations and Their Peoples." George Yancey, an African American, and Karen Chai Kim, a Korean American, joined Michael Emerson, a white, to form a multiracial team of sociologists exploring multiracial congregations.

The team spent three years in intensive research, studying both multiracial and uniracial congregations. Relying on studies that focused on when a transitional number is achieved, the team defined a multiracial congregation as a congregation in which *no one racial group accounts for 80 percent or more of the membership*. They created an extensive questionnaire and conducted over 2,500 telephone interviews with people of all races and beliefs in the United States. They also created a written survey that was then mailed to and completed by approximately five hundred Christian congregations across the country. In the third phase of the research process, the team traveled to four diverse metropolitan areas to observe the congregations firsthand.

During the extended site visits, the team conducted face-to-face interviews with nearly two hundred congregants and clergy, studied the histories of these congregations, and participated in activities such as Masses, worship services, meetings, and fellowship events. Part of this book is drawn from the results of this research.[6]

As a team, we realized that the answer to whether congregations should be multiracial or not is, at its root, a claim about what ought to be, relative to some standard. To answer our question, we needed to locate it within a particular tradition, one that has the power to answer what ought to be. The fundamental creed of the United States of America—that individuals are endowed with rights and freedoms and that there should be liberty and justice for all—does not have such power. At least in its current interpretation, it simply declares that within limits, people should be free to do as they wish and not restrict other people from doing the same. *Divided by Faith* showed the ways and reasons that this creed has led to numerous religious affiliations in the United States, resulting in about 90 percent of worshipers attending racially homogeneous congregations.

When religious people make choices based on their individual rights, they largely end up in homogeneous congregations. Answering the question about whether we ought to end up in uniracial congregations requires that we draw on a more powerful tradition. Given that overwhelmingly the largest percentage of religious people in the United States is Christian—nearly 90 percent at the time of this writing—it makes the most sense to draw directly on that tradition.

To do so, and to write this book, we needed a lead author trained in the Christian tradition and the issues of race. Ideally, the person also would have experience in uniracial and multiracial congregations. We found just such a person in the lead author, Curtiss Paul DeYoung, a "reconciliation theologian," trained at Howard University School of Divinity and author of the books *Coming Together: The Bible's Message in an Age of Diversity, Reconciliation: Our Greatest Challenge—Our Only Hope,* and *Beyond Rhetoric: Reconciliation as a Way of Life.* He also served as a senior pastor for a multiracial congregation and earlier had been on the pastoral staffs in both white and African American uniracial congregations.

Together the four of us set out to answer our question: Should Christian congregations be uniracial or multiracial (or does it even matter)? The result of this search led to our argument—that Christian congregations, when possible, should be multiracial. In arriving at this conclusion, we view the fact that there are four of us as a strength. We come from a variety of racial, economic, and religious backgrounds; grew up in different parts of the country; and come from very different families that have resided in the United States for different amounts of time. For example, some of us do not know exactly how many generations our families have been in the United States, whereas one team member remembers immigrating to the United States as a young child. Not only did we start out with varied backgrounds and experiences, but we also began with varying degrees of agreement with respect to the book's main argument. This diversity led us to sharpen our support for the final argument, and it forced us to seriously consider and address the arguments in favor of uniracial and uniethnic congregations. After carefully considering counterarguments, we arrived at three legitimate exceptions to our main argument, which we discuss in chapter eight.

This book is organized into four main sections. We begin by examining the original model for "doing church," exploring what the New Testament teaches. We then focus on churches in the United States, beginning in the early 1600s, comparing them to the New Testament standard. Though there is hope, much of what is presented in this section is shocking when held to the light of the New Testament model. In our third section, we carefully consider rationales for racially homogeneous churches, and in chapter eight we respond to these arguments. The final section presents a theology for multiracial congregations and, based on our three years of sociological research, offers practical advice on the promise and challenges of multiracial congregations.

This book, of course, is not the final word on the question of race and Christian congregations. We do hope, however, that it will serve as a benchmark for what will no doubt be a growing discussion and debate about the nature of congregations in the twenty-first century. Every piece of demographic evidence and every demographic projection suggest that the United States is more racially diverse than it has ever been but not as racially diverse as it will be in the coming years. We need to move beyond simply stating that Christian worship is the most segregated hour in the United States. What does the Christian tradition teach that we ought to do? This book is one attempt to answer this question.

I

BIBLICAL ANTECEDENTS FOR MULTIRACIAL CONGREGATIONS

1 | A HOUSE OF PRAYER FOR ALL THE NATIONS

The apartheid government of South Africa established three segregated communities on the south side of Johannesburg under the Group Areas Act: Soweto, Lenasia, and Eldoradopark. The white Afrikaner government reserved Soweto for blacks, Lenasia for Indians (from the country of India), and Eldoradopark for Coloureds (people of mixed race descent). Although the era of legalized separation ended in South Africa, the effects linger, as these three neighboring communities remain largely segregated. The Christian Revival Centre ministers in the city of Lenasia. Changes began to occur in this congregation when the members constructed a new church building in 2000. The Christian Revival Centre located their building at the edge of Lenasia and next to an informal settlement (a very poor shantytown). As they began their ministry in this new location, members of the congregation came to believe that God had called them to minister not only in the Indian community but also to the residents of this informal settlement who were black South Africans facing economic impoverishment.

To pursue this outreach the Christian Revival Centre invited a black South African evangelist to preach for two weeks of nightly services at the church. The congregation's Indian pastor privately hoped that this evangelist would decide to co-pastor the church with him. At the end of the two weeks, many blacks from the informal settlement began attending this church previously composed of Indians. During the last service the evangelist looked at the new attendees from the black community, pointed to the Indian pastor, and announced, "Here is your pastor." Then he looked at the pastor, pointed at the blacks in attendance, and said, "Here are your new members." After overcoming his initial shock and surprise, the pastor began to faithfully serve people in the informal settlement through visitation and pastoral care.

Immediately the leadership of the congregation discussed the issue of Sunday morning worship services. They decided to have two services. One service would continue in the traditional format of the congregation. A second service would seek to include members from the informal settlement in its design and leadership. This service would have more of a black South African flavor—in this case, a Zulu feel. Yet the pastor wondered if they took the easy way out.

A month or so later, one of the authors of this book—Curtiss Paul DeYoung—preached at the Christian Revival Centre during a Tuesday evening service that included both Indian and black members of the congregation. His sermon proclaimed that the story found in the Acts of the Apostles described how the first-century church moved from an ethnocentric congregation in Jerusalem to a multiethnic congregation in Antioch (Acts 2–13). The pastor phoned DeYoung after the service to inform him that all the members of the congregation's leadership council had attended the service. They went to their pastor after the service and said that the congregation must not take the easy road. They must have one service for everyone—and this meant incorporating Zulu musical styles into worship. While this might require great sacrifices for the Indian Christians in the congregation, God called the Christian Revival Centre to the ministry of reconciliation.

In the course of a few months they moved from being a congregation for Indians to a church that sought to embrace everyone in their community. The church leadership at the Christian Revival Centre in Lenasia decided that the power of God's call to unity far surpassed the challenge posed by generations of apartheid separation.[1] This story from a congregation located many miles and time zones from the United States invites us to revisit the Scriptures. The

Christian Revival Centre in Lenasia believed that the Bible instructed them to build a congregation that embraced all races. As we begin our focus on multiracial congregations in the United States, we start at what is, for Christians, the foundation: the message of Jesus and the life of the first-century church.

The first-century world as described in the New Testament did not experience racism in the same way it is understood today in the United States. People in that time did not have a history of European colonial expansion to the Americas that nearly decimated the indigenous population. Nor did they transport and enslave millions of people from the continent of Africa. The first-century church did not emerge in a world where political leaders, anthropologists, capitalists, theologians, and others participated in a process of creating a racial hierarchy that placed people with white skin and European ancestry in the superior position and relegated the inferior position to persons of color—indigenous people native to the Americas, persons of African descent who arrived as slaves, *mestizos* colonized in Mexico, and immigrants or refugees from Latin America, Asia, Africa, and the islands of the Pacific and Atlantic Oceans.

The world in which Jesus and members of the church lived did have distinctions that brought division and hierarchies that produced discrimination rooted in personal and societal understandings of ethnicity and culture. These differentiations often contained the same emotional and structural power to divide as race does today. This was particularly true of the divide between Jews and Gentiles (people from other nations). Biblical scholar Joachim Jeremias notes that the attitude of many Jews toward Gentiles in Jesus' time "was largely determined by the oppression which they had undergone at the hands of foreign nations, and by their fear of the increasing prevalence of mixed marriages."[2] To gain some fresh insights for our day, we will look closely at how the Bible presents Jesus and the first-century church navigating the separatist tendencies in their society.

It is not enough to understand how Jesus and the early church addressed preexisting bigotry in their day. What did Jesus envision as he developed a community of followers and how did his vision impact the makeup of the various congregations mentioned in the Bible? Was there an overarching vision of transformation and an intense experience of reconciliation that led to the birth of a new worldview regarding community? The Bible is a collection of documents that instruct Christians in how to live out their faith as individuals and in community. We believe that the Bible offers a rich multitude of antecedents for multiracial congregations in the twenty-first century. Therefore, in the first two chapters of *United by Faith* we lay a foundation for our thesis: when possible, congregations should strive to be multiracial. In chapter one we focus on the ministry and message of Jesus of Nazareth as a precursor to multiracial congregations. Chapter two examines the composition of the congregations of the first-century church. Their diversity of expression is noted as well as their commitment to implement the mandate of Jesus.

We begin by examining the social location of Jesus of Nazareth and his radical message and ministry. We seek to answer the question: Are what we call multiracial congregations today a hoped-for outcome of Jesus' life work? Our knowledge about Jesus comes primarily from the four New Testament Gospel writers. They wrote with the purpose of inviting people to embrace the faith understandings introduced by Jesus and taught by the early Christians. Therefore, the Gospel writers sifted through the oral accounts of Jesus' ministry and teachings to weave together Gospels that reflected the needs and interests of their particular audience.

The composition of the Gospels took place in the last half of the first century, decades after the crucifixion of Jesus. The early church experienced the deaths of key first-generation leaders in the church such as the apostles Peter, Paul, and James before the Gospels were complete. Given the time period in which they were written, the Gospels offer us a glimpse into the first-century church and how the meaning of Jesus' life and teaching guided its members' life together. The authors of Mark, Luke, Matthew, and John wrote to audiences from different social settings. So the common themes speak to the center of Jesus' message and the similarities of these divergent congregations. We offer an overview of the biblical material related to Jesus drawn from all four Gospels as it speaks to our focus on multiracial congregations.

The Inclusive Message of Jesus' Birth and Death Narratives

Two of the Gospel writers began their narrative of Jesus' life with stories of his birth. In the Gospel of Luke, Jesus' mother, Mary, was pregnant without the formality of marriage—an unwed mother. She gave birth to Jesus in the unacceptable and unappealing surroundings of a smelly, dirty livestock barn. Mary placed the baby Jesus in an unsanitary animal feeding trough that served as his crib. Poor shepherds, whose line of work was despised by many in society, served as the primary witnesses to this historic event.[3] The Gospel of Luke paints a picture of a Jesus who, even at his birth, experienced outsider status and whose presence attracted those who felt excluded.

The author of Luke also positioned the birth of Jesus in the context of the broader world. He noted that it took place while Caesar Augustus sat on the throne of the Roman Empire and Quirinius governed Syria. This signaled the readers of Luke that the arrival of Jesus also impacted a world beyond Israel. This point was confirmed shortly after Jesus' birth when his family brought him to Jerusalem to offer a sacrifice on his behalf. A devout man named Simeon took Jesus in his arms and declared, "My eyes have seen your salvation, which you have prepared in the presence of all peoples, a light for revelation to the Gentiles and for glory to your people Israel" (Luke 2:30–32). While the Gospel writer's second volume, Acts, recorded the culmination of this prophesy of the inclusion of Gentiles alongside Jews, it was first announced at the beginning of the Gospel of Luke—"a light for revelation to the Gentiles" and "for glory to your people Israel."

The Gospel writer who composed Matthew also began his book by foreshadowing the inclusive nature of the message of Jesus and the early church. He narrated the story of rich Magi from Asia coming to Bethlehem to pay respects and offer gifts to the infant Jesus—an allusion to the Gentile inclusion in God's salvation story. Biblical scholar Raymond Brown remarks, "The drama of Jew and Gentile believer is placed on the level of divine revelation in the Matthean infancy narrative."[4] Then Matthew's Gospel added the important episode when Jesus' family embarked on a journey through the night to the continent of Africa to secure refuge from the murderous threats of Rome's appointed governor Herod the Great. According to the Gospel of Matthew, Jesus lived in Egypt for a few years. As if to add further credence to this powerful image of unity in chapter two of Matthew, the author inserted a few comments for the readers. He noted, "This was to fulfill what had been spoken by the Lord through the prophet, 'Out of Egypt I have called my son'" (Matthew 2:15; see also Hosea 11:1).

Many African American preachers and others have used this passage to annul the message of white racists—"Out of Africa I have called my son."

At the end of the Gospels we observe once again the universality of the Jesus story as recorded by the writers. Both Jews and Gentiles embraced Jesus at his death. While Jesus was betrayed and denied by many members of his own ethnic group, several Jewish women were with him at the end, as was his disciple John, the son of Zebedee (John 19:25–27). An African named Simon of Cyrene carried his cross (Matthew 27: 32; Mark 15:21; Luke 23:26). The Roman governor Pilate ordered his execution, but a Roman centurion guarding Jesus at the cross stated, "Truly this man was God's Son!" (Mark 15:39; Matthew 27:54; see also Luke 23:47). Some Jewish religious leaders did plot Jesus' death, yet members of the Jewish ruling council named Joseph of Arimathea and Nicodemus made arrangements for his burial (Matthew 27: 57ff; Mark 15:43ff; Luke 23:50ff; John 19:38ff).

After reporting his resurrection, the Gospel writers recorded that Jesus declared, "repentance and forgiveness of sins is to be proclaimed in his name to all nations" (Luke 24:47). He commissioned his followers to "go therefore and make disciples of all nations" (Matthew 28:19; see Mark 16:15; Acts 1:8). The earthly life of Jesus of Nazareth began and ended with a worldview and mission that were inclusive. We suggest that the bookends of Jesus' life story display the message of the Gospels and provide a framework of inclusion for the congregations that were receiving and reading these first-century documents. We now examine what happens between those bookends.

Raised in "Galilee of the Gentiles"

Isaiah chapter nine states, "in the latter time he will make glorious the way of the sea, the land beyond the Jordan, Galilee of the nations" (9:1). This passage that spoke of messianic hopes became prophetic for those who believed in Jesus of Nazareth. For indeed Jesus the Jew was raised in Galilee of the nations (or the Gentiles).[5] The Gospel writers went to great lengths to inform their readers of the influence of Gentiles on the life of a Jewish Jesus. As we just noted, Matthew began his Gospel by having the child Jesus visited by Magi from Asia.

Then his family traveled out of Israel into Egypt to escape the threats from Herod. When detailing the beginning of Jesus' ministry, Matthew quoted Isaiah to introduce him as the one who was the fulfillment of prophecy, "Land of Zebulun, land of Naphtali, on the road by the sea, across the Jordan, Galilee of the Gentiles—the people who sat in darkness have seen a great light, and for those who sat in the region and shadow of death light has dawned" (Mt. 4:15–16).

The diverse mix of people in Galilee reflected the demographics of much of the Roman Empire. The Galilee in which Jesus grew up included Assyrians, Babylonians, Egyptians, Macedonians, Persians, Romans, Syrians, and indigenous Canaanites.[6] In the mind-set of first-century Jews, all these groups were Gentiles. Also, Greek cultural influences and Roman economic and administrative functions shaped Galilean society.[7] Jesus was raised in Galilee and influenced by this milieu. It is impossible to know how much contact Jesus had with the various ethnic groups in Galilee. He resided in rural Nazareth. As he worked with his father in construction he may have traveled to cities with active building projects such as Sepphoris or even Caesarea Philippi and Tiberias.[8] Here he would have certainly rubbed shoulders with Gentiles. The Gospel writers clearly wanted to highlight Jesus' Galilean roots. Historian Paul Barnett writes, "His home was not the sacred temple-city, Jerusalem, the world center for the rabbinic academies, but Nazareth in Galilee, a region surrounded by Greek states and permeated by Hellenism. It is appropriate that a message that was to be taken to the Gentile world should be centered on one who was nurtured and raised in Galilee of the Gentiles."[9]

A Radically Inclusive Fellowship

The Gospel writers wanted it to be known that Jesus was raised in an environment that maintained his own Jewish cultural and religious identity yet was enriched by the influence of various Gentile cultural elements. This prepared Jesus for a ministry that was radically inclusive. This is evident in his "congregation" of disciples. It began with his choice of twelve disciples that included both a tax collector and a zealot. Tax collectors were despised as collaborators with the Gentile enemy of Israel—the Roman Empire. Zealots were feared because of their militant views that called for the violent revolutionary overthrow of the Roman Empire. As biblical scholar Gerd Theissen notes, the fact that "both a tax-collector and a zealot, a resistance fighter, are included in the most intimate group of disciples . . . points to a readiness for reconciliation which transcends frontiers and culminates in the requirement to love one's enemy."[10] Jesus soon added a number of women just as diverse to his band of disciples including Mary called Magdalene, Joanna the wife of Herod's steward Chuza, Susanna, Salome, and Mary the mother of James and Joses (Luke 8:1–3; Mark 15:40–41).

Jesus' inclination toward building an inclusive fellowship was not limited to the entourage of disciples who traveled with him. He intentionally reached out broadly to all he encountered, inviting them to participate in the life of his "congregation" of followers. This is most apparent in what scholars have called his "table fellowship." Table fellowship symbolized those you found to be worthy of inclusion in your social circle. Whom you ate with made a statement about who were your friends. The Pharisees were considered a "table fellowship sect."[11] They used table fellowship to maintain the purity of their nation as well as to model what they believed should be the exclusive ethnocentric identity of Israel. Jesus disturbed and disrupted religious leaders of his time because he used table fellowship to model what he believed was the future of God's people (and who were included in that group). The author of the Gospel of Mark wrote, "And as he sat at dinner in Levi's house, many tax collectors and sinners were also sitting with Jesus and his disciples—for there were many who followed him. When the scribes of the Pharisees saw that he was eating with sinners and tax collectors, they said to his disciples, 'Why does he eat with tax collectors and sinners?'" (2:15–16).

Some religious leaders of Jesus' day defined their "congregation" by who was excluded from membership. There were long lists of those who could not meet the definition. Such lists included women, Samaritans, Gentiles, individuals with criminal records, anyone who was disabled or sick, tax collectors, and those considered "sinners." Also those with certain occupations were not counted as worthy: camel drivers, sailors, herdsmen, weavers, tailors, barbers, butchers, physicians, businesspeople, and many others.[12] The only people who qualified were healthy males of pure Hebrew ancestry who held respectable jobs and followed all the laws of the religion. This exclusive view also required that they avoid contact with those not considered worthy.

The attempt by some religious leaders to implement an exclusive approach to religious faith was challenged by the radically inclusive Jesus. Jesus broke all the rules that these religious leaders made to separate themselves from others. It clearly indicated his acceptance when Jesus publicly shared meals with tax collectors and those deemed sinners. For those who saw Jesus as a prophet or the Messiah, his invitation to dinner was equivalent to receiving an invitation to dine at God's table of inclusion.[13] Theologian Albert Nolan indicates the significance of such acts when he writes:

> It would be impossible to overestimate the impact these meals must have had upon the poor and the sinners. By accepting them as friends and equals Jesus had taken away their shame, humiliation and guilt. By showing them that they mattered to him as people he gave them a sense of dignity and released them from captivity. The physical contact which he must have had with them when reclining at the table and which he obviously never dreamed of disallowing must have made them feel clean and acceptable.[14]

The Gospels are filled with stories of Jesus touching those declared untouchable, speaking to those who were not to be spoken to, befriending those who were thought not to deserve a friend. The Gospel of Mark illustrates this well. Jesus said to a paralyzed man who had been lowered through the roof of a house, "I say to you, stand up, take your mat and go to your home" (2:11). Jesus walked up to Levi while he was sitting at his tax collector's booth and said, "Follow me" (2:14). Jesus saw Jairus' daughter lying dead in her bed, took her hand, and said, "Little girl, get up!" (5:41). A woman "suffering from hemorrhages for twelve years" touched Jesus (5:25). This woman was a person to be avoided and cast aside according to the purity laws of the religious leaders. She was a woman. She was sick and getting sicker. She was bleeding—emitting bodily fluids. When she touched the hem of Jesus' garment—therefore rendering Jesus no longer "pure" according to the rules of religion—Jesus embraced her as a daughter of God.

The author of the Gospel of Mark not only detailed the story of Jesus' ministry to those among his own ethnic group who were considered outcasts. He also recounted the stories of those times when Jesus stepped outside his own ethnic group and ministered in Gentile regions. Jesus reached out to a Gentile man who lived in the cemetery and called himself, "Legion" (5:1–20). Jesus cast the demon out of the daughter of a Greek woman from Syrian Phoenicia (7:24–30). Jesus put his fingers in the ears of a man living in the Gentile city of Decapolis and said, "Ephphatha"—which meant, "be opened" (7:34). At the culmination of what biblical scholar Brian Blount calls Mark's "virtual Jesus Gentile mission," Jesus fed four thousand Gentiles (8:1–9).[15] This story, which sounds like a repetition of a feeding of five thousand Jews two chapters prior (6:35–44), described a powerful demonstration of Jesus' vision of offering the same ministry to Gentiles that he offered to Jews. To make the point even more persuasive to his readers, the author of Mark used "the table language of the Last Supper" when he described how Jesus took seven loaves, gave thanks, broke them, and distributed the loaves to the people in an act that not only fed four thousand people but symbolized the inclusion of Gentiles at God's communion table.[16]

A House of Prayer for All the Nations

According to the Gospel writers, Jesus did not try to initiate a new religion as he invited Jews and neighboring Gentiles to join his radically inclusive "congregation" of followers. Jesus ultimately sought to transform the religion of his day. The context for Jesus' dramatic discourse and countercultural community building was a religion and a nation seeking renewal. After years of living under the oppressive rule of Rome, the people who lived there during the time of Jesus grasped for any sign of hope. Many of the religious leaders who were Jesus' harshest critics led a renewal movement, as we noted above, that proposed creating boundaries or rules that defined who could be included among the people of God. They believed that a separatist ethnocentric model would revive a religion and nation devastated by domination and occupation. As biblical scholar Marcus Borg writes, "Jesus did not simply accept the central role of table fellowship, but used it as a weapon. . . . It was a political act of national significance: to advocate and practice a different form of table fellowship was to protest against the present structures of Israel."[17]

In addition to his active table fellowship, Jesus preached his inclusive gospel in synagogues and in the temple in Jerusalem. He took his agenda for transformation into the very places where the renewal movement of some religious leaders attempted to gain a following for a separatist understanding of Israel's future identity. The author of Luke has Jesus begin his ministry by preaching in the synagogue in Nazareth (4:16–30). In this setting Jesus announced a ministry that included the poor and oppressed of Israel. Then Jesus used stories from the Hebrew Scriptures to imply that just as God had sent Israel's prophets Elijah and Elisha to minister to widows and lepers outside of Israel, his ministry would expand beyond the boundaries of Israel. This "implication" was enough to get him thrown out of the synagogue and nearly killed. Biblical scholar Howard Clark Kee states, "Jesus' initiative in reaching out to the outsiders corresponds with the nature and purpose of God, but it is resented and denounced by the traditionalists whose identity is based on the separatist features of Israelite law."[18]

The author of the Gospel of John also included a time when Jesus countered the influence of separatist religion. A woman from Samaria challenged Jesus to respond to the exclusiveness of the religion practiced by some. She said, "Our ancestors worshiped on this mountain, but you say that the place where people must worship is in Jerusalem" (4:20). Jesus responded, "Woman, believe me, the hour is coming when you will worship the Father neither on this mountain nor in Jerusalem. . . . But the hour is coming, and is now here, when the true worshipers will worship the Father in spirit and truth, for the Father seeks such as these to worship him" (4:21, 23). Jesus shared with this woman from Samaria his understanding that God's "congregation" included her, a Samaritan.

The dramatic confrontation that Jesus had with moneychangers in the temple was recorded by all the Gospel writers. The authors of Matthew, Mark, and Luke all included Jesus quoting from the prophet Isaiah (56:7) in their retelling. Only Mark included the entire quote. Jesus declared, "Is it not written, 'My house shall be called a house of prayer for all the nations?'" (Mark 11:17). The author of Mark understood that the last four words of that quote from Isaiah— *for all the nations*—summed up what caused the religious leaders to fear Jesus and look for a way to kill him (11:18).[19]

Jesus quoted the prophet Isaiah from the Hebrew Scriptures to announce and declare the purpose and the passion of his ministry. He stood in the temple area and proclaimed to all who could hear him what he understood to be the culmination of three years of preaching, teaching, healing, and ministering along the highways and byways of greater Palestine, "My house shall be called a house of prayer for all the nations." Brian Blount captures the writer of Mark's understanding of Jesus' message when he writes:

> In the Gospel of Mark, Jesus is a preacher of multicultural worship. He envisioned a future that was radically different from the one espoused by the Temple leadership of his present Jerusalem. The Temple presided over a world where non-Jewish ethnicities were condemned by the theological motifs of holiness and purity, and demonized by the myopic fever of messianic nationalism. Mark's Jesus offered a counter kingdom proposal: he foresaw a time when every people of every nation would call God's Temple their house of prayer.[20]

We conclude that Jesus' inclusive table fellowship and vision of a house of prayer that was for all the nations was a precursor to what we call multiracial congregations. Jesus' "congregation" of followers was multicultural. Jesus believed that this inclusive vision was rooted in the Hebrew Scriptures and was God's desire for the future. Also, given the Gospel writers' evident effort to include the influence of Gentiles on the life and ministry of Jesus the Jew, we believe that the congregations from which they wrote likely were diverse ethnically (and racially).

Perhaps the most interesting fact related to the message recorded by the Gospel writers was that they wrote during a time after the destruction of the temple in Jerusalem. Indeed the hour had come when true worshipers did not worship in the temple in Jerusalem but worshiped in spirit and truth (John 4:21, 23). The destruction of the temple in Jerusalem brought to an end what some had posited as their symbol of a faith that excluded people from other nations. Meanwhile, a "Jesus movement" of houses of prayer that included people from all nations emerged in Palestine and throughout Asia, Africa, and Europe. We now examine more closely what is known of the racial and cultural diversity of the congregations of the first-century church.

2 | CONGREGATIONS IN THE EARLY CHURCH

Christianity's first congregation emerged from an undistinguished group of Galilean followers of Jesus who gathered together in Jerusalem during the days following the drama of the Crucifixion and Resurrection. The death, resurrection, and ascension of Jesus ushered in a new era for his disciples. No longer did they have a human Jesus providing guidance. The mantle of leadership passed on to them. Those early followers faced the challenge of implementing Jesus' vision of a house of prayer for all the nations. So 120 of them gathered together in an upstairs room praying for wisdom and direction. Among those assembled were the twelve apostles minus Judas Iscariot who had betrayed Jesus. Matthias was there having been selected to replace Judas as a member of the twelve (Acts 1:15–26). Also in the room were the women disciples who had faithfully followed Jesus in his three years of ministry and fearlessly supported him through the ordeal of his death. Mary the mother of Jesus and other relatives joined the group as well (Acts 1:13–15). They were a congregation seeking an identity and purpose without the presence of their leader.

After several weeks of meeting together for prayer, an amazing and transforming event occurred on the day of Pentecost, interrupting those clandestine gatherings of spiritual discernment. According to the author of the Acts of the Apostles, the power of the Holy Spirit came upon those 120 Galileans praying in an upper room and propelled them out into the streets proclaiming the good news of Jesus Christ in the languages of the nations. "Jews from every nation under heaven living in Jerusalem" gathered and inquired as a result of this unusual occurrence (Acts 2:5). Individuals who relocated to Jerusalem from Jewish enclaves throughout the continents of Asia, Africa, and Europe heard the Gospel in the dialect of their local community in the country of their origin. The Spirit of Jesus supernaturally spoke through these Galilean disciples in the language of the house of prayer for all the nations. On the day of Pentecost the Jerusalem congregation grew from 120 Galilean Jews to over 3,000 multicultural, multilingual Jews (2:41). Several thousand more were added in the days that followed (4:4, 5:14, 6:7). The church was multicultural and multilingual from the first moment of its existence.

In this chapter we discover how the authors of the New Testament present the development of the church. The disciples of Jesus sought to embrace his inclusive vision in the congregations that emerged under their leadership. Congregations of the church of God from Jerusalem to Antioch to Rome embraced people from a wide range of ethnic backgrounds and cultural perspectives, becoming houses of prayer for all the nations. They were implementing Jesus' instruction to make disciples from all nations (Matthew 28:19–20). The diverse and inclusive nature of early congregations did not occur by accident. This outcome was the result of embracing the vision and strategy of Jesus. They even created a new language to describe their coming together in community; descriptors such as the church, the people of God, the body, and many others were used. The terms used by the early followers of Jesus Christ to describe themselves emphasized their inclusive posture. We first examine the diversity of the congregation in Jerusalem—the mother church of Christianity. We also look at the makeup of the congregations it spawned in greater Palestine. Then we study the great missionary-sending congregation in Antioch as well as congregations established by its leaders (Paul, Barnabus, Silas, etc.) and by others.

The Jerusalem Church

As noted at the beginning of this chapter, the congregation in Jerusalem began with a rich multicultural flavor. Yet many in

Jerusalem regarded the individuals in this culturally and linguistically diverse Jerusalem congregation as marginal persons.[1] Second-class Galilean Jews and migrant Hellenized Jews made up the membership of this first church. Not until chapter six of Acts does the author mention anyone from the mainstream of Jerusalem's life joining the congregation: "and a great many priests became obedient to the faith" (6:7). Many of the Jews who migrated to Jerusalem from the Diaspora spoke Greek. They worshiped in synagogues for Greek speakers and read from a Greek translation of the Scriptures called the *Septuagint.* So the Jerusalem congregation bridged a divide found in first-century Judaism—culture- and language-specific synagogues.[2]

The diversity of the Jerusalem congregation also expressed itself in opinions shaped by cultural experience. Biblical scholar Jerome Crowe notes:

> A Jew born and brought up in Jerusalem was likely to be characterized by an enthusiastic admiration for the Temple and its worship. Many migrants from the Diaspora shared this enthusiasm, though others clearly did not. . . . Jews born in Palestine may well have been prone to identify all Gentiles with those Gentiles they were most familiar with, the mercenary soldiers in the service of Rome who enforced an oppressive pagan regime. Jews from the Diaspora, from Antioch or North Africa or the great university city of Alexandria, were more likely to have an understanding of the positive values of Hellenistic culture and a sympathetic appreciation of its moral ideals.[3]

Although we may welcome such a wide diversity, differences also bring challenges, conflict, and tension. The Jerusalem congregation learned this early. In chapter six of Acts, the author informs the reader that the congregation stood on the verge of an ethnic conflict (6:1–6). A crisis emerged regarding social services provided to widows in the congregation. Some complained that the widows born and raised in Palestine were favored in the daily distribution of food over the Greek-speaking widows who immigrated to Israel from other parts of the Roman Empire. The leadership addressed the issue immediately before it might lead to ethnically divided congregations. Seven new leaders, "full of the Spirit and wisdom," were selected to oversee the ministry in question: Stephen, Philip, Prochorus, Nicanor, Timon, Parmenas, and Nicolaus (6:3, 5). They each bore Greek names. As biblical scholar Ben Witherington III notes, "This seems to suggest that the community as a whole, in order to avoid even the appearance of favoritism, named mostly if not exclusively Greek-speaking Jewish Christians to administer the food distribution."[4]

The author of Acts wisely included this incident to share with the broader church a lesson learned by this first congregation in Jerusalem. Congregations that preach the message of Jesus Christ will appeal to a diverse group of people. This should not be avoided. Yet good judgment is required in sustaining a congregation that the Gospel brings together. The Jerusalem congregation faced head-on the challenges posed by diversity with action that was prayerful, immediate, empowering, and that further implemented Jesus' vision of a house of prayer for all the nations. We shall discover later in this chapter that the early church encountered even more challenges in their efforts to reconcile diversity as they established congregations outside Jerusalem.

Congregations in Palestine and the Regions Beyond

The growth of the Jerusalem congregation was disrupted by the martyrdom of Stephen, one of the seven Greek-speaking leaders (Acts 8:1). Most of the Greek-speaking leaders (and probably many members) fled the city due to the extreme persecution that followed Stephen's death. Because these leaders took the message of the Gospel with them, the first-century church rapidly expanded its reach beyond Jerusalem and beyond Judaism. One of the seven Greek-speaking leaders—Philip—left Jerusalem and witnessed to an Ethiopian finance minister (8:26–40). One of the original twelve apostles—Peter—left Jerusalem and preached at the home of a Roman centurion (10:1–48). These two episodes in the life of the early believers dramatized and symbolized the future of the church.

In his final words to his disciples before ascending into heaven, Jesus proclaimed that they would be his "witnesses in Jerusalem, in all of Judea and Samaria, and to the ends of the earth" (Acts 1:8). Many Greek historians and writers considered Ethiopia (or Nubia) to be the ends of the earth since it was located outside the boundaries of the Roman Empire.[5] In chapter eight of Acts, when the Ethiopian finance minister from Queen Candace's Nubian Empire traveled the road leading through Gaza back to Africa, he initiated the response to Jesus' call to reach "the ends of the earth" and symbolized how far the church would expand its reach beyond Jerusalem. In chapter ten of Acts, Peter entered the home of a Roman military officer who lived in the city of Caesarea (named after the emperor of Rome). The Roman centurion named Cornelius enforced the police state that existed in Palestine. Peter preached at the home of Cornelius and the centurion's entire household converted to Christianity, showing how far the church would broaden its scope beyond of the boundaries of Jewish ethnic identity.

After the martyrdom of Stephen the church spread beyond the city of Jerusalem to Samaria, Galilee, and all of Palestine, where Greek culture and Gentile neighbors influenced resident Jews. This occurred just a few years after Jesus' resurrection. A strong possibility exists that many of these believers had followed Jesus during his earthly ministry. In chapter eight of Acts, Philip preached to people in Samaria (8:5–25). This was an amazing development given the animosity between Samaritans and Jews at the time. Yet it was consistent with the ministry of Jesus. Perhaps some of the Samaritans who responded to Philip's outreach had met Jesus when he spent two days in the region after encountering a woman at Jacob's well in the Samaritan city of Sychar. The congregation(s) founded in Samaria certainly included indigenous Samaritans. Perhaps some Hellenist Jews remained in Samaria as members.[6]

Not much is known about the makeup of congregations in Palestine. Clues in the Gospels and Acts reveal some interesting findings. Biblical scholar Raymond Brown suggested that the community that produced the writings attributed to the apostle John had "Samaritan elements" and was probably located in Palestine. His research led him to believe that the Johannine community "involved an originating group of Jewish Christians and a later group of Jewish Christians of anti-Temple persuasion with their Samaritan converts . . . (with) clear signs of a Gentile component among the recipients of the Gospel."[7] Brown's research paints a picture of congregations in Palestine in the latter part of the first century with all the cultural diversity of the Jerusalem congregation plus the addition of "Samaritan converts" and a "Gentile component."

It is possible that the first congregations in Galilee emerged after Pentecost in the same homes where Jesus spent time—those of Peter (Matthew 8:15), Mary and Martha (Luke 10:38f) and Simon the leper (Mark 14:3ff).[8] Galilee was a very diverse province. We should not be surprised to find that eventually these congregations would be diverse, especially since Jesus ministered to both Jews and Gentiles in the region during his days on earth. We have limited explicit information regarding congregations that existed in Palestine. Yet the research done by scholars like Raymond Brown points to congregations populated by culturally diverse Jews and Gentiles, as well as Samaritans.

This tendency toward congregations that reconciled Jews and Gentiles became the standard of the early church. While Jews often started congregations within their own ethnic group, soon Gentiles would join. This seems to be the case among the congregations that emerged along the Mediterranean coast.[9] This Jesus movement brought a Gospel that reconciled the differences and tensions often experienced in relationships between Jews and Gentiles. To those first hearing the message, the disciples of Jesus proclaimed "a universalistic Judaism, which was open to outsiders."[10] Eventually these congregations existed in a space outside both the world of Judaism and the varieties of religions and philosophies found in the Roman Empire.[11]

Biblical professor David Rhoads sums up the miracle of the first-century church:

> The early Christian movement meant nothing less than breaking down the dividing wall between Jews and Gentiles. And this universal vision was much more than the combining of two groups, for neither was monolithic. On the one side, Judaism was itself multiform in that era of history—both in Palestine with its various sectarian groups and among the communities of Jews dispersed throughout the Roman Empire and throughout the Parthian Empire to the east. On the other side, there was the multiplicity of Gentile nations. The Greek word *Gentiles* literally means nations. Across the ancient Mediterranean world, there was an incredible array of local ethnic communities, subcultures, and language groups within the aegis of the Roman Empire. That is, there were many "nations" within Northern Africa and the south; Palestine and the east; Asia Minor, Greece, and the north; Italy and the west; and on the islands in the Mediterranean Sea. The region around the Mediterranean Sea was multilingual, multiracial, and multiethnic, with many different religions and philosophies. These Jewish groups and Gentile nations comprised the multiplicity of cultures that Christianity sought to address and to embrace. In this multicultural arena, the diversity of early Christianity took shape.[12]

The Antioch Congregation

According to Acts, the first congregation to experience the reconciliation of Jews and Gentiles into one coherent faith community formed
in Antioch of Syria in the thirties. Antioch was the third largest city in
the Roman Empire, with a population of nearly half a million
people.[13] A wide cultural mix of peoples including Syrians, Romans,
Greeks, Arabs, Persians, Armenians, Parthians, Cappadocians, and
Jews made up Antioch's urban population.[14] One seventh of the
population was Jewish. A Jewish community had existed in Antioch
from the early days of the city.[15] The relative peace of the Jewish community was disrupted in the late thirties and early forties. Ethnic
tensions erupted between Jews and the majority Greco-Syrians. Mobs
attacked Jews and torched their synagogues.[16]

The problems faced by Antioch in the first century rival those of
any city in the world today. Most families lived in areas of extreme
population density that lacked adequate sanitation and water. This
condition led to disease and early death. Half the children died at
birth or in infancy. If a child did live, she or he often experienced the
death of at least one parent prior to becoming an adult. The housing
projects were overcrowded, dirty, and foul smelling, and they offered
no privacy. Crime ruled the streets. Yet more and more people found
their way to these crowded neighborhoods. Antioch was "a city repeatedly
smashed by cataclysmic catastrophes: where a resident could expect
literally to be homeless from time to time, providing that he or she
was among the survivors."[17]

Ethnic strife was intense. Enslaved persons composed close to one
third of Antioch's population, "many of whom had been deported
from their homeland in the wake of ruinous wars with no hope of
improving their position."[18] Race riots were common because so many
people of differing ethnic and cultural groups lived together in
cramped, overcrowded conditions.[19] Sociologist Rodney Stark adds
that Antioch was "a city filled with hatred and fear rooted in intense
ethnic antagonisms and exacerbated by a constant stream of strangers
. . . a city so lacking in stable networks of attachments that petty
incidents could prompt mob violence."[20]

Into this city arrived Greek-speaking Jewish Christians who left
Jerusalem during the persecution of the mid-thirties. They began

preaching to fellow Jews (Acts 11:19). Some of their Cyrenean and Cypriot leaders also preached to Greeks (11:20). This gave birth to the first congregation of followers of Jesus Christ that included both Jews and Gentiles. Over time it is quite probable that the wide cultural mix of people in Antioch was represented in the church.[21] The Jerusalem church sent Barnabus to provide leadership and a link with the mother church (11:24). Barnabus recruited Saul of Tarsus (later known as the apostle Paul) to join the leadership team (11:25–26). Three others also emerged as leaders: Simeon, who was called Niger, Lucius of Cyrene, and Manean, a member of the court of Herod the ruler (13:1).

The Antioch congregation selected a diverse leadership team in the early stages of their formation. Perhaps they had learned this from the Jerusalem congregation. Both Paul and Barnabus were Jews raised outside of Palestine and immersed in Greek culture, yet they were fluent in the traditions of Jerusalem. Saul spent his school years in Jerusalem under the watchful eye of the noted teacher Gamaliel. Both were bilingual, speaking Aramaic and Greek. Manean grew up in the household of Herod Antipas as a stepbrother.[22] This was the Herod who beheaded John the Baptist and interviewed Jesus during his trial. His nephew, Herod Agrippa, persecuted the church in Palestine even as Manean provided leadership in Antioch (Herod Agrippa martyred James, one of the original twelve disciples). Lucius of Cyrene came from North Africa, possibly one of the people who initially preached in Antioch. Simeon, called Niger (black), was most likely a black African.

The Antioch congregation lived out an inclusive table fellowship that emulated the social practices of Jesus. Each person who joined the fellowship felt affirmed for the culture of his or her background. Yet each also adopted a higher calling through allegiance to Jesus Christ. Jews and Gentiles continued to embrace their culture of origin but broke with certain cultural rules that inhibited their ability to live as one in Christ. For example, they ate and socialized together. While this was not permitted or approved of in society, in "the many house-congregations of Antioch . . . Jews and Gentiles, living together in crowded city quarters, freely mixed."[23] For Jewish Christians this required them to give up an understanding that their ethnic identity necessitated separation from Gentiles and to risk being seen as developing close relations with pagans.[24] In the midst of Antioch's extreme ethnic tensions "Christianity offered a new basis for social solidarity."[25]

Therefore the social commentators of the day in Antioch could not identify the followers of Jesus with any known group. The members of the Antioch congregation certainly did not practice pagan rites or emperor worship. Nor did they all live by Jewish cultural and religious standards. So they were called Christians or Christ followers (Acts 11:26). This name declared that they made up "a social but not an ethnic group."[26] As theologian Virgilio Elizondo states, the Christians "could not be classified according to the classification categories of either the pagans or the Jews. They were both and yet they were neither the one nor the other alone. They were the same and yet they lived differently. They were bound together by a new intimacy and mutual concern that went beyond normal, acceptable behavior within the empire."[27]

The Antioch Model Spreads

The Antioch congregation became the model for the expansion of the church in the first century. The foremost initiator of new congregations in this period—the apostle Paul—was mentored and sent forth by the leadership of the Antioch congregation. The congregations founded by Paul and his coworkers often started in a fashion similar to that of Antioch. They preached first to Jews and then to Gentiles. Paul's team of preachers started at the local synagogue. By preaching in the synagogues first they reached some Jews (Acts 13:5, 14; 14:1; 17:1, 10, 17; 18:4, 19; 19:8). Few Jews would have found these emerging communities of faith attractive had the outreach begun with Gentiles. The cultural and religious changes required to join an all-Gentile assembly would have proven difficult at this point. Also among those attending the synagogues were some Gentiles—called "God-fearers"—who embraced a monotheistic belief or were attracted to the moral vision of Judaism. Once God-fearing Gentiles became Christian converts they reached out to Gentiles who practiced pagan religions or emperor worship. Soon the congregations included Jews and people from many other nations. They were culturally diverse religious communities. This strategy based on the Antioch model of church development enabled congregations to be houses of prayer for all the nations. It also launched a fledgling movement for social unity rooted in local expressions of inclusive togetherness—congregations united by faith in Jesus Christ.

We do not know how the evangelism effort moved forward in each place where Paul preached and initiated congregations. Nor can we say for sure that every congregation included both Jews and Gentiles. Some areas did not have a Jewish population. But we can observe the inclusion of both Gentiles and Jews in most locales where Acts offers a description of events or a reference to the ethnic makeup of the congregation. After Paul and Barnabus were commissioned by the Antioch congregation to spread the word about Jesus Christ, they witnessed in synagogues and to Gentiles in Cyprus (Acts 13:4–12), Pisidian Antioch (13:14–52), and Iconium (14:1–5). The author of Acts even stated, "At Iconium Paul and Barnabus went as usual into the Jewish synagogue. There they spoke so effectively that a great number of Jews and Gentiles believed" (14:1, NIV).

When Paul, Silas, and Timothy traveled to the Roman colony of Philippi in the district of Macedonia they did not find a synagogue. Yet because of their strategic commitment to witness to Jews first they eventually located a group of Jewish women who prayed by a river on the Sabbath (Acts 16:11–15). A businesswoman named Lydia asked that she and her entire household be baptized. Soon a congregation developed at Lydia's home (16:40). The apostle Paul's team also proclaimed the Gospel in the Gentile sections of the city. Their bold preaching and the casting out of an evil spirit resulted in their arrest. Jail did not quiet Paul and Silas. Before they were released, the Roman jailer himself became a believer (16:16–39). The Gospel triumphed "in the midst of the Jewish meeting place, and in the midst of the Roman stronghold."[28] Therefore, the first congregation established by Paul on the continent of Europe was multicultural.

Paul and his associates continued to initiate multicultural congregations in Europe. After Philippi they went to the largest city in Macedonia (Acts 17:1–9). "After Paul and Silas had passed through Ampholis and Apollonia, they came to Thessalonica, where there was a synagogue of the Jews. And Paul went in, as was his custom, and on three Sabbath days argued with them from the scriptures" (17:1–2). Both Jews and Greeks believed. Biblical scholar F. F. Bruce responds to the notion that Paul established separate congregations for Jews and Gentiles because he wrote two separate letters to the Thessalonians. He writes, "The idea that a church planted by Paul comprised separate Jewish and Gentile sections is antecedently improbable."[29] Paul's team found similar success next in the Macedonian city of Beroea (17:10–15).

A very important congregation was established in Corinth, a city of nearly 100,000 people (Acts 18:1–18). Since Corinth was a Roman colony, many of its residents were Romans. Several were the descendants of relocated urban poor people from Rome. Yet there were also numerous people who were the descendants of "peoples conquered by the Romans . . . perhaps from Syria, Judea, Asia minor, and Greece itself."[30] Biblical scholar Ben Witherington III notes:

> The city was in many regards the best place possible in Greece for making contacts with all sorts of people and for founding a new religious group. Corinth was at the crossroads between the eastern and western portions of the Mediterranean, having ports on either side of the Isthmus of Corinth, and between the northern and southern regions of Greece. . . . Religiously, the city was pluralistic and included temples or shrines to traditional Greek gods and goddesses (including Aphrodite on the Acro-Corinth), recently founded Roman cults that included the practice of emperor worship, and a considerable and long-established Jewish colony. Here Paul was likely to meet people of varying social statuses and religious orientations who if converted could help establish a significant congregation in this place, not to mention many itinerant businessmen and businesswomen who if converted could help spread the word elsewhere in the Empire.[31]

The apostle Paul did establish such a congregation with the help of Silas, Timothy, and a couple—Priscilla and Aquila—who had relocated from the church in Rome due to persecution of Jews. Paul began with intense efforts every Sabbath in the synagogue. He soon left the synagogue because of strong opposition and began holding services right next door at the house of Titius Justus, a God-fearing Gentile convert. Meeting next door to the synagogue proved strategic in establishing a congregation that reached both Jews and Gentiles. It was not long until Crispus, the official of the synagogue, and his entire household became believers.

Paul established another important congregation in the city of Ephesus in western Asia (Acts 18:19–21; 19:1–20:1). Nearly a quarter of a million people lived in this city. Paul spent more time developing the congregation in Ephesus than in any other place. He stayed for about three years. He spoke in the synagogue for the first three months of his tenure. At several points the author of Acts clearly stated the multicultural nature of this congregation. He wrote that "all of the residents of Asia, both Jews and Greeks, heard the word of the Lord" (19:10; see also 19:17). On a return visit later, Paul declared to the members of the congregation in Ephesus, "I testified to both Jews and Greeks about repentance toward God and faith toward our Lord Jesus" (20:21). Witherington writes, "It is here in Ephesus that he has the longest stable period of ministry without trial or expulsion, here that he most fully carries out his commission to be a witness to all persons, both Jew and Gentile."[32] Paul was intent on ensuring that congregations of the church of God began and remained multicultural. For Paul, an ethnic group was not the basis for a church. Biblical scholar Wayne Meeks notes, "By the time the extant letters were written, the established pattern was instead to found in every city associations of believers in Christ, drawn from gentiles and Jews alike."[33]

The congregation in Rome probably started when Jewish "visitors from Rome," in Jerusalem for Pentecost, returned home (Acts 2:10). The congregation likely had close ties with the Jerusalem congregation. At some point early on, Gentiles joined the congregation. Then in the forties the emperor Claudius expelled all the Jews from Rome and the congregation was composed of only Gentiles (18:2). At Claudius' death the expulsion order was reversed and many Jews returned to Rome.[34] Many Christian Jews also returned to the congregation in Rome. By the time Paul wrote the church at Rome, it was culturally diverse. Paul's letter appealed to both Jews ("if you call yourself a Jew"—2:17) and Gentiles ("now I am speaking to you Gentiles"— 11:13). He wrote of God calling the congregation "not only from the Jews only but also from the Gentiles" (9:24). He noted his long-standing strategy for outreach, "I am not ashamed of the gospel; it is the power of God for salvation to everyone who has faith, to the Jew first and also to the Greek" (1:16).[35] The people whom Paul greets in his letter to the Roman congregation include an interesting mix of Greek,

Latin, and Jewish names (Romans 16:3-16).[36] When he later visited (Acts 28), the congregation was made up primarily of "lower-class immigrants, both Jews and Gentiles, organized in several quite diverse house church communities."[37]

The Church Struggles to Maintain Unity

The first-century church struggled to keep its Christ-inspired unity movement intact in the midst of such a wide diversity. The idea that Gentiles and Jews could or should worship and socialize together in the same congregation was foreign to the worldviews of most people. There were many challenges in crossing this cultural divide. Paul often reminded his congregations that there was no Jew or Gentile in Christ (Romans 10:12; 1 Corinthians 12:13; Galatians 3:28; Ephesians 2:11–26; Colossians 3:11). Some early church leaders did not easily grasp what developed at Antioch and in other congregations. By examining the accounts of the early church in Acts and Paul's recollection in his letter to the churches in the region of Galatia we observe three attempts by leaders in the first-century church to preserve the unity found in culturally diverse congregations.

After several years of ministry Paul visited Jerusalem to confer privately with the key leaders of the mother church: the apostles Peter (Cephas) and John, members of Jesus' original twelve disciples, and the apostle James (Galatians 2:1–10). Two members of Paul's multicultural leadership team, Barnabus, a Jew, and Titus, a Greek, accompanied him. This meeting of church leaders occurred so that Paul might, in a proactive fashion, broaden the awareness of the leadership in Jerusalem regarding this rapidly expanding movement of multicultural congregations. Paul described to the Jerusalem leaders how the grace of God permeated the ministry to the Gentiles. He received their blessing to continue in the same manner. The apostles in Jerusalem only asked that Paul and his associates "remember the poor," which Paul "was eager to do" (2:10). With this private assurance, Paul continued his ministry to reach Gentiles who would sit alongside Jews in his many congregations.

The private agreement was tested and challenged by an event that Paul described next in his letter to the Galatians (2:11–14). The apostle Peter visited the Antioch congregation. At first he enjoyed their unhindered table fellowship where Jews and Gentiles ate together. This was in violation of purity codes followed by many Jews of the time. Inclusive dining was the practice in the congregations founded by Paul and his associates. During Peter's visit some people from the Jerusalem congregation arrived. They presented themselves as representatives from the apostle James and promoted the view that Gentiles must first be circumcised before they could share table fellowship with Jews. Under their influence, Peter stopped eating with Gentiles in the Antioch congregation. It may have also caused a break in the sharing of Holy Communion with the Gentile members. Peter's action, in turn, prompted Barnabus and other Jewish Christians to follow his example. A real threat existed to the unity of the Antioch congregation. It could split into Jewish and Gentile factions. When Paul arrived on the scene he made his second attempt to preserve the unity of the church when he confronted Peter publicly on his behavior in Antioch.

We must first address the reason that Peter (and others) stopped eating with Gentiles if we are to understand what occurred at the Antioch congregation. The group from the congregation in Jerusalem believed that Gentiles must first become Jews culturally and religiously prior to embracing Christianity. According to Acts, a group of Pharisees who joined the Jerusalem church were proclaiming the view that Gentiles must be circumcised and embrace Jewish cultural practices (15:5). They visited Antioch to preach their message and to influence Peter.

The Jerusalem congregation's outreach to fellow Jews would have been made more difficult if Jewish converts believed they had to give up the ways of their tradition. This was particularly important if they were to reach those with a perspective that emphasized cultural purity. Peter may have perceived this as a practical issue of "how unrestricted table fellowship of Jews and Gentiles within the Christian community at Antioch would appear to non-Christian Jews of Palestine . . . when it was known back in Palestine that one of the 'pillars' of the Jerusalem church ate with Gentiles at Antioch in an unrestricted manner."[38] Peter may have viewed his actions as a pragmatic response that enabled the Jerusalem church to evangelize unencumbered by concerns about the cultural purity of Jewish Christians.

Their argument and its influence over Peter persuaded other

Jewish Christians in Antioch to imitate Peter's behavior. As biblical scholar F. F. Bruce notes:

> Even worse, if possible, than Peter's action in itself was the effect of his example on other Jewish Christians, and when even Barnabas— the last man of whom it might have been expected—was persuaded to join in withdrawing from table fellowship with Gentiles, what must the Gentile Christians have thought? They could draw only one conclusion: so long as they remained uncircumcised, they were at best second-class citizens in the new community.[39]

If Barnabus, the first pastor of a multicultural congregation and Paul's co-laborer in the mission to the Gentiles, changed his view, then what hope was there for a sustained witness to unity in Antioch?

Paul's response was swift and strong. He opposed Peter publicly (Galatians 2:11). Paul told Peter that such an action compromised "the truth of the Gospel" (2:14). It was hypocritical and heretical. Paul chose *not* to take what seemed the pragmatic course of action, that of "founding a separate and exclusively Gentile church." The apostle Paul "never wavered in his conviction that God was making a new creation by drawing into one church both Jews and Gentiles."[40] He believed that it was not enough just to maintain a spiritual unity in the universal church. Unity needed to be seen and experienced in the local congregation as well. The break in sharing meals together would end "the social unity of the church."[41] The apostle Paul could not stand by and allow the Christian church to lose its power to reconcile and therefore make void the truth of the gospel.

When Paul wrote his letter to the Galatians the issues that had surfaced in Antioch apparently were unresolved.[42] The fifteenth chapter of Acts also recounts the incident when those who claimed to represent James tried to influence the congregation in Antioch: "Unless you are circumcised, according to the custom taught by Moses, you cannot be saved" (15:1, NIV). The Antioch congregation appointed Paul and Barnabus to travel to Jerusalem and speak to the apostles on this issue. Barnabus' lapse under Peter's influence must have been momentary, as he is portrayed as defending the gospel of grace extended to the Gentiles. The crisis in Antioch had the potential to spread to the rest of the churches. This summit between leaders in Jerusalem and those from the Antioch congregation represented a third attempt by church leaders to preserve the unity of the early church (Acts 15:1-31).[43]

Both sides presented their views in the meeting. Then Peter took the floor and defended the position of Paul and Barnabus, noting that he (Peter) was used by God to begin the outreach to Gentiles. Peter stated:

> And God, who knows the human heart, testified to them by giving them the Holy Spirit, just as he did to us; and in cleansing their hearts he made no distinction between them and us. Now therefore why are you putting God to the test by placing on the neck of the disciples a yoke that neither our ancestors nor we have been able to bear? On the contrary, we believe that we will be saved through the grace of the Lord Jesus, just as they will (Acts 15:8–11).

Paul's rebuke of Peter must have awakened him to the truth of the gospel. It is possible that "Peter may have used at the council the argument for freedom which Paul had impressed upon him so recently in the Antioch dispute."[44]

By this time James was the primary leader in the life of the Jerusalem congregation. He followed Peter's eloquent defense of multicultural congregations by declaring: "Therefore I have reached the decision that we should not trouble those Gentiles who are turning to God" (Acts 15:19). James then set the following terms for Gentile believers: they were to avoid food offered to idols, not eat meat of strangled animals or blood, and abstain from sexual immorality (15:20). F. F. Bruce notes, "These requirements may have been intended to facilitate social intercourse between Jewish and Gentile Christians. Some Gentile practices were specially offensive to Jews, and if these practices were given up, Jewish Christians would feel that an obstacle in the way of table fellowship and the like with their Gentile brethren had been removed."[45] A letter was sent to the congregation in Antioch and other congregations with Gentile members saying that circumcision was not required and that, if they could embrace a few suggestions for change in social practices to accommodate Jewish believers, table fellowship should resume (15:23–29). The decision at the Jerusalem council preserved the unity of the Antioch congregation and that of the church at large.[46] It also empowered Paul and others to forge ahead in their ministry of reconciliation. The result was the founding of multicultural congregations wherever they went. The struggle to maintain unity in Antioch reminds us that racial reconciliation and multiracial congregations often come at a cost and with sacrifice.

Conclusion

The early congregations of the church of God were culturally diverse. In Jerusalem they bridged the diversity of culture found among the Jewish people of the time. Outside Jerusalem, congregations bridged the separation between Jews, Samaritans, and Gentiles. Followers of Jesus Christ continued to establish multicultural congregations beyond the time recorded in the New Testament into the second century. Their broad inclusiveness decreased only when the church became more aligned and identified with the Roman Empire and the culture of the elite.[47] The faith that united the early followers of Jesus was co-opted and the church became divided by faith.

We have discovered that the early followers of Jesus embraced his vision of a house of prayer for all the nations and implemented this in their congregations. Biblical scholar Gerd Theissen sums up well the optimism of these early believers:

> How could the Jesus movement cherish the hope of permeating the whole of society with this pattern? Was that not to expect a miracle? And indeed a miracle is what they hoped for. The Jesus movement believed in miracles, in the realization of what appeared to be impossible. . . . Now if the movement had at its disposal powers which foretold a complete change in the world, might it also have confidence in ethical extremes? Would not the faith which moves mountains (Mark 11:23) also be capable of changing the human heart? If so many miracles had taken place, would not the miracle of love be possible also? We should not underestimate the encouraging effect of miracles.[48]

So for Theissen and us, the basic question is this: "How were relatively stable and sturdy communities with considerable inner cohesion formed from a mixture of ethnic, social and religious groups? How did Jews and Gentiles, Greeks and barbarians, slaves and freemen, men and women, come to form a new unity in Christ?"[49] We declare that the first-century church was united by faith! This unity occurred as local congregations strategically implemented Jesus' vision of a house of prayer for all the nations. Together these congregations produced a movement for social unity across the great divide of culture, tradition, class, and race. Ultimately, the unity of the first-century church was the result of the miracle of reconciliation—a conversion from their ethnocentrism to the intention, practice, and vision of Jesus.

II

MULTIRACIAL
CONGREGATIONS
IN THE UNITED STATES

3 | CONGREGATIONS AND THE COLOR LINE (1600–1940)

As citizens of the twenty-first century, it is difficult to fully comprehend and imagine the horrible human tragedy of slavery in North America. Human beings were kidnapped from their homes in Africa by fellow human beings and crammed into ships where they endured appalling conditions as they made their way to the "new world." Many people of African descent died during this passage by sea. Others jumped into the ocean determined never to be anyone's slave. Most endured intense suffering and deprivation with little or no knowledge of what awaited them at the end of the journey. Some of these individuals transported to North America found strength to survive in their faith. Persons who practiced Islam and indigenous African religions were among the millions kidnapped and carried to the shores of what would become the United States of America. Some persons sold into slavery might have been members of ancient Christian churches in Africa or converts from European missionary activity on the shores of the African continent.[1]

The first interracial worship experiences among whites and Africans on the North American continent probably took place without the knowledge of either group. Many of the slaveholders, who purchased African people on their arrival in the colonies, belonged to

Christian churches. Because of language differences it is quite possible that slaveholding Europeans and enslaved Africans stood next to each other praying to God without any awareness of their shared moment of worship. Sociologist C. Eric Lincoln further dramatized this image of the first meetings of whites and Africans in North America:

> Chained neck to neck, wrist to wrist, and ankle to ankle, and shipped off into a new kind of Babylonian captivity in Christian America, the Africans left their gods but not their God. Muslim and heathen alike, and possibly some Christians as well, chained body to body between decks four feet high; if they survived the darkness, the filth, the horror, and the degradation of the "middle passage," they would arrive by and by in the land of the American Christians: the Congregationalists, the Presbyterians, the Roman Catholics, the Quakers, the Lutherans, the Baptists, the Methodists, and, of course, the Anglicans—once removed. There they would eventually meet the white man's God.[2]

The mental image of enslaved Africans and slaveholding Europeans standing side by side simultaneously calling out to the same God in prayer and worship is a far cry from the first-century church that embraced the notion that in Christ there was no slave nor free, Jew nor Gentile, male or female (Galatians 3:28). Yet this troubling mental image characterizes the religious relationship between persons of color and whites throughout the history of the United States.

We now look at the history of interracial worship and multiracial congregations from the 1600s to the 1940s. We are aware that neither racism nor the division by race that besets congregations originated in the United States. The development of racism and beliefs in white superiority predate the time period we are about to discuss. Even the fragmentation of the church by race, culture, and class has its genesis in a much earlier time. Certainly the theology that provided the underpinnings for racism in the United States has antecedents in prior eras. We do not have adequate space to offer a history of the church between the first and seventeenth centuries. Several volumes would be needed. Our goal is to compare the message of Jesus and the Christian faith of first-century congregations as described in the New Testament with that of congregations that have existed in the United States since the beginning of the European colonial era in the 1600s.

We have discovered that periodically the spirit of the first-century church broke through the confines of the dominant white racism to produce historic seasons of reconciliation. For short moments in time it appeared that the realization of Jesus' vision of a house of prayer for all the nations was at hand. Then racism reared its ugly head and extinguished the flames of unity. Before we pursue our premise that congregations should be multiracial when possible, we must first pause and honestly assess the history of such efforts in the United States.

Early Colonial America

Segregation by race with whites in the dominant position was not predetermined to become the identifying feature of social life throughout the history of the United States. Initially the British colonies in North America experienced a division based on a class distinction between indentured servants and free persons. The servant class included Native Americans, African Americans, and European whites. In August 1619 the first Africans arrived in what would become the United States. It appears they were captured and enslaved by Spanish merchants (they all had Spanish names) and then stolen by the crew of a Dutch ship. When they set foot in North America they were classified as indentured servants—not slaves.[3] Indentured servants were not locked into a lifetime of servanthood. They could earn their freedom after working three to seven years and thereby change their status and the future of their children. At this time the class of free persons consisted principally of British whites, joined by African Americans who had earned their freedom. The skin color of a person did not doom her or him to slavery.

While we could debate the morality of class distinctions, we simply want to make the point that race was not a defining factor and class was fluid. The lack of a socially constructed racial separation— which is prevalent for much of the history of the European presence in North America—was most evident among the servant class. Historian Lerone Bennett Jr. notes:

> Working together in the same fields, sharing the same huts, the same situation, and the same grievances, the first black and white Americans, aristocrats excepted, developed strong bonds of sympathy and mutuality. They ran away together, played together and

revolted together. They mated and married, siring a sizeable mixed population. In the process the black and white servants—the majority of the colonial population—created a racial wonderland that seems somehow un-American in its lack of obsession about race and color.[4]

This apparent lack of racism among the servant class also proved true in some local congregations. Among the original group of twenty Africans arriving in 1619 were Antoney and Isabella. They married and gave birth to a son named William. This first child of African descent born in North America—the first true African American—was baptized into the "white" Anglican Church.[5] Another example from the 1600s occurred in the Anglican church of Elizabeth River, Virginia. In 1649 a couple from the congregation faced punishment for fornication. A man named William Watts, a white and formerly a servant, and a woman named Mary, an African and a servant, both received punishment based on their actions and not their race. Soon such an act could bring death for the African person.[6] It is important to note that congregations were not yet segregated into separate white and black churches.

Europeans did not invite Native Americans into congregations as they did African Americans during this early colonial period. Europeans treated Native Americans as "the other" in matters of faith. All contact was from a distance. The British attempted limited evangelization among Indians. These efforts were kept separate from any outreach to persons of European descent. One strategy developed a number of segregated towns of "praying Indians."[7] These newly formed villages housed Christian Native Americans "to remove the Indian person from relationship to the tribal group in order to associate him or her with the artificial community of Christ."[8] The evangelism of Native Americans by whites during the colonial period served to isolate Native American converts from Indians practicing traditional religions and also from white Christians.

The separation of whites from persons of color increased in colonial society during the 1660s. The growth of a capitalist economy and the demand for sugar and tobacco in the world market caused the development of a permanent institution of slavery for persons of African descent and required the creation of the philosophy and the practice of white supremacy. African Americans became the people chosen for enslavement by default. Native Americans could easily escape into the surrounding forests and whites could blend into the dominant population. Persons of African descent did not have these options. Also the prevailing attitude was that Africans were cheaper to purchase than white indentured servants and there was a whole continent full of Africans to exploit.[9]

The Atlantic slave trade produced one of the most brutal chapters in human history. From the very beginning of the travesty, European nations sought to assign some redeeming value to this economic transaction. They tried to convince themselves that "the cruelty inherent in enslaving fellow human beings" was eased because Africans would now become Christians.[10] They were unaware that some may have been Christians in Africa before arriving on the shores of North America. British leaders charged their citizens in North America to provide instruction to enslaved Africans in the Christian religion. Often this imperative was disregarded. Historian of religion Albert J. Raboteau writes:

> The danger beneath the arguments for slave conversion which many masters feared was the egalitarianism implicit in Christianity. The most serious obstacle to the missionary's access to the slaves was the slaveholder's vague awareness that a Christian slave would have some claim to fellowship, a claim that threatened the security of the master-slave hierarchy.[11]

Enslaved Africans also often disregarded the instruction. Theologian Gayraud Wilmore estimates that in the 150 years following the arrival of the first Africans on North American soil only 6 percent embraced Christianity.[12]

The population of African Americans remained small in the North. When a free black became a Christian he or she usually entered a white congregation; however, white congregations often implemented segregation through the use of the "Negro pew"—separate seating for blacks. Despite the small number of African Americans, some northerners did own slaves. Even pastors benefited from the institution of slavery. During the first half of the 1700s in the North "ministers often felt the need to have slaves in their own households and sometimes found them provided by thoughtful congregations as part of the parsonage furnishings. . . . Scores of New England ministers, including Cotton Mather and Jonathan Edwards, owned slaves in this period."[13]

Biracial Congregations

In the 1700s there was a significant increase in the slave trade bringing more Africans to live in the colonies. Also the legalization of lifetime slavery for Africans and their offspring was fully implemented. In the 1740s an evangelical movement called "The Great Awakening," sparked by the revivalist preaching of George Whitefield and others, drew poor whites and this growing population of enslaved African Americans into the Christian faith in large numbers. The primary beneficiaries of this revival were the Methodists and the Baptists. More and more African Americans joined in the services held at white congregations or at camp meetings. C. Eric Lincoln noted, "What the Africans found in the camp meetings of the Great Awakening was *acceptance and involvement as human beings.*"[14]

Biracial congregations of whites and African Americans emerged out of these camp meeting revivals. During the second half of the eighteenth century some amazing possibilities presented themselves in these congregations. African Americans and whites worshiped together. Enslaved African Americans were also offered the right hand of fellowship. This ritual of membership occurred during a Sunday service. Members of the congregation would pass by the new member shaking hands with her or him as a symbol of welcome to the congregational family.[15] African Americans and whites even addressed each other as family using the terms "brother" and "sister."[16] Historian John B. Boles writes:

> This equality in the terms of address may seem insignificant today, but in an age when only whites were accorded the titles of Mr. and Mrs., and it was taboo for a white to so address a black, any form of address that smacked of equality was notable. Behind it lay the familial idea, accepted by whites in principle if not always in practice, that in the sight of God all were equal and were members of His spiritual family.[17]

Some white ministers preached against slavery and freed the enslaved African Americans they owned.[18] One enslaved African recounted, "I had recently joined the Methodist Church and from the sermon I heard, I felt that God had made all men free and equal, and that I ought not to be a slave."[19] Even more startling was the fact that

African Americans served in pastoral roles at some biracial congregations. Historian Nathan Hatch notes, "For a brief interlude, white evangelicals endorsed the desire of converts to exercise their preaching talents, and black preaching became a regular occurrence in Baptist and Methodist communions. In a variety of churches at the end of the century, black pastors even served racially mixed congregations."[20] When the pastor of a mixed-race Baptist congregation in Virginia resigned from leadership the church invited an African American man to preach for them. The church was so delighted with his sermons that they paid for freedom for the man and his family. In another case an African American man—William Leman—pastored a white Baptist church in Virginia.[21] In yet another, Henry Evans—a free black—was licensed to preach by the Methodists. He started the first Methodist church in Fayetteville, North Carolina. Initially he preached only to African Americans. Soon some whites discovered his preaching and began attending. It was not long until the whites "crowded out" the blacks from their seats. The congregation received a white pastor but Evans remained as an assistant until his death.[22]

Whites who were poor or lower class and did not own enslaved African Americans primarily populated these biracial congregations, which "enabled them to see blacks as potential fellow believers in a way that white worshipers in more elite churches seldom could."[23] These egalitarian tendencies were similar to those experienced by whites and Africans who were indentured servants. When examined through the lenses of twenty-first century sensibilities, these biracial congregations would probably fail the test of what we would desire in multiracial congregations. But given the context of "absolute domination," the fact that African Americans could freely worship and participate in a near equal manner was amazing and significant.[24] As historian Randy J. Sparks states:

> Even though the biracial churches never succeeded in merging the slave and white communities, this failure should not negate the churches' positive accomplishments. The churches played an important role in the lives of hundreds of slaves. White church members sometimes rose above their prejudices and recognized blacks as fellow children of God with souls equal to their own. When a congregation gathered by the riverside and sang and prayed as blacks and whites were ritually immersed, race could be temporarily transcended.[25]

John Boles adds, "Without claiming too much or failing to recognize the multitude of ways slaves were not accorded genuine equality in these biracial churches, it is still fair to say that nowhere else in southern society were they treated so nearly as equals."[26]

We have found very little evidence of a similar experience for Native Americans participating with whites in multiracial congregations. Choctaw pastor and historian Homer Noley notes a few cases among Methodists in the early 1800s. Methodists began an outreach in the Great Lakes region to reach whites in the area. Yet Mohawks were evangelized in the same proportion as whites. A year or so later it was "reported that the mission house was usually filled for worship services. The membership of the Mission Society, however, was forty-four, of whom seven were white."[27] Also in the Great Lakes region among the Chippewa it was reported that "Methodist class was also initiated. Before long the Methodist class had grown to fifty-nine members, nineteen of whom were whites." The ministry staff "included three Indian exhorters and an interpreter."[28] It appears that such instances were rare and of limited duration.

Segregation in Biracial Congregations

In writing about Southern Baptists, historian Paul Harvey captures the essence of why biracial congregations eventually failed:

> In the late eighteenth century, a moment of opportunity for a biracial religious order seemed fleetingly to present itself. . . . But this apparent opening was illusory. It quickly became evident that whites valued the blossoming of their evangelical institutions and would make the necessary moral accommodations to maximize their growth. Southern Baptists never accepted their African American coreligionists as equals. They lacked the will, the fortitude, the theology, and the intellectual tools to even contemplate doing so.[29]

The early embrace of African Americans by whites faltered as societal norms pressed into the sacred sanctuaries of southern congregations. Many found interracial worship distasteful and refused to submit to African American leadership.[30] Soon whites "created a pattern of social intercourse within those churches that respected racial distinctions."[31]

After a brief fling with racial reconciliation, most whites returned to their marriage to racism. Biracial congregations soon separated the races in all aspects of church life. Separate seating was instituted in most congregations. African Americans were relegated to back pews, galleries, roof pews, separate balconies, standing along the rear wall, or even listening from outside the building.[32] Blacks were seated "farther up, out, or back than the lowliest white servant."[33] Some congregations had separate entrances for whites and blacks.[34] African Americans received communion "from a black assistant who served their segregated area."[35] According to theologian Dwight Perry, "Some congregations even erected dividers several feet high so Blacks were not physically mingling with the White congregants."[36] In many congregations African Americans outnumbered whites in attendance. When this became uncomfortable for whites, they instituted separate services—and sometimes formed separate congregations (under the rule of whites).[37] Albert Raboteau declares:

> It was in this context also that the white and black members of mixed churches in the antebellum South struggled with the tension between Christian fellowship and the system of slavery. Fellowship required that all church members be treated alike; slavery demanded that black members, even the free, be treated differently. . . . This tension revealed the irreducible gap between the slave's religion and that of his master. The slave knew that no matter how sincerely religious his master might be, his religion did not countenance the freedom of his slave. This was, after all was said and done, the limit to Christian fellowship. The division went deep; it extended as far as the interpretation of the Bible and the understanding of the Gospel.[38]

This tension and division that Raboteau describes led African Americans to create parallel opportunities for worship and fellowship. Enslaved persons of African descent developed their own unique forms of Christian interpretation and practice that spoke to the conditions created by racism. Sociologist E. Franklin Frazier called this the "invisible institution."[39] In secret places away from the view of the slaveholder African Americans formed their own religious communities. These were precursors to African American congregations and denominations.[40]

The Catholic Experience

Thus far our focus on biracial congregations has been within Protestantism. The Roman Catholic Church also provided ministry to

African Americans held as slaves by their members, primarily in Maryland and Louisiana.[41] Many priests owned enslaved African Americans (as did some religious communities). Like Protestants, Catholic congregations practiced an internal segregation of separate and inferior seating status for African Americans.[42] The Mass was adapted to accommodate the racism of the time. Historian Randall Miller writes:

> The white Catholics of St. Martin's Church in St. Martinsville, Louisiana, for example, imposed distinctions in the church between whites and all "colored" parishioners when approaching the table or adoring the cross. Free persons of color were not to make their devotions until all the whites had completed theirs, and the black slaves had to wait for the free persons of color to finish before they could fulfill their duties. The priest admitting a slave to communion needed the permission of the master.[43]

African Americans served in pastoral roles in some biracial Protestant congregations. This did not occur in Catholic congregations. African Americans were not invited to enter the priesthood. Historian Stephen Ochs explains why:

> American Catholics viewed the priest as a mediator between God and humanity; he held the keys to the kingdom of heaven. . . . The priest, therefore, did more than preach; he shared in the priesthood of Christ. Upon ordination by a bishop, he received supernatural powers to change bread and wine into the body and blood of Christ during the sacrifice of the Mass and to forgive sins in the sacrament of penance. Acting as Christ's representative the priest baptized, celebrated Mass, forgave sins, anointed the sick, buried the dead, and preached the gospel. . . . The exalted view of priesthood shared by most white Catholics precluded in their minds the possibility of black priests. Sharing the prevailing racist ideology of their fellow countrymen, most white Catholics regarded blacks as inferior to caucasians and therefore unfit to serve as priests. Moreover, the ordination of blacks to the sacred priesthood would, at least implicitly, threaten white supremacy in the church, for it would clearly trumpet the moral and intellectual equality of blacks and whites.[44]

As victims of prejudice, most Catholic Church leaders did not want to risk their own tenuous existence by challenging racism against African Americans, particularly in the South. The majority of Catholics accepted the prevailing racist notions about blacks.[45] James, Alexander, and Patrick Healy—three brothers—were ordained to the priesthood between 1854 and 1864. They were the mixed-race offspring of an Irish slave owner and his enslaved mixed-race mistress. The Healy brothers went to seminary in Canada and Europe since no Catholic seminary in the United States accepted persons with African blood running through their veins. They were ordained in Europe since no bishop in the United States would ordain them. They each served the church in the United States but were considered aberrations and "near white."[46]

The Quakers

The Quakers were by far the most militant religious group addressing the evils of slavery. Once they decided that slavery was morally wrong, they freed the enslaved Africans they owned and in many cases compensated the persons who had served them as slaves. Paying such reparations was unheard of.[47] The Quakers also organized to fight against slavery as an institution in the United States. It is surprising then to find very limited involvement by African Americans in the meetinghouses of the Society of Friends. One reason for this lack of multiracial congregations could be that the Quakers' radical commitment to fight slavery allowed them less access to enslaved persons. Also they did not evangelize African Americans; and prejudice still infected some Quakers—an occasional Friends meeting maintained separate seating by race, and African Americans were often denied membership.[48] Historian Forrest Wood offers another reason that may explain the small number of African American Quakers:

> It seems that for almost everyone the worst thing about slavery . . . was that slaveholders were committing a sin, and any person who did not speak out against bondage was no less guilty in the eyes of God. . . . Needless to say, what was glaringly absent from most of these expressions on the sinfulness of owning slaves was a concern for the suffering of the enslaved. If slavery was an abomination for the slaveholder, *what was it for the slave?* Bondage was a horrible violation of the humanity of what would ultimately be an estimated ten million Africans and their descendants, but these pious spokesmen for Christ saw it mainly as a collective sin that white society must exorcise in order to avoid God's wrath. In other words, they saw *themselves* as victims.[49]

The Church Splits

Given the racism found in most of Christianity it comes as no surprise that the church split along racial lines. That process began in November of 1787 when African American leaders Richard Allen and Absalom Jones left St. George Methodist Episcopal Church in Philadelphia, Pennsylvania, in protest of newly enforced segregation measures. Some of the most noted champions of freedom in the United States, including George Washington and Thomas Jefferson, provided financial assistance to help construct a new church building for Allen's followers.[50] Apparently it did not cross the minds of Washington and Jefferson to challenge the racist practices of the Methodist Episcopal Church. Richard Allen led the formation of an African American Methodist denomination in 1816 called the African Methodist Episcopal Church (AME). A few years later in 1820 another African American Methodist denomination emerged when African Americans left a Methodist Episcopal congregation in New York City. It was named the African Methodist Episcopal Zion Church (AMEZ). Within other denominations in the North, separate congregations for blacks emerged around the same time.

Several predominantly white denominations split over the issue of slavery in the years preceding the Civil War. The Methodist Episcopal Church split in 1844 because of a debate over slave ownership. The southern congregations left and established the Methodist Episcopal Church, South. In 1837 and again in 1857 the Presbyterian Church split. Slavery was one of the issues that predicated the split. In 1845 southerners among the American Baptists left and created the Southern Baptist Convention because of disagreements over the morality of slavery. The Episcopal church overall did not embrace abolition. Historian Gardiner Shattuck Jr. writes, "Abhorring ecclesiastical schisms more than the suffering of people held in bondage, white Episcopalians had argued that slavery was a purely political question and, as such, beyond the church's concern."[51] But they were forced to create a new southern denomination during the secession of the eleven southern states from the Union—Protestant Episcopal Church in the Confederate States of America.

At the conclusion of the Civil War there was a "mass exodus" of African Americans from white denominations and biracial congregations.[52] The Congregationalist denomination resisted segregation in local congregations into the early 1880s but finally caved in to pressure.[53] Many African Americans left the Roman Catholic Church after their emancipation and joined with emerging black Protestant denominations.[54] John Boles offers a powerful summary of what occurred:

> Of course, that freedpersons wanted to leave the biracial churches is a commentary on the less-than-complete equality they had enjoyed in them. Blacks had a strong sense of racial identity, reinforced by their having been slaves and, within the confines of the churches, by their segregated seating. The complete sermons they had heard for years, not just the self-serving words the white ministers directed specifically at them, had engendered in blacks a sense of their moral worth and equality in the sight of God. The biracial churches simultaneously nurtured this sense of moral equality and thwarted it by their conformity to the demands of the slave society. Black participation in the biracial churches—as preachers, deacons, stewards, and Sunday school teachers—had given them practical leadership and administrative experience, as had their islands of autonomy within the demographically biracial churches. Theologically and experientially blacks were ready to seize the moment offered by emancipation to withdraw from their old allegiances and create autonomous denominations. No better evidence of the freedom slaves had not enjoyed in the biracial churches exists than the rapidity with which blacks sought to establish separate denominations after the Civil War.[55]

Opportunities for Racial Reconciliation

Attempts were made during the period of Reconstruction after the Civil War to cross the racial divide in Christianity. The pervasiveness of white racism and the strong desire for freedom among African Americans allowed for little success.[56] Then in the early 1880s a movement emerged in the midwest section of the United States. It was called the Evening Light Saints by some and the Church of God Reformation Movement by others. Presently the group is identified as the Church of God (Anderson, Indiana). Their message was holiness and unity and their spirit was nondenominational. The Church of God defined the concept of holiness in relational terms. They suggested that if individuals embraced the holiness of God they would be able to love each other more perfectly. This perfection in love would automatically lead to unity. The message of unity attracted women who felt called to ministry and African Americans who hungered for a Christianity that could cross the racial divide.[57] Church historian Douglas Strong calls the early Church of God "a radical antidenominational, racially inclusive, egalitarian Holiness group."[58]

The early leaders of the Church of God were fearless in their attempts to preach and practice a message of unity. The church's foremost leader was a brave white minister named Daniel S. Warner. He did not recognize societal barriers. One example was his partnership in leading revivals with Julia A. J. Foote, an African Methodist Episcopal Church preacher who promoted a holiness message. In Warner's ministry with Foote he crossed the boundaries of race, gender, and denomination.[59] Warner refused to tone down his message when preaching in the segregated South. He and his entourage experienced persecution as a result. On one occasion they were attacked by a mob while preaching in Mississippi. Church of God historian Charles E. Brown stated that Warner was "rigid and stern" in his commitment "for justice for the Negro."[60] Another example of the fearless preaching by Church of God ministers occurred at the 1897 Alabama State Camp Meeting. Both African Americans and whites gathered for the services. As an acknowledgment of the legally mandated segregation of the races, a rope extended through the middle of the tent. During one service Lena Shoffner preached from Ephesians 2 about tearing down the "middle wall of partition." Someone from the crowd did exactly what she called for and the rope was removed. Whites and African Americans knelt together in prayer. Later that night a mob dynamited the camp meeting grounds.[61]

In the South in the late 1800s it was nearly impossible to establish a local congregation that was multiracial due to legal segregation. The early Church of God leaders often defied segregation laws by holding interracial worship events. Also African American and white ministers coordinated their efforts in establishing congregations.[62] Meanwhile across the North the Church of God established several multiracial congregations. In places where both whites and African Americans joined the Church of God movement they entered one unified congregation. These efforts at unity were not without critics. By the turn of the century, with the death of first-generation leaders (Warner died in 1895), the Church of God's commitment to racial inclusiveness started to waver. White leaders in the church began to make exceptions to the message of racial unity in the case of evangelism, fellowship, and marriage.[63] In 1909, interracial congregations split by race in Pittsburgh and New York City. This continued throughout the North over the next few years with the racial division of nearly all of the multiracial congregations of the Church of God.[64]

Another major racial rift occurred in the Church of God in 1912 at the annual national convention in Anderson, Indiana. An informal group of white leaders encouraged African American leaders to establish their own national event. The stated reason was that the large numbers of African Americans in attendance deterred whites from attending.[65] This tragic occurrence further severed relationships across racial lines in the Church of God and eventually led to an internal schism. Many African Americans organized themselves under the name National Association of the Church of God. Rather than starting a new African American denomination, African American leaders established a separate organization to empower their ministry. Similar to the "invisible institution" during the days of slavery, the National Association of the Church of God developed as a parallel organization offering a Christian witness counter to the racism in the Church of God.

Even today the Church of God as a national body is more demographically multiracial than most denominations.[66] Yet locally most of its congregations are segregated by race and nationally its leaders collaborate from the context of segregated organizations. Former church official David Telfer sums up the heartbreaking impact on the church at large:

> By 1910, the Church of God was in a position unique in American Christianity. A significant percentage of its national membership included black Christians who were participating freely at the local and national levels of the church. At that time, there were predominantly white and predominantly black church groups in America, but there were few interracial church groups that had black members in large percentages, which was a truer reflection of the ratio of blacks to whites in the population of the United States at the time. If the Church of God reformation movement had not given in to the

prevailing social pressures of the 1910s, it might have had a profound witness to the nation and other American churches on the issue of black-white relationships. This is an opportunity the church has not had in the years since.[67]

As the Church of God struggled with its practice of racial unity, a brief and unusual experiment addressing racism occurred in the Roman Catholic Church. A missionary organization called the St. Joseph's Society of the Sacred Heart for Foreign Missions was established in England in 1866. An outgrowth of this group in the United States emerged as an independent entity in 1893 under the same name without the "Foreign Missions" designation. They came to be known as the Josephites. Their commission was to reach African Americans in the United States.[68] Their first superior general, John R. Slattery, led the community from 1893 to 1904. Under Slattery's leadership this mandate to reach African Americans was taken a step further. He began to recruit African Americans to attend the Josephites' seminary and then enter the priesthood. Soon a few of these recruits were ordained to serve as priests. As we noted above, Catholics have a very high view of the priestly role. John Slattery's empowerment of African Americans as priests produced angry responses from other priests and Catholic members at large. This overwhelmingly negative response caused Slattery to lose his faith in the Church. In 1904 he left his position as superior general of the Josephites and in 1906 he left the Catholic Church completely.[69] As soon as a breakthrough for racial reconciliation began to lift its head, racism scored a knockout.

Yet another opportunity for the emergence of multiracial Christianity erupted in 1906 in Los Angeles, California. An ordained minister of the Church of God (Anderson, Indiana), William Seymour, was at the center of what many have called the birth of the modern Pentecostal movement. Seymour began his involvement with the Church of God in Cincinnati, Ohio, at the turn of the century. He embraced their message of holiness and unity and traveled with other Church of God ministers preaching about reconciliation. In 1905, William Seymour learned of Charles Parham, a white Holiness preacher who was among the first to speak in tongues in the twentieth-century reemergence of Pentecostalism. Seymour attended a ten-week training course offered by Parham and became convinced of the importance of speaking in tongues as the evidence of the baptism of the Holy Spirit. (Due to Parham's racism, Seymour, who was African American, sat outside the door of the room listening to the teaching.) Seymour's newly acquired emphasis on speaking in tongues led to his departure from the Church of God (Anderson, Indiana), which did not approve of such phenomena.[70]

William Seymour eventually found his way to Los Angeles. His preaching emphasis on speaking in tongues made it difficult for him to find a church that embraced him (although he had not yet received the manifestation himself). Eventually he was invited to preach in various individuals' homes. His emerging house congregation began with a few African Americans. In March 1906 some whites joined the congregation. On April 9, 1906, a revival began when Seymour and others began speaking in tongues. News of this event spread quickly. The crowds grew so rapidly that within a week the revivalists relocated to an abandoned building on Azusa Street that at one time had housed an African Methodist Episcopal congregation. Thus came the name, Azusa Street Revival. The congregation took the name Azusa Street Apostolic Faith Mission.[71]

The gatherings were quite amazing because of their diversity. African Americans and whites attended in similar numbers. People of Hispanic, Asian American, and Native American backgrounds as well as from other ethnic groups were often present. Regarding the presence of Hispanics, Eldin Villafañe notes:

> Hispanics have been part and parcel of the Pentecostal Movement since its inception. The Azusa Street revival drew a significant number of Hispanics living in the Los Angeles area. Victor De León tells us that ". . . no one was surprised to see Mexicans around the Azusa street meeting even though the number was not large. Many of them were well-to-do ranchers and very devout Catholics. Nonetheless there were some who had recently arrived from Mexico, and by the turn of the century they found themselves displaced in an environment controlled by the Gringo culture and language." The names of Luis López and Juan Navarro are noted as early participants of the Azusa Street revival, thus among the first Hispanic Pentecostals. Juan Navarro was the first preacher.[72]

It was very unusual and highly significant that an African American was the pastor of this multiracial congregation and revival.

Also, William Seymour empowered women and people of all races into leadership in the worship services and in the administration of the congregation. Strong writes:

> The congregants at Azusa transcended the social distinctions commonly adhered to by the broader culture. They denied the divisiveness of denominations. They washed each other's feet in the manner of the early church. . . . Blacks held positions of spiritual leadership over whites. Women preached to men. Children exhorted their elders. Mexican Americans testified to English-speakers in their own Spanish language—and in unknown languages.[73]

Frank Bartleman, a minister in Los Angeles, remarked, "The 'color line' was washed away in the blood."[74]

The services at the multiracial Azusa Street Apostolic Faith Mission continued for over three years, with three services a day, every day of the week. Pentecostal historian Vinson Synan notes:

> The Azusa Street movement seems to have been a merger of white American holiness religion with worship styles derived from the African-American Christian tradition, which had developed since the days of chattel slavery in the South. The expressive worship and praise at Azusa Street, which included shouting and dancing, had been common among Appalachian whites as well as southern blacks. The admixture of tongues and other charisms with southern black and white music and worship styles created a new and indigenous form of Pentecostalism. . . . The interracial aspects of Azusa Street were a striking exception to the racism and segregation of the times. The phenomenon of blacks and whites worshiping together under a black pastor seemed incredible to many observers.[75]

The Azusa Street Revival ended in 1909 (with a brief resurgence in 1911–1912). The multiracial nature of this congregation proved difficult to sustain when the excitement of revival died down. Racism played a role in the demise of the congregation's multiracial makeup. Many white Pentecostals abhorred the interracial gatherings and spoke against Seymour. There were disputes about approaches to leadership, which had racial overtones. Seymour further isolated himself from the growing Pentecostal movement when he renounced his view that speaking in tongues was the initial evidence of the presence of the Holy Spirit. He believed that the presence of the Holy

Spirit produced unity. When Seymour observed racist whites speaking in tongues he certainly had to change his perspective regarding this as evidence of the Holy Spirit.[76] The Azusa Street congregation eventually became a small predominantly African American congregation.

The Church Splits Again

Pentecostal denominations emerged from the Azusa Street Revival. Several ministers who received the baptism of the Holy Spirit at the Azusa Street Revival returned to their denominations and brought the message of speaking in tongues with them. Others impacted by the revival began new denominations. William Seymour did not launch a denomination. His nondenominational roots from his days in the Church of God (Anderson, Indiana) were deep. Many of these Pentecostal denominations began as interracial groups. Yet all the denominations split by race within a few years.

The Fire-Baptized Holiness Church began in 1898 as a multiracial denomination, became Pentecostal as a result of the Azusa Street Revival, but had split racially by 1908. The Church of God in Christ incorporated in 1897. Charles H. Mason, bishop of the Church of God in Christ, attended the revival and left with a multiracial commitment. The Church of God in Christ was the only Pentecostal denomination at the time that could legally credential ministers. Hundreds of ministers, both African American and white, joined the denomination. There were about as many white congregations as African American congregations in the Church of God in Christ during the first few years following the Azusa Street Revival. Yet in 1914, many white Church of God in Christ ministers left and joined with other white ministers to form the Assemblies of God denomination. The Pentecostal Assemblies of the World was a multiracial denomination from 1919 to 1924. In the years from 1924 to 1937 many whites departed, leaving it a predominantly African American denomination. Most of these multiracial denominations had racially separate congregations.[77] The Assemblies of God experienced another racial split in the 1920s when many Hispanic congregations left and started their own denomination—*Asamblea de Iglesias Cristianos*.[78] The reason stated by their leader, Francisco Olazabal, was "because the 'gringos' had control."[79]

Rituals of Racism

In the 1920s a number of preachers were very active in white supremacist organizations. Approximately forty thousand ministers were members of the Ku Klux Klan with Protestant ministers serving as Grand
Dragons in Pennsylvania, Texas, North Dakota, and Colorado. In his
book *Rituals of Blood: Consequences of Slavery in Two American
Centuries,* social critic and scholar Orlando Patterson quotes Wyn
Wade describing the religious nature of Klan activities:

> The Klan's cross burnings in the 1920s were invariably constrained
> by a strict Christian ritual. The ceremony opened with a prayer. . . .
> The multitude then sang, "Onward Christian Soldiers!" After the
> hymn, the cross was lit and the explosion of kerosene and the rush
> of flames over the timbers were thrilling, to say the least. . . .
> Children sometimes wet their pants. . . . Bathed in warmth, left arm
> outstretched toward the blazing icon and voices raised in "The Old
> Rugged Cross," Klansmen felt as one body. These were moments
> they would always remember.[80]

Lynchings also had the feel of a religious worship service. The
white victimizers would preach sermons and whip the crowd into a
frenzied state. The African American victims would often pray to
God, quote Scripture, or sing a hymn. One person who had been tied
to a tree was heard singing the hymn, "Nearer My God to Thee" as he
burned to death.[81] The troubling image of enslaved Africans and
European slaveholders standing side by side praying, with which we
began this chapter, was repeated in the equally disturbing lynchings.

Conclusion

As we have noted in this chapter, there were some brilliant moments
when reconciliation was being practiced. At times it seemed as though
the diverse congregations of the first-century church might reappear. But
racism could not be kept at bay. The institutionalization of slavery disrupted the time of indentured servants worshiping together without
regard to color. Separate seating and other segregation measures defeat-
ed the egalitarian implications of the biracial congregations emerging
from the Great Awakening revivals. A second generation of leadership in
the Church of God (Anderson, Indiana) fell prey to societal norms and

interracial congregations split by race. The Roman Catholic Church could not embrace the thought of African Americans representing Christ as priests at the altar. Racial discord sabotaged the multiracial congregation and revival that exploded on Azusa Street. The possibility of multiracial congregations was minimized when most denominations divided by race. Segregation in the United States and in local congregations was fully entrenched by the second quarter of the twentieth century.

Church historian Lester B. Scherer's comments regarding the period of 1619–1819 are applicable to this entire chapter. He writes:

> Christian faith and community usually displayed no special potency for insulating white people from the prevailing attitudes toward black people. . . . Christian instruction did not dissolve the prejudices; the ecstasy of conversion in the revival services did not expel them. In Christian imagination the blacks were a people apart, to be assessed by different criteria from whites. That perception tainted all approaches to black people, even those designed to relieve or liberate them. . . . The same defect of imagination that made it possible to enslave Africans in the first place made it virtually impossible for whites to envision them as authentic co-members of any community, including a Christian congregation. . . . The behavior of white people at the point of congregational life is significant because it shows how they really felt. Expelling slaveholders would have carried a grave political threat to the survival of the church; but seating free blacks indiscriminately would not. The threat was rather a personal one, for there was in church membership the expectation of warm mutual respect and sometimes of chaste intimacy. White Christians could sometimes manage pity for blacks but rarely respect or intimacy. Christian fellowship stopped at the color line.[82]

The history of the church in the United States leads one to believe that sustaining multiracial congregations is a near impossibility due to racism. One wonders, what happened to the faith that could reconcile people in the first century? Christianity in the United States became a principal divider of people by race. People believed they were saved and sanctified, born again, received into the mystical Body of Christ, baptized in the Spirit, and speaking in tongues. Yet they could not believe that God was able to reconcile people across racial lines. Perhaps W. E. B. DuBois was right when he wrote in 1929, "The American Church of Christ is Jim Crowed from top to bottom. No other institution in America is built so thoroughly or more absolutely on the color line. Everybody knows this."[83]

4 | THE EMERGENCE OF MULTIRACIAL CONGREGATIONS (1940–2000)

A small group of African American religious leaders made a pilgrimage to India in 1935. Among those on the journey was mystic theologian Howard Thurman, who would become the foremost proponent of racial reconciliation in the United States from the 1940s through the 1970s. Thurman was in his mid-thirties and a professor at Howard University in Washington, D.C. The most memorable exchange on this trip was a conversation between the African American delegation and Mohandas Gandhi. When responding to a question regarding race relations in the United States, the Mahatma stated that it would be through the African American struggle for freedom in the United States that "the unadulterated message of nonviolence" would reach the world.[1] Looking back on the twentieth century, Gandhi's words proved true. The rise of Martin Luther King Jr. and the civil rights movement influenced freedom movements in South Africa, a divided Germany, China, and elsewhere.

While in India, Howard Thurman was asked repeatedly, "Why is the church powerless before the color bar?" In reflecting on this question, Thurman wrote, "All answers had to be defensive because there was not a *single instance* known to me in which a local church had a completely integrated membership. The color bar was honored in the practice of the Christian religion."[2] While in the Khyber Pass and before leaving India, Thurman and his wife, Sue, paused to reflect on the events of their trip. The Thurmans experienced a mystical moment of vision and insight. As Howard Thurman described the encounter,

> We saw clearly what we must do somehow when we returned to America. We knew that we must test whether a religious fellowship could be developed in America that was capable of cutting across all racial barriers, with a carry-over into the common life, a fellowship that would alter the behavior patterns of those involved. It became imperative now to find out if experiences of spiritual unity among people could be more compelling than the experiences which divide them.[3]

Beginning in the 1940s, the twentieth century became a time for experimentation with multiracial congregations and racial reconciliation. In this chapter we examine some of these endeavors, starting with Howard Thurman's attempt to realize his vision.

The Church for the Fellowship of All Peoples

Nearly ten years after the visionary experience in the Khyber Pass in India, Howard Thurman embraced an opportunity to make this vision a reality in the setting of a local congregation—the Church for the Fellowship of All Peoples in San Francisco, California.[4] Many consider this congregation the first truly integrated congregation in the United States. Former president of Morehouse College Benjamin Mays wrote, "At the time it was the only integrated congregation in both leadership and membership in America."[5] The idea for this congregation originated with a white ordained Presbyterian minister and professor named Alfred G. Fisk. In the early 1940s, he and a few other people organized worship services in an area of the city inhabited predominantly by African Americans. These worship services were interracial gatherings. The emerging congregation called themselves the Neighborhood Church.

Alfred Fisk served as a part-time pastor for the congregation. Yet he recognized the need for a co-pastor who was African American. He requested that Howard Thurman recommend an African American theology student who could serve as a part-time co-pastor. Thurman first tried to help Fisk find someone. The more Thurman looked, the more he began to sense a personal interest in the position. Thurman wrote, "I felt a touch on my shoulder that was one with the creative encounter with the Khyber Pass dream of several years earlier."[6] So he finally wrote and informed Fisk that he would like to be considered for the co-pastor position. The Thurman family arrived in San Francisco in the summer of 1944. The inaugural service for the newly named Church for the Fellowship of all Peoples occurred in October of 1944. Thurman soon became a full-time pastor with Fisk serving in a part-time capacity. They alternated their preaching in order to maintain an interracial character in the pulpit. This provided a rich image for promoting a new way of life together in a local congregation.

While the Presbyterian denomination had invested much in the development of this congregation, ultimately Fellowship Church determined that the best choice was not to affiliate with any denomination. This enabled the congregation to develop an "interracial, interdenominational, and international quality."[7] As Thurman stated, "Fellowship Church was a unique idea, fresh, untried. There were no precedents and no traditions to aid in structuring the present or gauging the future."[8] Yet Thurman felt he had two insights from his experience to aid him: "a profound conviction that meaningful and creative experiences between peoples can be more compelling than all the ideas, concepts, faiths, fears, ideologies, and prejudices that divide them; and absolute faith that if such experiences can be multiplied and sustained over a time interval of sufficient duration *any* barrier that separates one person from another can be undermined and eliminated."[9]

The vision of Fellowship Church attracted many people. The congregation began with less than fifty members but grew to about 350 resident members. Two types of membership were available. Resident membership was for those who participated full time in the life of the congregation. For persons who wanted to affiliate with the vision of Fellowship Church and support it but lived too far away or did not choose to leave their denominational church, the congregation offered the option of becoming members-at-large. Over a thousand people from across the nation and around the world selected this designation, including Mary MacLeod Bethune, Eleanor Roosevelt, and Alan Paton.

The resident membership of Fellowship Church was always multiracial. During Howard Thurman's nine-year tenure, the congregation was about 60 percent white, 35 percent African American, and 5 percent Asian and Hispanic. In the years since Thurman departed to become the Dean of Chapel and Professor of Spiritual Disciplines at Boston University (where he would encounter a doctoral student named Martin Luther King Jr.), the congregation fluctuated in membership. When doctoral student Barnett Grier did a study of the congregation in 1982 the average Sunday attendance was thirty-five persons with a racial composition of 50 percent African American, 47 percent white, and 3 percent other racial groups.[10] In 1997, a newsletter of a neighborhood organization where the church building is located described the congregation as having fewer than one hundred members.[11]

The development of the Church for the Fellowship of all Peoples in San Francisco was a breakthrough in Christianity and in the belief that multiracial congregations were possible in the United States. It still serves as a signpost for anyone stepping out in faith to believe that first-century Christianity can be reproduced. Theologian Luther Smith Jr. writes, "Fellowship Church's importance to American Christianity is not in being the progenitor of a major denominational or ecclesiastical movement, but in possibilities it demonstrated for inclusive church worship and fellowship."[12] Thurman scholar Alton B. Pollard III summarized the impact of Fellowship Church:

> For Thurman, this was the chance to conclusively determine whether institutional religion could develop a model which annealed separations rooted in socio-economic standing, gender, age, denomination, and race. He was particularly hopeful for the dissolution of barriers of race and culture within Fellowship Church, thereby serving as a decisive conduit for societal change. . . . The degree of cooperation realized within the congregation caused it to often be singled out as an unusual, unique and even "peculiar" church. And yet this was precisely what caused Thurman so much anguish, because in his estimation it was not Fellowship Church but American Christianity which was the "peculiar institution."[13]

Other Congregations in the United States

Most congregations in the 1940s and 1950s were not like Fellowship Church. Sociologist Frank Loescher did a study in 1946 of local congregations and their racial composition. He estimated that only about eight thousand African Americans of the eight million who were Protestants attended interracial congregations—that is, one tenth of 1 percent of African American Protestants. Most were members of African American denominations and the remainder were involved in uniracial African American congregations of other denominations.[14] Loescher observed that congregations "resisted" the migration of African Americans into white neighborhoods. When transition occurred, most of these congregations sold their buildings to an African American church and fled the neighborhood.[15] A study done by the Southern Regional Council in 1959 reported that there were "no more than twenty white churches" with African American participants in eleven southern states. Of these, 75 percent were Unitarian congregations. Therefore only five or six white Christian congregations in the South had any African Americans attending Sunday worship services.[16]

Fellowship Church was not the only congregation experimenting with racial reconciliation in the 1940s and 1950s. Historian David Reimers, in *White Protestantism and the Negro,* draws attention to a few other congregations with similar aspirations including the South Berkeley Community Church in Berkeley, California; South Congregational Church in Chicago, Illinois; All Peoples' Christian Church and Community Center in Los Angeles, California; First Presbyterian Church in Chicago, Illinois; and West Cincinnati–St. Barnabus Church in Cincinnati, Ohio.[17] These congregations were white churches inviting the participation of African Americans as members and in some cases on the pastoral staff. There were also some predominantly African American congregations that embraced whites into their membership. Bidwell Presbyterian Church in Pittsburgh, Pennsylvania, and Metropolitan Church of God in Detroit, Michigan, were two such congregations.[18]

Another congregation noted by Reimers was the East Harlem Protestant Parish in New York City.[19] This congregation was launched in 1948 by four denominations (later eight participated). The congregation was founded to witness to the Gospel's call to minister among the poor. Yet their interracial composition (African Americans, Puerto Ricans, and whites) and racially diverse pastoral team offered the community another powerful witness. George Webber, one of the founders of the East Harlem Protestant Parish, writes:

> When in America the churches are divided along racial lines, the power of the gospel to overcome our human differences is denied. But when by the grace of God a congregation, set in the midst of our broken, hostile world, does by its life together truly overcome this disunity, it is an incredible witness to the miracle of the gospel. . . . I am persuaded that in East Harlem our churches would have grown far more quickly had we been willing to appeal to one racial group rather than to seek always to reflect the racial composition of the community. . . . Clearly when a church does stand fast and in its life brings together people of different races, the world does not ignore the witness.[20]

The Catholic Church began to integrate its congregations more aggressively in the 1950s.[21] Prior to the turn of the century the Josephites order ordained African Americans as priests under the leadership of John Slattery. There was much resistance in the church to Slattery. He left his leadership post and eventually the Catholic Church as a result. But the Josephites continued to ordain African Americans. In the early 1950s, Catholic Bishops in the South responded to pressure from African American priests and began to address segregation in Louisiana, North Carolina, Mississippi, Texas, and elsewhere. They ended segregation in seating, confessional, and communion; also, segregated congregations and schools were challenged to integrate. When Joseph F. Rummel, archbishop of New Orleans, declared that segregation was "sinful and morally wrong," he faced criticism from politicians in Louisiana and Mississippi.[22]

Archbishop Rummel received more than verbal criticism when he sent African American priests to say Mass in his Louisiana parishes. In October of 1955, Gerald Lewis was sent to preside at the Mass held in St. Cecilia's Chapel in Jesuit Bend, Louisiana. He arrived on Saturday. After midnight he received an anonymous phone call warning him not to say Mass at the church. Lewis ignored the threat. When he arrived at the church, three congregation members accompanied by two police officers informed him that he could not enter the building. They would not allow an African American priest to say Mass. The archbishop considered this action an insult to the priesthood and suspended Mass at St. Cecilia's until the congregation would agree to accept any priest sent, no matter what race. Rummel received support for his actions from national civil rights leaders such as A. Philip Randolph and from the Vatican.

By November, the crisis exploded when one white segregationist "formed a citizens' council to keep black priests from offering Mass in the area." The group developed a petition declaring that integration contradicted church teaching. One person stated, "If no white priest is available, let the church remain closed."[23] The church remained closed for two and one-half years. Finally a few white church members signed a document saying they would accept whatever priest was sent to their congregation. Rummel decided that a few people in agreement constituted progress. St. Cecilia's Chapel reopened on Easter Sunday in 1958 with fifty-five whites and twenty-five African Americans attending Mass. Two months later St. Cecilia's Chapel was destroyed by a hurricane.

Civil Rights Activism

Many Protestant congregations also resisted racial integration. The civil rights movement in the 1950s and 1960s encouraged church leaders to bring attention to this matter in the southern United States. In the spirit of the sit-ins and the freedom rides, a movement of "church visits" gained momentum.[24] The premise of these church visits was that either an interracial team or a group of African Americans would arrive for worship on Sunday morning at segregated white congregations to see whether they would be seated. In most cases, they were not. As a part of the civil rights actions that occurred in Birmingham, Alabama, during the spring of 1963, groups of African Americans (sometimes with whites) attempted to attend worship services during Holy Week. They were not allowed to worship with white churchgoers.

Shortly thereafter, a white Methodist clergyman and former student of Howard Thurman, Ed King, decided to launch similar actions in Jackson, Mississippi. African Americans arrived to attend worship services in June 1963 at two all-white congregations: First Baptist

Church and Galloway Memorial Methodist Church. They were not allowed into the church buildings. The pastor at Galloway Church, W. B. Selah, was troubled when he learned of this occurrence. He informed his congregation "there can be no color bar in a Christian church."[25] The congregants of Galloway Memorial Methodist Church held to the policy they had approved earlier that year:

> It is not un-Christian that we prefer to remain an all-white congregation. The practice of the separation of the races in Galloway Memorial Methodist Church is a time-honored tradition. We earnestly hope that the perpetuation of that tradition will never be impaired.[26]

Selah would not compromise his faith and the message of Jesus Christ. So he requested that the bishop appoint him to another congregation.

Ed King continued to organize groups to attend services at white congregations in Jackson. These groups were blocked from entrance and often arrested by police. By the summer of 1964, over forty individuals had been arrested for "disturbing a worship service."[27] Even Methodist Church bishops could not gain entrance to Methodist congregations if they were African American, or white and accompanying a group with African Americans. In one case, a member of Galloway Memorial Methodist Church was arrested. A white science teacher from a local college had joined the church hoping to influence the congregation's attitudes regarding racial separation. In October of 1963, he invited an African American student and two white Methodist clergy visiting from out of state to visit the Sunday School class he taught. They entered the congregation without difficulty. Soon several police officers arrived on the scene and proceeded to arrest the African American student, the two white clergy, and the science teacher who was a member of the congregation. Theologian and historian Charles Marsh reflects on this incident, "Although many people had certainly been arrested for praying and worshiping God in prohibited places, no one in the civil rights movement (or perhaps in the history of the Christian church) has ever been arrested for the crime of attending his own church."[28]

Similar events were transpiring in other places through the efforts of the Episcopal Society for Cultural and Racial Unity (ESCRU).[29]

The ESCRU would often conduct church visits to segregated white Episcopal congregations while involved in civil rights campaigns sponsored by the Southern Christian Leadership Conference—headed by Martin Luther King Jr. In May of 1965, a group of African American Episcopalians attempted to attend a worship service in St. Augustine, Florida. The ushers blocked them from entering. Then a member of the group directed the ushers' attention to a church sign that stated, "The Episcopal Church Welcomes You." One usher responded that the message on the sign did not include African Americans. When the rector of the congregation learned what was occurring on the steps of his church, he declared that as rector he could admit anyone to worship and then escorted the African American Episcopalians into the sanctuary. The rector soon lost his job.[30]

The ESCRU also showed up at an all-white Episcopalian congregation in Selma, Alabama, during the civil rights campaign sponsored by the Southern Christian Leadership Conference and the Student Nonviolent Coordinating Committee. Again, African American visitors and whites accompanying them were not allowed to take a seat in the church. On one visit, a white suffragan bishop from Michigan, Kim Meyers, attempted to enter the congregation on a Sunday, "arguing that—as a bishop—he had a moral right to celebrate the Eucharist at the altar of any Episcopal parish he visited."[31] Because of his civil rights involvement, he was not allowed access. So as Myers and two hundred others who had gathered in Selma for the civil rights action campaign stood outside this congregation, he "recited the penitential office from the Prayer Book."[32] Then they marched to the Brown Chapel AME Church where the civil rights activists were convening and celebrated the Eucharist outside on the sidewalk with the press capturing the moment. The Episcopal congregation finally relented and allowed African Americans to attend if they would "sit at the back of the church and take communion only after all whites in the congregation had received it."[33] The ESCRU appealed to the bishop who oversaw the congregations in Selma, with no success. So members of the ESCRU carried signs outside the diocesan headquarters "proclaiming that white Episcopalians in Selma had resurrected the 'slave gallery' custom of antebellum times."[34]

Multiracial Congregations Today

The civil rights movement of the 1950s and 1960s in the United States brought greater awareness to the church's role in racial division and its potential for racial reconciliation. In New York City, the Riverside Church provided movement leaders with a national pulpit when Martin Luther King Jr. gave his speech against the Vietnam War in 1967 and James Forman delivered the Black Manifesto in 1969. The Riverside Church was well suited for this role, having become multiracial in the 1950s (see chapter five for an extended discussion). The last forty years have seen the rise of some large multiracial congregations. In the mid-1960s, the Glide Memorial United Methodist Church in San Francisco, California, modeled the vision and philosophy of the civil rights movement and worldwide liberation struggles when it began to embrace all kinds of people. Under the pastoral leadership of Cecil Williams, the congregation became home to thousands of people from all races and cultures. The congregation is particularly well known for its recovery ministries.[35]

In the 1970s, the multiracial spirit of the Azusa Street Revival returned to some congregations within Pentecostalism. One such place was the Brooklyn Tabernacle in New York City. Jim Cymbala arrived as the pastor at the small congregation in 1971. During the thirty years of Cymbala's leadership, the congregation has grown to nearly ten thousand members. The congregation also is home to the Grammy Award–winning Brooklyn Tabernacle Choir directed by his wife, Carol Cymbala. This choir developed a very engaging form of multicultural worship.[36] Another example of the Azusa spirit in Pentecostalism emerged in the mid-1990s when Ché Ahn launched the multiethnic, multiracial Harvest Rock Church in Pasadena, California. The congregation began in 1994 in Ahn's living room. By 1995, three other congregations had merged with the original group.[37] The spirit of reconciliation also impacted Pentecostalism's denominational arrangements. In 1948 the Pentecostal Fellowship of North America (PFNA) was established as an organization to represent Pentecostals. Unfortunately, it included only white denominations. In 1994, in what was dubbed the "Memphis Miracle," the PFNA was disbanded and a new inclusive organization called the Pentecostal and Charismatic Churches of North America was formed. The first leader of the new group was the bishop of the predominantly African American denomination, the Church of God in Christ.[38]

The Church of God (Anderson, Indiana) also saw its vision of unity reemerge in some congregations.[39] Four examples of this are congregations pastored by Daniel Harden (white Anglo), Gayle Salter (African American), Ed Davila (Hispanic), and Paul Sheppard (African American). Their stories illustrate the many ways congregations become multiracial. The long-term pastorate of Daniel Harden at the Kendall Church of God in Miami, Florida, has resulted in a congregation of nearly six hundred people from a wide range of racial and cultural groups. The congregation has changed from the primarily white congregation that existed when Harden arrived in 1981 to one in which the largest group of people is from the West Indies. The racial makeup of the congregation is 50 percent Jamaican, 12 percent Hispanic, 10 percent white Anglo, 9 percent Haitian, 8 percent African American, 7 percent Islanders (other West Indians), and 4 percent Asians and others. Harden believes that pastoral visitation was significant in the development of the Kendall congregation. "I personally visited in the home of families that visited our church. It was like magic. When a family of color found that the pastor came to their home, they saw that as acceptance." The Kendall Church of God describes itself as a congregation that is "international, intercultural, interdenominational, and interesting."[40]

Gayle Salter and Ed Davila both pioneered multiracial congregations. In 1988, Gayle Salter started the Eastside Church of God in Warren, Ohio. From the beginning she did not narrow her vision to one group of people. For much of the history of the congregation the racial makeup was nearly evenly divided among African Americans and whites. At this writing the congregation is approximately 65 percent white and 35 percent African American. For many whites, Salter was their first African American pastor and for most members of the congregation she was their first female pastor.[41] In 1995, Ed Davila launched the River City Christian Outreach in San Antonio, Texas, a congregation of less than one hundred members now nearly evenly divided among Latinos, African Americans, and whites. Like Gayle Salter, when Davila sought to start a congregation he did not target a certain racial group. Initially the congregation was mostly Hispanics and whites. In recent years, the River City church has become the home of African Americans as well. Ed Davila and the leadership are intentional about being relevant to the diversity in the congregation.[42]

One of the fastest growing congregations in the Church of God (Anderson, Indiana) is the Abundant Life Christian Fellowship in Menlo Park, California.[43] In 1989, Paul Sheppard assumed the pastorate of a small congregation of thirty-four African Americans. The congregation had grown to three hundred members by 1996 and now has nearly 2,500 active members. Sheppard notes, "What was once a small Black church has evolved into a thriving multi-ethnic family of believers." The congregation's racial makeup is approximately 55 percent African American, 35 percent white, 15 percent Asian, and 5 percent Hispanic, Pacific Islander, Arabs, and people from India. The staff at the Abundant Life congregation is very diverse and representative of the racial makeup of the congregation.

Abundant Life Christian Fellowship did not set out to be multiracial. In fact, they assumed that they would reach primarily African Americans. They discovered that their "plain, practical, and humorous" Bible teaching, soulful worship, friendly people, flexible dress code, ninety-minute worship services, and lack of "churchy" language, appealed to a wide range of people. Paul Sheppard notes:

> Once the diversity began, we learned to welcome it, celebrate it, and be intentional about addressing the problems it creates. For instance, over the years we've convened informal racial reconciliation forums so that members could dialogue, admit their struggles, confess wrong attitudes, encourage each other, and pray for genuine unity. In addition I tactfully confront and challenge the narrowness and bigotry of White, conservative evangelicals whenever the text I'm covering allows for it (e.g., political decisions that have racial undertones, the so called "even playing field" that has made affirmative action unnecessary, etc.).

Several books by pastors of multiracial congregations were published in the 1990s. The two Pentecostal pastors noted above were among these: Jim Cymbala of the Brooklyn Tabernacle wrote *Fresh Wind, Fresh Fire,* and Ché Ahn of Harvest Rock Church wrote *Into the Fire: How You Can Enter Renewal and Catch God's Holy Fire.* Also,

Ken Hutcherson of Antioch Bible Church in East Seattle, Washington, wrote *Here Comes the Bride;* Norman Anthony Peart of Grace Bible Fellowship in Cary, North Carolina, wrote *Separate No More: Understanding and Developing Racial Reconciliation in Your Church;* and Stephen A. Rhodes, pastor of Culmore United Methodist Church in Falls Church, Virginia, from 1991 to 1999, wrote *Where the Nations Meet: The Church in a Multicultural World.*[44]

Multiracial congregations are still few and far between. In our work with the Multiracial Congregations Project we discovered that only 5½ percent of Christian congregations in the United States are multiracial (less than 80 percent of the membership is from any one racial group). Their rarity means they remain front-page news. In 1999, *USA Weekend* featured Unity Baptist Church of St. Paul, Minnesota, as its cover story. The article detailed the merger of an African American Baptist congregation and a white Baptist congregation.[45] In 2000, the *New York Times* used the story of the multiracial Assembly of God Tabernacle in Decatur, Georgia, to describe the state of race relations in the United States.[46]

The twenty-first century holds the potential to be the century of the multiracial congregation, despite the relatively small percentage such churches represent among total congregations. The broad population shifts taking place in the United States are expected by the midpoint of the century to produce a country with a racial demographic that is very diverse and without a numeric majority. Such changes produce settings with an increased possibility for multiracial congregations. A movement toward more multiracial congregations must be the cutting edge for ministry and growth in this century. We look inside the life of four such congregations to gain a glimpse of what is possible for the future of the Christian church.

5 | A CLOSER LOOK AT FOUR MULTIRACIAL CONGREGATIONS

On Sunday, September 23, 2001, thousands of people—of all races and religions—gathered at Yankee Stadium in New York City to pray and to mourn the tragic losses of the September 11 terrorist attacks on the World Trade Center and the Pentagon. Celebrity host Oprah Winfrey was on the stage, along with a veritable "who's who" of the New York community: Senator Hillary Rodham Clinton, former president Bill Clinton, Governor George Pataki, and Mayor Rudolph Giuliani. The true leaders of this ceremony were another group of influential New Yorkers—the clergy. Among the clergy was James A. Forbes Jr., senior pastor of the Riverside Church in the city of New York. It was only fitting that Forbes participated in the ceremony because the historic Riverside Church has been and continues to be among the most prominent churches in the nation. Riverside Church is also one of the oldest and largest multiracial congregations in the country. Its commitment to internal reconciliation has prepared the congregation to go out into public places that need healing. Multiracial congregations will be called on in the years ahead to use their experience to provide a healing salve for the wounds of racial division, cultural misunderstandings, and even the lingering pain of traumatic events.

During the course of our extensive site visits and interviews with church members and clergy, we identified a number of congregations that fit our criteria for being considered "multiracial." We define a multiracial church as a congregation in which no one racial group is 80 percent or more of the people. We use the cutoff of 20 percent of the people of a different race or races because this is the point of critical mass. Mathematically, assuming people randomly meet twenty others in the congregation, each person has a 99 percent chance of meeting someone of another race. In many of these congregations, we found sincere efforts on the part of the clergy as well as members to truly integrate the congregation despite racial and ethnic differences. Multiracial congregations can be found in various denominations having memberships of less than 100 to some with several thousand.

We highlight four of these efforts to share some of the work that is being done for the sake of unity. Nevertheless, we must acknowledge that these congregations, like all organizations, are inherently imperfect. Although we focus on positive efforts on the part of the churches, we know that not everyone has had positive experiences in multiracial congregations. In fact, we have heard of persistent racial insensitivity as well as continuing de facto segregation by race and ethnic group within some technically "multiracial" congregations. These are certainly causes for concern and in chapters six, seven, eight, and ten we address these issues. But in this chapter we focus on the "sincere efforts" made by four congregations, which go far above and beyond the norm of congregations in the United States. They have made an important first step, or series of first steps, and we discuss them here.

It so happens that all four of the congregations we describe here evolved from all-white churches. As we have shown earlier there are many models for developing multiracial congregations. They can emerge from congregations serving persons of color reaching out to a different racial group, through mergers of uniracial congregations, or by starting a new congregation with the intent of its being multiracial. All these models can be successful. The four congregations chosen for closer examination here were selected on the basis of certain criteria. They have a history of being multiracial for a number of years and through more than one pastoral administration. That is, they have demonstrated that their multiracial character is more than a phase in the congregation's life based on the whim of certain leaders or the midpoint of a neighborhood transition. Given the racism in the United States, this criterion meant that most of the choices would be congregations that were originally populated by whites. Also there is variation by region and denomination in the selections. We begin with the Riverside Church.

The Riverside Church of New York City

The Riverside Church in New York City is an interdenominational, liberal, mainline Protestant church, born out of the modernist movement of the earlier twentieth century.[1] The church has been self-characterized as "interdenominational, interracial, and international," but it maintains affiliations with the American Baptist Churches as well as the United Church of Christ. The church began as the Fifth Avenue Baptist Church in Manhattan, a congregation whose members were predominantly wealthy and white. In Fifth Avenue Baptist's quest for a new pastor, lay leader John D. Rockefeller Jr. became determined to hire Harry Emerson Fosdick, who was a strong advocate of the liberal tradition. He had gained fame and notoriety for his stance against fundamentalists as illustrated by his sermon "Shall the Fundamentalists Win?" Fosdick, one of the nation's most prominent preachers at the time, declined the offer several times, noting that he did not want to be merely a "private chaplain to a fairly small group of extremely wealthy people in Manhattan's most affluent residential neighborhood."[2] In response, Rockefeller proposed that a new, larger church be built in Morningside Heights, thereby allowing Fosdick to reach a larger metropolitan audience and opening up the congregation to those of different cultures and classes. Thus, from the beginning, there was a vision that the church would overcome barriers of race and class. Nevertheless, this vision would take many years to come to fruition.

Construction of the new church building began in 1927 and was largely funded by Rockefeller himself. When a 1928 fire caused a major setback in construction, Rabbi Nathan Krass helped the congregation by arranging for it to meet in Temple Emanuel for one year. When the first Sunday service was held at the new church on October 5, 1930, six thousand people sought to attend. *The Christian*

Century heralded it as "an event of arresting importance in American church life."[3] Fosdick became a major preaching personality and best-selling author who attracted large crowds to his Sunday services. His new ministry in the very large and expensive Gothic church located across from Grant's Tomb on the banks of the Hudson River heightened national interest. Furthermore, the church was also seen as an attempt to take the gospel to the most difficult of mission fields—higher education. The new church's location next to great centers of learning enhanced its far-reaching potential.

The Riverside Church's location has been important in its development and history. In the area immediately surrounding the church are such prominent centers of learning as Columbia University, the Manhattan School of Music, Jewish Theological Seminary, and Union Theological Seminary. Riverside has had a close relationship with its neighbors, drawing many pastors, staff, and members from their faculty and student bodies. The church also became international in the sense that it has reached out to international students in these institutions since the 1930s through language and assistance programs. The church's Morningside Heights location means that it also borders Harlem, the most famous African American neighborhood in the United States.

Although the church was founded by predominantly white, upper-class, liberal Protestants, many African Americans and Hispanics joined the church during the tenure of the second senior pastor, Scottish preacher Robert James McCracken. Former Morehouse University president Benjamin E. Mays confirmed this in his 1957 book, *Seeking to Be Christian in Race Relations:* "For many years Riverside Church in New York City has been open to all races."[4] When McCracken retired from the pulpit in 1967, he was remembered for his stands against McCarthyism, conformism, and the religion of Positive Thinking in the 1950s. He was also honored for his early support of the civil rights movement and early opposition to the war in Vietnam. In fact, Martin Luther King Jr. took his stand against the war in Vietnam from McCracken's Riverside Church pulpit. McCracken provided strong moral leadership on the racial issues confronting Riverside. His sermon "Discrimination—the Shame of Sunday Morning" appeared in *The Pulpit* in February 1955 and was widely noted. McCracken preached an evangelical faith that crossed racial lines, class, and language and sought to "transform unjust social structures rather than to accommodate them."[5]

Decades after McCracken's tenure, his student from Union Theological Seminary, James A. Forbes Jr., preaches on Sundays at 10:45 A.M. to over two thousand people in the magnificent Riverside Church complex. Forbes was chosen in 1989 from over two hundred applicants, and with his selection became Riverside's first African American senior pastor. During Forbes's student days at Union Theological Seminary, he served in a summer internship at a predominantly white church in North Carolina as part of an experiment in interracial pastorates.[6] This experience certainly laid a foundation for what awaited him as the pastor of Riverside. Forbes returned to Union Theological Seminary as a professor of homiletics in 1976 and was a frequent and popular guest preacher at Riverside. He is known for his eloquent and moving sermons, having built a national reputation as a "preacher's preacher."

On an average Sunday, about 2,200 worshipers fill the church. As they enter the church doors, members and visitors alike are heartily greeted by a team of ushers. Despite the large size, the church members exude a warmth that immediately puts visitors at ease. Congregants sit integrated in the pews and they hug and greet one another by name during the time in the service when they "pass the peace." People of different races and ages sit in their Sunday dress attire, with some of the black women wearing hats. While regular members tend to dress more formally, backpack-toting tourists in shorts and T-shirts are also completely at ease. Although the congregation is racially integrated, its members tend to be middle class. One cannot exactly tell the membership composition of the church by merely attending services. On any given Sunday, nearly one third of those in attendance are visitors. Because more of the visitors tend to be white, a casual Sunday observer would be led to believe that the church is about half white and half African American.

When James Forbes arrived at Riverside, the congregation was approximately 60 percent white and 40 percent African American. Within a few years, the ratio became 50 percent white and 50 percent African American. Today, the congregational membership seems to have stabilized at about 65 percent African American and 35 percent white, with a "sprinkling" of people of Asian and Latino backgrounds.

The main choir is about 75 percent white and 25 percent African American, while the inspirational choir is 95 percent African American and 5 percent white. The ushers are predominantly African American, as are the staff members. The church elected its first African American deacon in 1958 and its first African American trustee in 1970. It hired its first African American minister in 1960 and its first African American administrator in 1975, with Forbes becoming its first African American senior pastor in 1989. The Hispanic Ministry began in the late 1950s and the Black Christian Caucus began in the late 1960s. According to Forbes, most of the racial integration that has occurred within the church is due to demographic factors. The neighborhood itself has been open to a variety of racial groups by virtue of mixed-race housing projects for all economic levels and institutions of higher education.

From its founding, however, the church was open to different groups and was especially active in the fight for civil rights. Two significant events in the struggle for human rights in the Christian Church in the United States occurred at Riverside Church. In 1969, James Forman disrupted a Sunday service and delivered the "Black Manifesto," calling for reparations for slavery from white churches.[7] Forbes recounts the church's racial history as it relates to African Americans:

> This church was always on the edge first of charity toward and then later openness to blacks slowly coming in to this congregation. I would say the demographics would, I believe, be the major factor in the shift to integrated leadership. Black members kept coming. By the time my candidacy came up, I was elected (so far as I could tell) almost unanimously. It was probably because this congregation had wrestled with the Black Manifesto being presented here in 1969. King was assassinated in '68 and in '69 James Forman delivered his manifesto here challenging white churches to give money back for reparations, and Riverside Church did raise money to help contribute toward black causes.

Interestingly, in 1981, the Coalition of Hispanic Christian Leadership interrupted a panel discussion on liberation theology at the Riverside Church Conference on the Church and the City because there were no Latinos on the program. The coalition called their document the "Riverside Manifesto."[8]

The church continued its tradition of reaching out to the community in the wake of the tragedies of September 11, 2001. Church members worked with a mosque in the area, supporting the Muslim community through this disaster. Riverside members attended Islamic services and they invited a Muslim professor to teach at Riverside. Members demonstrated their support by escorting Muslim children to school. The church's social justice ministry organized an emergency response team in conjunction with the Episcopal diocese in New York City to help support volunteers at Ground Zero. Riverside also joined a group of New York churches in sharing the responsibility of cooking and cleaning for New York City firefighters. The church members themselves were touched by the tragedies and the church stood up as a whole to meet the needs of the community.

The progressive decline in the proportion of white members and staff over the years is a manifestation of the degree of accommodation and conflict that has occurred at Riverside since James Forbes's arrival. Although Forbes was welcomed enthusiastically by most of the congregation, the church has had to come to terms with racial and cultural differences. For example, Forbes preaches in the oral tradition, which is typical in African American churches. Not only are sermons in the oral tradition longer than those in predominantly white congregations, but they also elicit a response from the congregation. When Forbes began preaching, some members were uncomfortable with the "Amens" and the clapping during the sermons. The church even held meetings about the matter, during which white members asked their pastor to discourage people from responding during his sermons. They noted that the responses made them feel like they were at a "show" and prevented them from hearing the sermon itself. This is an example of the clashes and misunderstandings that can occur within a multiracial congregation.

Another difficulty in becoming multiracial came in the form of determining the length of the worship service. The white members were used to services that lasted about one hour. The black members were used to longer services. The church settled on a compromise of about one and one-half hours for each service. The congregation engaged in similar disputes over the style of music as well as the method of greeting visitors and even in the level of formality in the church. Forbes eloquently states his "75 percent" philosophy on compromise and on the comfort level at a church:

A truly diverse congregation where anybody enjoys more than 75 percent of what's going on is not thoroughly integrated. So that if you're going to be an integrated church you have to be prepared to think, "hey, this is great, I enjoyed at least 75 percent of it," because 25 percent you should grant for somebody's precious liturgical expression that is probably odious to you; otherwise it's not integrating. So an integrating church is characterized by the need to be content with less than total satisfaction with everything. You have to factor in a willingness to absorb some things that are not dear to you but may be precious to some of those coming in.

Thus, the Riverside Church has learned to compromise and allow room for different groups to find comfort in different elements and traditions. Today, the services are reminiscent of a high church style; there are no "Amens" and no clapping during the sermons. The church seems to have achieved a comfortable equilibrium between the styles of the different groups. One visitor admits, "It was weird being in a black church that wasn't very 'black.' You can really sense the compromise between black and white styles. Very high church and friendly at the same time. A tangible mixing of different styles."

The stated mission of the Riverside Church is to "serve God through word and witness; to treat all human beings as sisters and brothers; and to foster responsible stewardship of all God's creation." Staying true to its liberal Protestant roots, the Riverside Church welcomes "all persons, celebrating the diversity found in a congregation broadly inclusive of persons from different backgrounds of race, economic class, religion, culture, ethnicity, gender, age, and sexual orientation."[9] The Riverside Church in New York City is an example of a successful multiracial congregation that is bound together by theological liberalism, a legacy of tolerance and inclusion, a tradition of community outreach, a conscientious leadership, and a healthy sense of compromise for the sake of unity.

The church also illustrates the importance of the senior pastor. It is under James Forbes's tenure that a majority of the church membership became African American, and it is uncertain how the membership will change with the appointment of his successor. Forbes himself acknowledges that the congregation will surely increase the percentage of African Americans if his successor is also black. Thus, the choice of Forbes's successor is a crucial one. He notes, "It will be important to see what white people do and how black people finally come to value multicultural [integration] and to see what sacrifices, even if they have power, they are willing to make." According to Forbes, a goal of this church is to "become so convinced that multiracial is the wave of the future, that we develop teams that can go out and help congregations that would like to move toward that."

The Mosaic Church of Los Angeles, California

On the opposite coast from the Riverside Church there is a multiracial congregation named Mosaic whose major goal is to evangelize the urban areas and the arts and entertainment district.[10] The Mosaic church is in Los Angeles, one of the most racially diverse cities in the United States. Furthermore, the arts and entertainment community of that city is one of the most racially diverse subcultures of that metropolitan area. In seeking to serve its desired population, Mosaic has attracted and maintained a highly multiracial congregation.

But Mosaic's focus has not always been on these multiracial populations. This Southern Baptist congregation initially was predominantly white—even though it was located in a Hispanic neighborhood. The church remained mostly white until the arrival of Tom Wolf as senior pastor in 1971. Wolf motivated the church to aggressively evangelize their Hispanic neighbors. The racial mix of the church changed to being predominantly Latino—with whites making up about 20 to 30 percent of the congregation. Under Wolf's leadership, the church grew from an average attendance of forty to about five hundred worshipers.

In 1996 Tom Wolf, who had previously stepped down from the head pastorship, left the church to serve in the mission field. With Wolf's departure, Erwin McManus, a Hispanic born in El Salvador, became more firmly established as Mosaic's senior pastor. Under his guidance, the nature of the multiracial atmosphere of the church changed in several ways. First, under Wolf the leadership of the church was generally made up of whites—despite their numerical minority. McManus took steps to integrate the leadership of the congregation and this multiracial leadership served to attract more persons of color. Second, a significant Asian American population developed in a neighborhood that is relatively close to the church.

McManus encouraged the members of the church to reach out to that community, enabling Mosaic to expand its largely white–Hispanic racial mix to one that today is roughly 30 percent white, 30 percent Asian American, 30 percent Latino, and 10 percent from other racial groups. Finally, the church under Tom Wolf had a powerful emphasis on international missions, and local ministry was deemphasized relative to overseas mission work. International missions are still important at Mosaic, but local ministry has since gained a higher priority. Mosaic's concept of local ministry extended the outreach efforts of the church beyond the local community so that the congregation could serve the greater Los Angeles urban area.

Erwin McManus developed a philosophy of ministry that emphasizes evangelism, cultural relevancy, and artistic creativity to meet the goal of bringing the Christian faith to these groups. Evangelism offers a core commitment to a Christian reality and reinforces the institutional loyalty of the church members—which may help attendees to overlook any racial contentions that develop within the church.[11] The emphasis on cultural relevancy gives the individuals in Mosaic the freedom to experiment with the cultural methods they use in evangelism. This emphasis on relevancy has made the church extremely appealing to young people. According to McManus, more than 90 percent of the attendees are under the age of forty-five. Mosaic is a church willing to adapt to modern cultural conventions, as long as this adaptation does not contradict the evangelical Christian message they promote.

Artistic creativity provides an innovative way to deliver their evangelical message. Members are encouraged to utilize a variety of artistic talents and training in worship and outreach programs. For example, rather than adapting the music style of other Christian traditions (e.g., contemporary praise, traditional anthems), the worship music of Mosaic is generally written by the members of this church—allowing those attendees an avenue of creativity. To say that the church has a contemporary worship style would be an understatement, as avant-garde is a better way to describe the worship atmosphere. This sort of artistic expression resonates with the members of the arts/entertainment community that leaders of Mosaic hope to reach.

A Mosaic ministry called "Urban" is a worship service that takes place on Sunday nights in a downtown Los Angeles nightclub. This setting provides an atmosphere that is relaxed and welcoming for many people who are uncomfortable in traditional church settings. Mosaic's normal Sunday morning service contains novel worship music and drama skits performed by church attendees. Such artistic innovation is also a part of Urban but the service is geared toward reaching an even younger audience. Instead of traditional ministries aimed at middle-age couples and their families (e.g., youth ministry, childcare), Urban focuses on creating an atmosphere that is comfortable for its young worshipers. The décor in the nightclub is likely to be familiar to many of the attendees at Urban, although such a décor would likely make older worshipers less comfortable. After the service, strobe lights come on and Christian rock music blares from the loud-speakers, which also gives the service a Generation X feel. Urban is a clear example of culturally relevant evangelism done with artistic creativity and an excellent representation of the philosophy devised by McManus.

While Mosaic's efforts to alter its delivery of the evangelistic message and its worship style are not done specifically to develop a multiracial ministry, the population reached by these ministries is multiracial. Handling racial and cultural diversity is not an after-thought for the leadership of Mosaic but rather is perceived as an opportunity for further ministry. McManus has emphasized the importance of learning the strengths and weakness of each culture so that his church members can better minister to people from those cultures. McManus argues that this leadership is important since it allows the church to provide representation for different racial groups. This sort of honest assessment should lead to deeper racial under-standing and acceptance instead of mere superficial racial toleration.

Mosaic illustrates that multiracial congregations have a potential for growth that may be absent in uniracial churches. Since McManus became the senior pastor, the church's weekend worship has grown from five hundred to roughly 1,200 attendees. A major reason this congregation has experienced such a robust growth is its ability to attract individuals who are more comfortable in a multiracial environ-ment than in uniracial settings. In interviews, Mosaic church members indicated that after attending this church, many of them would avoid attending a uniracial congregation. In fact, because the members of Mosaic tend to be very young (the average age of a Mosaic church member is thirty-three), several of them have never known what it is like to attend a uniracial church. Most of these individuals have grown up in a multiracial social environment and the church becomes an extension of their own personal experiences.

This is not to say that Mosaic is unable to attract individuals who live in racially segregated environments. A young Chinese American woman interviewed had very few non-Chinese friends before joining Mosaic. Yet even for her, the multiracial nature of the church was one of the features that attracted her to Mosaic. Although Mosaic attempts to reach out to individuals in a multiracial environment, its vibrant and racially diverse atmosphere also has the potential for attracting individuals from a more racially segregated social environment. One of the lessons to learn from Mosaic is that a multiracial congregation possesses the potential for drawing individuals who are comfortable with a multiracial social atmosphere and individuals from a uniracial social atmosphere who become interested in surrounding themselves with people of other races.

The direction Mosaic has taken led to the development of a highly multiracial Christian community of mostly young adults. Interracial friendships and marriages are common within this church. Racial differences probably matter less because the church attendees share similarities in many nonracial characteristics such as youth, Christian commitment, urban culture, and interest in the arts. Furthermore, like many within the younger cohort, most of the church members grew up being exposed to individuals of different races. Another important lesson to learn from Mosaic is that it is a mistake to think of multiracial congregations as static institutions. Multiracial churches can evolve and change over time to become even more racially and culturally diverse. The changes initiated by Erwin McManus have helped to further diversify an already multiracial congregation and to produce a church that is primed to minister in the twenty-first century.

St. Pius X Catholic Church of Beaumont, Texas

In areas with progressive populations such as Los Angeles and New York City one would expect to find some multiracial congregations. It seems less likely to discover a thriving multiracial congregation in Beaumont, Texas. Beaumont is an unpretentious city of 114,000 people. Although the city is located in Texas, it is just twenty-five miles from Louisiana, and the city's Roman Catholic population has a significant percentage of people from southern Louisiana. Because Louisiana has the largest percentage of black Catholics in the nation, Beaumont has a number of African American Catholics. In fact, there are at least two African American congregations in the community.

Located on nine acres of wooded land on the northeast side of Beaumont, St. Pius X Catholic Church is a humble congregation that has quietly done something unique.[12] It has been racially integrated for at least forty years, yet the people of this church do not seem to know how rare this is. What they do know is that St. Pius is their home congregation and the people here are their friends. With increasing integration over the years, St. Pius currently is about 50 percent African American, 45 percent white, and 5 percent Hispanic and Filipino. Its boards, councils, committees, and friendship circles look much like the larger church.

St. Pius was established in 1954 as the post–World War II population boom and migration that characterized much of the United States was shaping Beaumont as well. Because of population growth to the Northeast side, particularly of Italians, the Diocese of Beaumont decided a new congregation was necessary. Nick Perusina was selected as the founding pastor. A parish pastor for ten years in Beaumont by that time, Perusina had been introduced to race issues very early in his ministry. As reported in the book *The Diocese of Beaumont: The Catholic Story of Southeast Texas,* "A race riot broke out within a few weeks of his arrival and much time was spent counseling both black and white families."[13] Such experiences as this race riot in the city had an important influence on him, and when he began the new congregation, he wanted it to be open to all, even during this era of racial segregation by law.

According to reports from long-time members, the church began with mostly Italians and some Louisiana French Catholics. But within a few years, the first African American Catholics began coming to St. Pius. No one seemed to know for sure when this first occurred, but we interviewed an African American congregant who has been at St. Pius since 1961, and she said there were a few other black members when she arrived. They appeared to arrive for two main reasons: St. Pius had something the nearby African American church did not—air conditioning (no small thing in this subtropical climate)—and Nick Perusina and the people of St. Pius were open and accepting.

Perusina was known for being open-minded and avant-garde. As one member who had been at St. Pius since its founding told us, "Father Perusina was a nonconformist. Just to give you an idea, we had altar girls here before the Vatican ever allowed it. We, the laity, were actually leading people in responses before other people were doing it. The best word to describe him was nonconformist. He was at times eccentric. But his piety and love for others overcame his eccentricities!" We found confirmation for what this congregant told us. According to written reports, St. Pius was the site of many innovations: it was the first to adopt changes from the Second Vatican Council, the first congregation to have a married deacon, the first to have a full-time social worker, the first to use lay people to distribute Communion at Mass and for home visitations, and Perusina was the first priest to join the Beaumont Ministerial Alliance.[14]

He was also known for being someone who cared for all people in the community. Because of the leadership of their pastor, St. Pius parishioners were used to nonconformity in their church, so it did not strike them as odd or offensive when African American Catholics began coming to St. Pius. By all reports, the change in racial makeup was gradual and seen as natural. The teachings of the Church and Perusina supported the racial changes and almost no whites left the congregation.

Delilah, a black member who has been at St. Pius since 1961, had many positive words to say about Perusina. She and her husband had moved from Louisiana and decided to try air-conditioned St. Pius one sweltering summer day. As was the case for all African Americans in the South at the time, Delilah grew up in strictly segregated environments. But just a year or two after her arrival, Perusina asked her to teach a religious education class. This meant she would be teaching white people, people with whom she was not allowed to sit in movie theaters and restaurants. According to Delilah:

> I was skeptical because of the fact that (in the outside world) we were called Negroes, and considered low class. And I was uncomfortable because I didn't have a very good competence level. I had

very low self-esteem because of what it [the racial system] had done. But with Father Perusina and some of the ladies here, I worked through it. I then realized, I can do this! And over the years my husband and I have continued to be involved. And I sit back now on Sundays and realize . . . it's beautiful, all the groups we have here, and I also realize, this parish is a part of me. I have given myself here and this is my parish and these are my friends.

Nick Perusina was the pastor of St. Pius until 1978, nearly a quarter of a century. In the letter appointing him to a new congregation due to the recently introduced rule of tenure limits for pastors, the bishop wrote: "You formed a truly loving, Christian community. Your sensitivity for social concerns has won admiration and affection."[15] In 2000, one member reflected on the racial mix, "I would give credit to our first pastor. He prepared us. I mean, to him, everybody was God's people."

Since his departure, St. Pius has had three other pastors: John DiStefano, Salvador Culotta, and currently, Francis X. Conroy. All have overseen both the spiritual growth and the growth of racial diversity in the congregation. A new church building, built in a modified Spanish architecture, was opened in 1980. The congregation wanted to do something to represent its people. As described by DiStefano, "the racial blending of the parish . . . is represented by the faceted stained glass windows at the entrance of the building."[16] This stained glass window is created with multiple colors mixed together around a center point.

After more than forty years of being an integrated community, St. Pius has forged deep bonds across racial boundaries. Every person we interviewed at St. Pius said they loved the diversity of the church. An African American woman told us, "We have a friendly group here, the blacks and whites. And, you know, we're sincere. We get along well. . . . This helps make our parish more united, and we work well together. This is home." A white woman in her seventies said, "It just feels like home. You know, all the people, the black and the white, we've worked together from the beginning, and we work together now." A white man told us that he particularly appreciates the depth of the bonds across race, "Some churches that are mixed, the whites sit in one place, and the blacks in another. We don't do that here. We are spread out all over. I mean I can sit in any pew and I'll be with black persons. Or any black person can sit in any pew and there will be white persons. It's a diverse congregation in every pew. We get to know each other because we are all here together."

We interviewed an African American couple in their forties who were relatively new to the congregation and an older white man who had been at St. Pius for most of its existence. As we sat around a conference table together, the African American couple told us they were looking for a multicultural church so they tried St. Pius. They loved being part of this community. Then the woman said, "May I say something about Jim [the white man being interviewed]? When we first came here he was so friendly to us. I would say that he was a person who made us feel really welcome." To which Jim replied, "She is being kind. That goes on throughout the parish. That's just one example of many of what's going on. Everybody's welcome."

Over the years, the surrounding neighborhood has changed. According to our analysis of census data, the neighborhood is now approximately 90 percent African American. The challenge facing St. Pius, an aging church, is to bring new growth and attract younger people. With that in mind, Francis X. Conroy became the pastor in January of 2000. Conroy, the son of Irish immigrants, grew up in Boston, and spent many years as an Air Force chaplain, literally traveling around the world. It was a life he very much liked. As he told us, "I loved the style of life. I loved intermingling with all kinds of people." It was a life he had hoped to continue, but when there was a need in the Diocese of Beaumont, first for a pastor in nearby Orange, Texas, and then at St. Pius, out of obedience to God and the bishop, he agreed to serve these congregations.

We first met with him just a few short months after his arrival at St. Pius. He is known as someone dedicated to getting people committed to and excited about their parish—a fire starter. He was able to bring new, dynamic life to his previous congregation and has high hopes for the same at St. Pius. He spoke with us about plans to get more programs going at St. Pius and for making St. Pius once again a center for spiritual and social activity. Within the first few months he made changes to the sidewalks and church, making St. Pius wheelchair accessible. He told us of meetings scheduled with members to get more activities going for youth.

Revisiting St. Pius a year later, we could already see changes. For example, the back page of the church bulletin, covered the year before with advertisements for local businesses, was now entirely devoted to announcing youth events, including religious education classes, a choir, planning for a Christmas cantata, and other youth activities. He also had told of his plan to start a monthly breakfast where people could come together outside of Mass and other traditional activities. A year later, not only had he started the breakfast but its attendance was averaging 125 people each month. Now Conroy is planning to start a monthly dinner as well. The people of St. Pius are excited by the energy their pastor has brought and they are full of much hope for the future of St. Pius. Over forty years of being an integrated community has forged deep bonds across racial boundaries and together they look forward to the next forty years.

Park Avenue United Methodist Church of Minneapolis, Minnesota

Moving from the South to the Midwest, our final congregation is found in the city of Minneapolis, Minnesota. At its inception in 1894, Park Avenue United Methodist Church was a white congregation.[17] Beginning in the 1960s, Park Avenue Church took a journey that transformed it into a congregation that currently has a racial make up of approximately 60 percent whites, 35 percent African Americans, 5 percent Latinos, and a few Asians and Native Americans. Three services accommodate the nearly 1,300 worshipers who attend every Sunday, with the third service being a bilingual service in Spanish and English. Many whites moved to the suburbs in the 1960s. The congregation decided to remain in the community rather than follow its members to the suburbs. This decision caused many people to transfer their memberships to other congregations. It also meant that Park Avenue Church had to reach its neighbors who were often African Americans.

The senior pastor during this transition was C. Philip Hinerman. He came to Park Avenue Church in 1952 and served the congregation for over thirty-five years. His commitment to a racially inclusive congregation anchored the church in the midst of dramatic change. One of the congregation's strategies for reaching the neighborhood was to develop a stellar youth program. In 1967 Hinerman hired a youth pastor named Arthur Erickson and commissioned him to serve half time in the church and half time in the community. Erickson used his Young Life background in youth programming to develop a nationally recognized summer youth program that reached a wide range of young people from the community. In 1973 he launched a one-week summer music and preaching festival called "Soul Liberation" that was held in the parking lot behind the church building. Musical artists like Andrae Crouch, the Second Chapter of Acts, Take 6, Barry McGuire, Salvador, Bebe and Cece Winans, and many others have graced the stage of the Soul Liberation Festival alongside preachers such as Tom Skinner, Tony Campolo, Juan Carlos Ortiz, John Perkins, Barbara Williams Skinner, and a host of other noted speakers. The youth program and the Soul Liberation Festival served as vehicles for demonstrating to people in the neighborhood that Park Avenue United Methodist Church welcomed them to join the church family. C. Philip Hinerman and Arthur Erickson weathered the storms of change together for twenty years as Park Avenue Church began to reflect the makeup of its urban community.

Robert Stamps was selected as the next senior pastor when Hinerman retired in 1988. Stamps brought a style that integrated a flair for high church reflection and Pentecostal emotion. A white man, he was also very comfortable in African American contexts because of his experience in multiracial settings. Stamps quickly recognized the need to recruit African Americans for the pastoral staff. Up to this point, only white clergy had served the growing multiracial congregation. So Stamps hired two young seminary trained African Americans who were in the ordination process to serve with him: Keith Johnson and Christopher McNair. Johnson had joined the congregation as a youth and then moved away from Minneapolis to attend seminary. McNair, a native Texan, had previously served as an intern with the congregation. Eventually Stamps realized that he would need to share the pulpit on a regular basis in order to model and empower racial reconciliation. This was a great sacrifice for Stamps, who loved to preach. Soon Johnson began to alternate Sundays with Stamps, in a fashion similar to the approach used by Howard Thurman and Alfred Fisk at the Church for the Fellowship of All Peoples.

Robert Stamps also realized that music and worship were critical components in sustaining a multiracial congregation. So he recruited Tom Fitch, a unique white musician who was able to bridge the worlds of black gospel and classical anthems. Fitch had intended to be a classical pianist when he started college, but one day while in college he heard the sounds of an African American gospel choir emanating from the school's music building. Fitch immediately enrolled in the course. He remarked: "I heard them singing about Jesus in a way that touched me very deeply, and that gave me the courage to believe that I might somehow belong with them."[18] Tom Fitch continued his classical training while at the same time playing piano and directing choirs at predominantly African American congregations. When Fitch arrived in Minneapolis, he became the architect of a new way of doing music and worship at Park Avenue United Methodist Church. Soon the congregation had a music program that integrated a wide range of musical styles on a Sunday morning, including black gospel, classical anthems, traditional hymns, contemporary praise, reggae, country, rap, and the occasional Latin and African sounds. To this day, the congregation sings a gospel version of the "Gloria Patria" that was composed shortly after Fitch's arrival.

The Methodist bishop appointed current senior pastor Mark Horst in 1994, following the departure of Robert Stamps. Horst, who is white, continued the established preaching tradition and alternated with Keith Johnson. Horst also worked hard to embrace the challenge of leading a multiracial congregation. Even though he had a background in urban and multicultural settings, he made himself vulnerable at many points to grow in his leadership abilities. He even invited one of the leading African American preachers in the area to critique his preaching and coach him in ways to connect with this diverse congregation. Horst's first years at the church saw much transition. Arthur Erickson and Christopher McNair left Park Avenue Church toward the end of the Stamps pastorate. Erickson started a community development organization and McNair initiated a youth development program. Park Avenue Church has a long tradition of entrepreneurial staff and lay leaders starting new ministries. Keith Johnson, the congregation's associate pastor, was the next to leave the staff to establish a ministry to professional athletes. Then in 1997 music minister Tom Fitch died of cancer and the congregation entered a period of grief.

Also during the early days of the Horst pastorate, racism moved to the forefront of discussion in the congregation. While the congregation had been multiracial for a number of years, conversations on race were often sidelined in favor of the perspective of just living together as a color-blind community. Mark Horst encouraged the congregation to take off the blinders and see color and race. He believed the congregation needed to deal directly with issues that emerged because of differences. One example of this clash of perspectives erupted in the congregation when Keith Johnson decided to attend the October 1995 Million Man March in Washington, D.C., which had been called by Louis Farrakhan of the Nation of Islam and others. Some church members were displeased with Johnson's decision to attend. Like many African American men who attended, Johnson returned home having experienced a sense of exhilaration and affirmation as an African American male.

On his return, Johnson invited African American men to meet with him and plan for ways to address the unique issues facing young black males in the community. Some were concerned that this action created internal segregation in the congregation. Others noted that if the African American men in the congregation wanted separation, they would be attending primarily African American congregations. The group eventually disbanded because of the controversy. Yet it signaled to the congregation that diverse views were held on the issue of racism. Ever since, the congregation has sought to bring discussions of race and reconciliation to the forefront of the church's agenda. As Mark Horst says, "Being an intentionally diverse congregation means you've got to talk about your differences. It means you've got to welcome differences."[19]

The congregation is known in Minneapolis for the number of interracial couples and multiracial families that attend. In a February 2002 front page story in the *Star Tribune* newspaper about the high per capita number of multiracial couples and families in Minnesota, the couples interviewed for the article were mostly members of Park Avenue Church. The congregation was featured in an accompanying article. Throughout the years, the multiracial composition of the congregation and its inclusive spirit have drawn a number of interracial couples and their children, as well as white families who have adopted children of different races. This in turn has made the congregation even more multiracial.

During the last five years, Horst has continued the emphasis on a multiracial pastoral team. He hired two African American associate pastors and preaches alternately with both of them. The dreadlock-wearing Peter Singletary arrived first. Efrem Smith, who was hired next, also directs the outreach arm of the congregation—the Park Avenue Foundation. Horst focused on making sure the broader staff and lay leadership of the congregation represented the constituency served by the congregation. After a long search process, the congregation welcomed Keith McCutcheon as its first African American director of music. Presently, the entire church staff and lay leadership more closely reflect the diversity of the congregation. Horst has also encouraged the leadership in the congregation to examine and address power issues that are a part of race. A commitment to having representational leadership and dismantling white privilege go hand in hand with developing an authentic multiracial congregation—particularly when that congregation began as a predominantly white congregation. As Horst likes to say, "It is not enough to open the doors of the church. We need to rearrange the furniture."[20]

While Park Avenue United Methodist Church was working hard to build an inclusive congregation that embraced African Americans and whites, the neighborhood began to go through another transformation. A number of Hispanic families moved into the area. At the turn of the century, the congregation has had to learn how to reach and welcome its newest neighbors. Some of the staff and lay volunteers speak Spanish; also some Latinos have joined the staff. As noted earlier, the third Sunday service is bilingual with a focus on music with more of a Latin feel. Mark Horst is taking Spanish classes. The congregation gave him a two-month leave at the beginning of 2001 to take language classes in Guatemala. When the senior pastor learns a new language to communicate with the newest neighbors, that makes a major statement to Latinos in the community and to the congregation.

The future of Park Avenue United Methodist Church may have been captured in a Sunday service in February 2002. Four preachers from the congregation approached the pulpit, each speaking for five to seven minutes about the Samaritan woman and Jesus from the Gospel of John. Associate pastor Efrem Smith started off the "tag team" sermon. Senior pastor Mark Horst followed him. Then Cecilia Williams, a minister in the congregation and a seminary student, offered her word. Finally Juan Lopez, a minister from Colombia (South America) and a member of the Park Avenue congregation, concluded the message through an interpreter. When Smith started his part of the round robin preaching he took a drink from the one glass of water sitting on the pulpit for the preachers. When Horst stood to take a turn he noted that in the ministry of reconciliation you may have to drink from someone else's glass. He also took a drink from the same glass of water. Then Williams reminded the church that they were talking about living water and she took a drink from the glass. Lopez followed suit during his turn. The image of four persons of different heritages—African American, white, biracial, and Latino—sharing the Word and a drink portrays quite well the present reality and future hope of Park Avenue United Methodist Church in Minneapolis, Minnesota. As the pastors often declare from the pulpit, "What God is trying to do at Park Avenue Church is a sneak preview of heaven."

Conclusion

Thus far we have been building a case for the biblical mandate for and the viability of multiracial congregations. We have just examined in more depth four congregations that have made significant steps toward integrating different races in one house of worship. Although they are not perfect, they demonstrate that multiracial congregations are an attainable goal. The four congregations became multiracial in four different ways. They were connected to different denominations: Roman Catholic, Southern Baptist, United Methodist, and American Baptist/United Church of Christ. Their theology ranged from conservative to liberal. The congregations were located in the East, West, South, and northern Midwest. The racial makeup, membership size, and average parishioner age all differed from congregation to congregation. The current pastors in these four churches are African American, white, and Latino. There is no set formula or ideal setting for developing multiracial congregations.

We argue that when possible congregations should strive to become multiracial, but this view is not universally held and certainly not widely practiced. In chapters six and seven we examine the arguments for and the theologies behind the prevailing reality of congregations separated by race, culture, and ethnicity. In chapter eight we offer our responses to these arguments.

III

RATIONALES FOR AND RESPONSES TO THE RACIAL SEGREGATION OF CONGREGATIONS

6 | Rejecting the White Man's Religion

In the late 1700s, Christian members of the Delawares, a Native American tribal group, moved to a new "praying town" in what is now the state of Ohio. These towns were places established for Native Americans who converted to Christianity. After conversion they were forced to live in a Christian community exclusively for Native Americans. This group of Delawares voluntarily chose to move to Sandusky to keep peace with white farmers in the area. The move took place after the Delawares had already planted their fields. So at harvest time, they returned to the fields so they could provide for their families. A white military brigade from Fort Pitt met them. The Native Americans calmly explained why they were there and surrendered. The white military officer in charge, Colonel David Williamson, ordered the band restrained. Not wanting to waste ammunition, the militiamen cruelly beat the Delaware Christians to death with clubs. They then scalped and burned twenty-nine men, twenty-seven women, and thirty-four children. Eyewitnesses reported that these peaceful Christians of Native American descent did not resist but rather sang hymns and offered prayers to God as they were slaughtered so viciously.[1]

The segregation of the church did not happen in a vacuum.

Historical events and societal phenomena influenced and shaped a religion in which segregation by race is the predominant form of community experienced in local Christian congregations in the United States. We have written this book to suggest that the multiracial congregation is the New Testament model, practically viable, and a vehicle for racial reconciliation. Yet we know that we do not live in a utopian society with a guiltless history. In this chapter and the following one, we present the long history of and valid reasons for racial separation in Christianity. We do our best to make a persuasive case for uniracial congregations. Then in chapter eight we respond from a multiracial congregation perspective to the issues raised. We begin with why Native Americans and African Americans often support racially segregated religious institutions. To do this, it is important to understand the ways Native Americans were "evangelized" and the historical importance of the black church and how segregation has served that church. It is also vital to comprehend how the actions of the dominant group in society created an environment in which many Native Americans and African Americans would value a segregated Christian faith. In the following chapter we examine Asian American, Hispanic, and white perspectives on separation.

A History of Brutality

Historian Vine DeLoria writes, "I was brought up in the Christian faith but with a strong family recognition or admission that the old Sioux ways had a validity in and of themselves. I attended a Lutheran seminary and received a degree in theology. Yet, I have in my lifetime concluded that Christianity is the chief evil ever to have been loosed on the planet."[2] DeLoria's view of Christianity is not an isolated perspective of a fringe element. He represents a significant and perhaps majority view among Native Americans. Many who consider themselves followers of Jesus Christ also resonate with DeLoria's statement as an accurate appraisal of the Christianity brought by Europeans to the Americas. The history of brutality, as evidenced by the opening story in this chapter, is a central reason that many Native Americans have sought separation from European-inspired forms of Christian faith.

The cruel and abusive treatment of Native American Christians runs throughout the history of the United States. We offer a few more brief examples of this brutal and genocidal behavior. In 1838 sixteen thousand members of the Cherokee Nation were driven from Georgia to what is today Oklahoma. Christian Native Americans sang hymns in the Cherokee language as they walked a path called by some the Trail of Tears. One song they sang was the Cherokee translation of "Guide Me, O Thou Great Jehovah." A verse says:

> Take me and guide me, Jehovah, as I am walking through this barren land. I am weak, but thou art mighty. Ever help us. Open unto us thy healing waters. Let the fiery cloud go before us and continue thy help. Help us when we come to the Jordan River and we shall sing thy praise eternally.

One fourth of those who were "forcibly marched" the nine hundred miles died while their hymns resonated heavenward.[3]

In 1844, Elijah Heading, a Cayuse, was traveling home from a journey to purchase cattle with members of several tribes. They were attacked by a group of horse thieves. The group defended themselves and even captured some of the horses. On the trip home, Heading stopped at a fort where there was a church. Since he was a Christian he decided to attend a worship service. As he entered the church building, a white man came over and charged Elijah Heading with stealing his horse. Heading explained the circumstances surrounding his trip and the horses. He offered to speak with him further after he spent some time in prayer. Heading descended to his knees and began to pray. The white man took out his gun and shot Elijah Heading in the back of his head while he was praying to God.[4]

In 1862 a violent uprising occurred in Minnesota after whites broke several treaties with Native Americans and dismissed their requests for food to feed hungry families. In response, there were random killings of whites. Tensions mounted and soon broke out in battle with the Native American contingent led by Little Crow, an Episcopalian. There were professed Christians on both sides. The battle ended when Native Americans either fled or surrendered. Over three hundred of the prisoners of war were found guilty and sentenced to death. President Abraham Lincoln intervened and reduced the number by nearly 90 percent. White settlers attacked the remaining Native Americans held captive and killed an infant.

One day after Christmas, "the greatest mass execution in United States history" occurred as thirty-eight of these Sioux Indians were hanged in Mankato, Minnesota. Many were Christians, and they began to sing hymns as the nooses were tightened around their necks. They held hands and continued singing to God when the trap door beneath them opened and their bodies dropped. It was discovered later that some of the thirty-eight executed were innocent.[5] Reminiscent of the lynching of African Americans, Native American Christians sang hymns and prayed to God while they were brutalized and killed by whites who often claimed the same faith. Many Native Americans have rejected Christianity or developed indigenous forms because they did not find "liberation in the gospel of Jesus Christ" presented to them by whites. Instead they have experienced "continued bondage to a culture that is both alien and alienating, and even genocidal against American Indian peoples."[6]

Making Native Americans White

United States president Andrew Jackson stated, "What good man would prefer a country covered with forests and ranged by a few thousand savages to our extensive Republic, studded with cities, towns, and prosperous farms . . . filled with all the blessings of liberty, civilization, and religion?"[7] Early colonial Puritan minister Cotton Mather said, "the best thing we can do for our Indians is to Anglicize them." He believed that the languages of Native Americans were "ill suited" to "the design of Christianity."[8] Even in recent years, Native American Christian minister Richard Twiss relates, "One day when my oldest son, Andrew, was eight years old, he spent several hours playing at the house of his friend Aaron, who is White. Later, after Andrew left, Aaron asked his mom and dad, 'Did you know that Andrew Twiss is half Indian and half human?'"[9]

Beyond the physical violence waged against Native Americans in the United States, there has been a concentrated effort to strip away Native American culture and belief systems and assimilate Indians into white culture and understandings of Christianity. Native Americans have often been viewed as subhuman or not culturally worthy of Christianity. White missionaries and pastors have played a role in efforts to anglicize Native Americans. As Choctaw pastor and historian

Homer Noley notes, "On the one hand, church denominations geared themselves up to take the souls of Native American peoples into a brotherhood of love and peace; on the other hand, they were a part of a white nationalist movement that geared itself up to take away the land and livelihood of Native American people by treachery and force."[10] Native Americans have sought to distance themselves from the adherents of a "white" Christianity in the United States, fearing that they would be ethnically cleansed.

The fact that a few Native Americans embraced the Christian faith leads us to believe that some efforts were positive. During the early years after the arrival of Europeans on American soil, a missionary from the Congregational Church named John Elliot evangelized among Native Americans. Starting in 1631, Elliot served as a pastor to arriving European immigrants in what is now Massachusetts, and by 1646, he also reached out to Native Americans in the region. Elliot took the time to learn the languages of the tribes he ministered among, and he trained tribal leaders to carry on the work. John Elliot was unusual in his willingness to empower Native American leaders to run their own congregations. By 1665 Elliot had established fourteen "praying towns" with a total population of converts numbering around four thousand. These communities were all run by indigenous leaders.[11]

In contrast to John Elliot, most white missionaries did not learn the various tribal languages and depended on interpreters. Historian Homer Noley states:

> There are numerous stories of Native Christian leaders carrying the gospel among the original inhabitants of this land. These leaders, although they were the true vehicle through whom the message of Christianity took root among the Native people, have very seldom been lifted up and given due recognition for their work. Historically, the church has credited White missionaries with accomplishing the spread of Christianity among this land's Native peoples. . . . All through the history of European missions to the Native peoples of the Americas, a primary role player in the spread of the church has been the interpreter. . . . The interpreter was the preacher who was heard and understood by the Native listener, because the interpreter was himself a fellow tribesman who spoke the Native language.[12]

What success there was in true conversions to Christian faith came from the work of Native American interpreters and a few attempts by whites to actually understand the culture of Native Americans.

Although the "praying towns" instituted by John Elliot and others initially seemed to be vehicles of empowerment, more often this model was used to separate Native Americans from the mainstream and "bring praying Indians more firmly under the control of Elliot and the Puritans, so that they might more readily abandon their pagan way of life and learn English 'civilized' behavior."[13] According to Osage/Cherokee religion professor George Tinker, praying towns could not be sustained due to these ulterior motives. The Native American converts joined the battle against the English and rejected Christianity.[14] Tinker notes, "Eventually it becomes clear that civilizing—that is, europeaniz-ing—Indian people evidently took precedence over conversion, or was the proof of conversion. Indeed, the two discrete acts seem to have been thoroughly intermingled in the minds of the missionaries."[15]

Today, many denominations have developed indigenous leadership in Native American communities. Yet these leaders remain accountable to a white power structure and church organization.[16] Other denominations continue to treat Native American congrega-tions as mission placements primarily served by white ministers.[17] The impression in both cases is that Native Americans need the involve-ment of whites to be considered authentically Christian. Some Native American scholars have raised the question, "Can one be Christian and Indian simultaneously in contemporary society?"[18] Vine DeLoria rec-ommends that the denominations "assist in the creation of a national Indian Christian Church. Such a church would incorporate all existing missions and programs into one national church to be wholly in the hands of Indian people."[19]

Separation for Cultural Survival

Another reason Native Americans promote separation is the unique-ness of Indian cultures and spirituality.[20] It is questionable whether Native American cultural categories can be integrated with Western perspectives. One clear difference is that many Native Americans have traditionally believed that God's presence is found in sacred places and experiences. In fact, "their whole cultural and social structure was and still is infused with a spirituality that cannot be separated from the rest of the community's life at any point."[21] A Western perspective places more emphasis on the timeline of events in history when God acted. The Western perspective asks *"When?"* The Native American perspective asks *"Where?"* In the history of the United States there was no regard for Native American people's connection to particular sacred places when they were resettled or forcibly moved to new homelands. Praying towns could not replace the land where tribes had lived and worshiped God for generations.

Another cultural distinctive that impacts religious faith is that Native American societies are usually structured by an understanding of kinship in which all created beings are in relationship to the Creator and all of the created are in relationship with each other. As George Tinker writes, "Each Native American tribal community in North America had a relationship with God as Creator that was healthy and responsible long before they knew of or confessed the gospel of Jesus Christ."[22] While each person has a unique identity, one's meaning in life is found in one's relationship with the entire community. All of creation is respected and valued. This also leads to a lack of hierarchy in relationships, including marriage.

While it might be possible for Native Americans to form multiracial congregations with other persons of color, it seems nearly impossible to bridge the gap with whites. Richard Twiss writes:

> Many Natives through the centuries have been offended by the rejection of Indian culture as pagan because it strikes at the heart of who they are as a people. . . . Native expressions of Christ and His kingdom are all but absent from the mainstream of the White church in America—this despite nearly five centuries of unabated missionary activity! . . . An authentic Native American cultural expression of Christianity has not been allowed to develop; the very idea has been rejected. Is it any wonder many Native people view Christianity as the White man's religion and blame Christians for the loss of their own culture and identity?[23]

The Origins of the African American Church

Like Native Americans, African Americans have endured a horrific history at the hands of whites who claimed to be Christians. White "Christianity" was used to maintain the oppressive racial hierarchical system of slavery. Whites did not hesitate to use "Christian" teaching to support notions of white superiority.[24] In response to this oppressive reality and with a desire to experience God in the midst of tragic circumstances, African Americans set up separate religious institutions that authenticated rather than legitimized their sufferings. Sociologist C. Eric Lincoln noted:

> While it is true that race was certainly a factor in the peculiar circumstances under which the Black Church did in fact develop in America, it was a problem originating in the White Church, from which black Christians finally felt compelled to withdraw if their faith and their humanity were not to be forever compromised. Racial exclusiveness has never been a factor of consequence in the Black Church. It was not the motivating impetus, nor is it the sustaining principle on which the Black Church rests and pursues its calling. . . . The fundamentals of the faith did not turn on race or ethnicity, but on spiritual essence. Thus did the Black Church achieve its own identity and conceive its own mission. In the pursuit of that mission, the Black Church can say of itself, in contrast to other communions, that at no time in its history has the Black Church closed its doors or denied its fellowship to people who were not black. Nor has it ever limited its concern to people who are.[25]

African American congregations began as "secret prayer and praise meetings" that helped keep "enslaved Africans alive by keeping alive the roots of their African experience."[26] From this "invisible institution" emerged congregations.[27] These separate Christian congregations played a valuable role in helping African Americans survive the horrors of slavery and provided a common base of unity and solidarity given the tremendous cultural diversity of the various African nations represented among those enslaved.[28] Many of the early southern African American religious institutions were completely independent of denominations. In the North blacks faced continuing obstacles in their desire to work with white Methodists and in 1816 decided to form the African Methodist Episcopal Church, shortly thereafter followed by the formation of the African Methodist Episcopal Zion Church. In the West the earliest all-black Baptist associations formed later in the nineteenth century. Both white and African American Christians institutionalized the segregated nature of the United States within their religious organizations very early in the nation's history.

Another reason for separation was that whites supported their notions of racial superiority with racist interpretations of the Bible, such as the Hamitic curse. This curse comes from Genesis 10:6–20 where Put, Mizraim, and Cush, three sons of Ham, are said to represent the people of Africa. Thus the origin of Africans was interpreted as the result of divine punishment. A closer look at the text reveals that Ham was not cursed. Rather it was his son Canaan, who represented the Canaanite people. Under such a false construction it becomes easy to relegate an entire group of individuals to second-class or even property status.[29]

Support was also drawn from the lack of overt condemnation of slavery within the Scriptures. It was argued that a lack of clear condemnation revealed that God allowed slavery between "inferior" and "superior" groups. "White" Christianity legitimated slavery by postulating that whites brought salvation to Africans by enslaving them and transporting them over to North America to be Christianized.[30] Although some early missionaries denounced slavery because of concerns about the ownership of Christians by other Christians, they eventually compromised their beliefs in order to gain the opportunity to convert Africans to Christianity and to avoid disrupting a society built on a racist premise.[31] Many of these missionaries eventually stopped any condemnation of slavery to retain their access to enslaved Africans.[32] African Americans used an interpretation of Christianity that ran counter to that of their oppressors to strengthen their resolve during times of harsh repression. Theologian Kelly Brown Douglas writes that blacks understood Jesus Christ in a very different way from most whites. African Americans "understood that Christ was against White racism and for Black freedom."[33]

Christian congregations were also among the first institutions in society where African Americans had relative freedom from the control of whites. African American congregations were places where political and social leadership developed and the interests of the black community were furthered. African American congregations were "the cultural womb of the black community," giving birth to many of the vital institutions within the African American community such as schools, banks, insurance companies, and low-income housing.[34] The African American church served as the hub of a "parallel community within broader white society."[35]

One example of how the African American form of Christianity, which emerged from separate African American congregations, contributed to the resistance of slavery can be seen in the nature of the black spiritual. Spirituals allowed African Americans to express their frustration with societal oppression and aid those who desired to escape. Some black spirituals served as songs of acceptable and thinly veiled protest.[36] These songs also possessed an African rhythm that created ties within their Christian faith to their African culture.

This type of radical Christianity was possible only because African Americans kept white racist notions out of their religious expressions. The separation of pre–Civil War African American congregations from the dominant white culture was vital in helping the church challenge the racism of that day. The institution of slavery was challenged intellectually and political action was planned in African American congregations. These congregations helped African Americans survive the dehumanization of slavery.[37] Clearly African American congregations benefited from this separation from whites. The division allowed African Americans to become leaders in their own communities and devise strategies to protest their enslavement.

From Civil War to Civil Rights

The valuable leadership role played by the African American church in the community of enslaved Africans persisted after the Civil War. The church continued to be the center of economic and social activity for African Americans and provided a meeting place for many other social organizations within the African American community. African American pastors had key leadership roles in African American communities. They served as pastor and community leader, preacher and social justice activist. Preaching professor Henry Mitchell notes, "The central figure in the black church is the black preacher. He has no exact counterpart in the white church, and to attempt to see the white minister on the same plane is to risk confusion, for the black preacher includes a dimension peculiar to the black experience."[38] The circumstances and the separation created the unique role of the African American preacher—a role still necessary in present-day society that could easily be lost in multiracial congregations.

The African American church continued to produce revolutionary leaders after the Civil War. Henry McNeal Turner, a bishop of the African Methodist Episcopal Church, developed an early version of black theology. Turner advocated the migration of blacks to Africa since he felt that the United States would never grant equality to African Americans. He raised the idea of reparations to finance this migration. Despite his radical ideology, Turner did not reject his Christian roots. He believed that God allowed Africans to be transported to the United States—but only temporarily—to equip them for a great missionary crusade to Africa.

The tradition of social and political activism within the African American church emerged again during the civil rights movement. In 1942 the Congress of Racial Equality (CORE) was formed. Although it was officially a secular organization, the early leaders of CORE were influenced by the African American church, which provided an ideological framework for the innovative use of nonviolent protest.[39] Also, A. Philip Randolph made use of black churches to organize his black labor union, the Brotherhood of Sleeping Car Porters. The time spent organizing in church meetings was one of the reasons Randolph was able to maintain this union.[40] Activists such as Randolph who appealed to a Christian ethic to justify their social and political positions prepared many blacks for Martin Luther King Jr.'s call for political and social reform. Theoretically King's emphasis on the supernatural and social progressiveness should have attracted white Christians with either Evangelical or mainline Protestant theological orientations—making a general multiracial Christian movement possible. However, despite King's tendency to adhere to the belief that the civil rights movement was a result of God's action, the movement did not attract Evangelical whites as easily as it attracted theological liberals. Many Evangelicals stayed away from the civil rights movement due to their beliefs that Christians should not become entangled in the affairs of the world.

Even today African Americans often have more traditional theological beliefs than mainline Protestant white Christians,[41] yet they possess more progressive social and political ideas than Evangelical white Christians.[42] This distinction has led to the development of an African American form of Christianity qualitatively different from either mainline Protestantism or white Evangelicalism. Beyond the need for congregations and denominations that are totally committed to the interests of African Americans, this qualitative difference is an argument for religious segregation in the black community since it means that African Americans in white churches will be either a theological or political mismatch for the rest of the congregation.

Of course, not all African Americans possess a conservative theological orientation. The radicalism of early African American ministers lives on in liberation theologies such as James Cone's "Black Theology."[43] Cone focuses on the empowerment of African Americans and the need for blacks to reject Eurocentric culture, since this culture has built the oppressive institutions from which African Americans suffer. He encourages African Americans to celebrate their own culture and community and not depend on approval by the dominant white society. This progressive tradition of the African American church reinforces the desire for separate congregations.

James Cone does not reject the biblical call for reconciliation with whites as would black separatist groups like the Nation of Islam. What he asks is that whites fully identify with oppressed African Americans and stand against white oppressors.[44] Many African American leaders do not expect this to happen; therefore, there continues to be a need for African American congregations. As sociologist Andrew Billingsley states, "It became clear to black and white Christians alike that there were serious incongruities in the white church's faith and practice which could not be reconciled short of exhaustive spiritual and moral overhaul and reconstruction. Although some individuals and even some churches recognized the depravity of Christian racism, so drastic a reform was nowhere on the agenda of the white church."[45] African American congregations are still needed to look after the interests of African Americans without undue interference from whites.

A final reason for separation of Christianity by race is racially divided denominations. As sociologist C. Eric Lincoln wrote:

> None of the Black communions would ever be very likely to be comfortable with any plans that would exchange their autonomy for white control and direction. Black Christians have had a bitter experience with religion in the white man's Church, and that experience transcended slavery and freedom alike. Wherever white Christians and Black Christians had come in contact with each other in America, Black Christians had been demeaned by the white man's presumption of racial superiority. In their own churches

in their own denominational structures, Black Christians had become accustomed to a sense of dignity and self-fulfillment impossible to even contemplate in the white Church in America. The Black Church created its own literature, established its own publishing houses, elected its own bishops and other administrators, founded its own colleges and seminaries, and developed its own unique style of worship.[46]

Summary and Conclusion

Our analysis of the history of Christianity among Native Americans and African Americans has generated several reasons for the continuing desire by many within these groups to maintain separation. Separate congregations provide a place to embrace and nurture culture. Native American cultures are distinct from those of whites in the United States. These unique features enrich the lives of Native Americans and resonate with the rhythms of a communal spiritual life. The cultural style of whites can inhibit the faith development of Native Americans. This same need is evident among African Americans. Worship in many African American settings is passionate and therapeutic. The African American preacher plays a unique role in the life of the community, and both African American and Native American congregations are virtual community centers in many neighborhoods.

Also, in many cases, African American forms of Christianity are either more theologically conservative or more politically progressive than the variations of Christianity found in the white community. This combination means that while black churches can work with mainline white churches on political issues and Evangelical churches on theological issues, neither mainline nor Evangelical white churches are places where African American Christians can consistently feel comfortable. The African American Christian experience is a unique one, not easily duplicated within multiracial congregations.

Another reason for racial separation is the belief among some African American and Native American Christians that white culture in the United States is oppressive, and even evil. This notion is generally found in the more radical versions of black theology or in the views of someone like Vine DeLoria. These perspectives possess great appeal. Such a mistrust of white Christians makes multiracial congregations nearly impossible.

The historic and present pervasiveness of racism in society means that African American and Native American congregations are important places for the affirmation of one's humanity. In fact, the denial of the basic humanity of persons who were not white in the United States birthed this separation. Among Native Americans the history of brutality and the attempts to ethnically cleanse Indians and assimilate them into white society have fostered a strong desire for separation. C. Eric Lincoln expressed similar thoughts regarding African Americans: "There was no room in the White Church for the black Christians who needed to be persons as well as believers. In consequence, even in the face of the formidable odds that would seek to suppress it, control it, or laugh it to scorn, the Black Church was as inevitable as religion itself."[47] Also African American and Native American congregations provide a place of refuge from racism. It is not unusual for middle-class African Americans living in the suburbs to seek out an urban African American congregation. When these African Americans attend integrated schools, work in multiracial environments, and/or live in integrated neighborhoods, they may perceive themselves as being constantly surrounded by whites. The African American congregation allows Sunday to be the one day of the week where such individuals can find a refuge from whites.

African American and Native American congregations are not only places of refuge from racism, they are places that fight against the continuing impact of racism in the United States. African American congregations have historically been places blacks can meet in relative safety from prying white eyes. As a result, it is common for the social and political leaders of African American resistance to come from the religious community. For African Americans and Native Americans to have a place of refuge and to fight white racism, separate congregations are essential.

7 | SEPARATE BUT EQUAL

The ethnic church in this country is an abomination to the all-encompassing gospel message. Eleven o'clock on Sunday mornings is the most segregated hour in America. We should all go to the same church." So proclaimed a seminary professor while Ken Uyeda Fong sat in class. When the class paused for a break, Pastor Fong went to his professor and inquired if he planned to begin attending the Asian American congregation where Fong was a member. The professor answered, "Why, no, I meant for you to come to our church." Ken Fong writes, "This fine Christian gentleman and world-class theologian could clearly imagine the cultural peculiarities of our church, but he was blind to those of his own."[1]

Would separation in the church occur even without racism? Do our cultural differences require it? As we noted, separate Native American and African American congregations emerged as a result of racism. Even without the horrible histories delineated, would Native Americans and African Americans prefer to worship in separate congregations for cultural reasons? While racism remains a significant reason Hispanic and Asian American communities give for separation, culture and ethnicity are more central concerns. We continue to explore the reasons for uniracial congregations by examining perspectives found in Latino, Asian American, and white communities.

A Unique History and Culture

As with Native American and African American churches, to understand arguments for separate Hispanic congregations, we must examine the genesis and unique historical development of Latin American peoples. Because people exist in social contexts, they carry with them collective memories, beliefs, and practices that in good part define who they are. In brief, when we bring people together with different identities, collective memories, and histories we put them at risk for losing their identities and their faith, and possibly allow the world to lose their unique perspective on God.

An essential concept in understanding Latino life and faith is *mestizaje:* the mixture of human groups.[2] Hispanic peoples came into being in the early sixteenth century in an often violent conquering of native peoples by the Spaniards. Latinos were created out of the miscegenation of the Spaniards, Amerindians, and Africans. In the United States the government classifies Hispanics as an ethnic group made up of many racial clusters. Yet in many ways "Latino" operates as a racial category—and Hispanics do experience racism. The reasons given for separate Hispanic congregations are similar to those given by other racial groups.

Part of the Latino experience of being conquered included the strong religious and cultural influences of the Spaniards. This effect was far-reaching; today, nearly 90 percent of Latinos are Roman Catholic, and even in the United States, with its robust Protestant flavor, over 80 percent of Hispanics are Catholic.[3] As more and more Hispanics embrace Protestantism—especially Evangelicalism and Pentecostalism—the impact of their Spanish Catholic past still has influence. But the religion and culture of Latinos differ from the religion and the culture of the Spaniards. These new peoples of the new world emerged from unique experiences and histories including not only the Spanish conquest of the sixteenth century but also the Nordic assaults of the nineteenth century and the marriage of Catholicism with ancient Amerindian religions.

Out of this history, they developed a faith with distinctive practices. The faith of Hispanics is often more devotional and communitarian, and it places much more emphasis on what can be called popular religion, the religion as developed and actually practiced by lay people, apart from formal theology.[4] Because Hispanic beginnings and life have been marked profoundly by plunder, slavery, oppression, poverty, and suffering, Christian faith has developed in such a way as to speak to these realities. Emphasizing symbols, dramas, and stories, Latino forms of Christianity reveal a predisposition toward the oral, visual, and dramatic. Two symbols from Spanish Catholicism were adapted to become central communicators of this faith: the Crucified Christ and the Virgin Mary. This contrasts with much of Christianity in the United States that is heavily influenced by the Protestantism of its European colonizers and immigrants.

Symbols of Faith

When one examines portraits or sculptures of Jesus crucified, as created by Latin American and Hispanic Catholics, these depictions communicate, in theologian Orlando Espín's words, "real suffering, real torture, and real death."[5] These depictions do so to identify Jesus with the real experiences of many Latinos. As Latinos struggle and suffer, often last in the world pecking order and at the bottom of the socioeconomic ladder in the United States, so too does their God. Jesus Christ's suffering at the hands of the Romans and "religious" leaders expressed his solidarity with all who have been oppressed, despised, mistreated, and rejected by the powerful.

Beyond the Crucified Christ, one cannot find a more powerful religious symbol and source of comfort among many Latino Catholics than the Virgin Mary. The most powerful, most influential account is of Our Lady of Guadalupe, and she has remained central throughout the centuries. According to tradition, in 1531 the Virgin Mary appeared at Tepeyac, a hill northwest of Mexico City, to Juan Diego, a poor native. Identifying herself as the Mother of the True God, she told Juan Diego to have a temple built on the site. As evidence of her appearance, she left an image of herself—which looks like an indigenous woman—imprinted miraculously on his robe, a poor quality cactus cloth. Many believe that the robe should have deteriorated in twenty years, but it shows no signs of decay 470 years later. It is said that the image even reflects in her eyes what was in front of her in 1531. Today, the Basilica built in honor of the Virgin of Guadalupe attracts over ten million visitors a year, making it, outside the Vatican, the most visited Catholic church in the world.[6]

For Latino Catholics, the belief that the holy mother of God appeared to a poor peasant in a land now populated with *mestizos* gives them a unique place in the faith, a special bond of caring. The Virgin of Guadalupe is particularly revered among Catholics of Mexican descent. She is credited with miracles, she is prayed to, she is trusted in, and whole art forms—such as Hispanic retablos (paintings of a scene from life with people communicating thanks to Mary, who is depicted in the upper-left-hand corner)—have developed around her.

Unique Theology

Because of this unique history, collective memory, and adaptation of religious symbols to speak specifically to their historical and cultural experience (which we have only touched on here), Catholic and Protestant Hispanic theologians often argue that Latinos must create their own theology and must practice their own faith. In addition to emphasizing the common conquest experiences and popular religion, these theologies usually include the concepts of survival and liberation. Because Latinos are often poor and lacking in political power, "the issues of survival put into question and judge as false all theologies and spiritualities that consider themselves apolitical."[7] Only dominant groups are in a position to say that faith and politics are unrelated, or should be. As such, Hispanics in the United States must control their own religious worship if they are to avoid being swallowed whole by the massive assimilating giant called the dominant culture. In the words of theologian Virgil Elizondo:

> Fundamental core religious symbols provide the ultimate root of the group's identity because they mediate the absolute. They are the final tangible expressions of the absolute. . . . They are the ultimate justification of the worldvision of the group and the force that cements all the elements of the life of the group into a cohesive, meaningful, and tangible world order. When such symbols are discredited or destroyed, nothing makes sense anymore. The worldvision moves from order into chaos, from significant mystery into a meaningless confusion.[8]

Put directly, assimilation murders the group. It silences its world-view and destroys its rich history, collective memory, and methods of religious belief and practice. But even if the group were somehow able to survive in the context of multiracial congregations, such an arrangement is often viewed as oppressive. Again, in the words of Virgil Elizondo, it is

> not sufficient to simply use Spanish in the liturgy, create our own music, and get more people involved in the work of the church. . . . We [need] both practical know-how so that we [can] make the structures of our society work in favor of our people and we [need] to create a new knowledge about ourselves, our social situation, and our religious beliefs.[9]

To be under the watchful, controlling eye of people who invented and benefit from the oppressive structures of society is to fail to gain true freedom in Christ. Christ came to liberate people, to announce supernatural unity while respecting and celebrating particularity. These views, common among many Latino and Latin American theologians, coalesce into liberation theology.

According to liberation theology, the gospel must be contextualized to cultural groups and their situations.[10] Ultimately, for each cultural group, the gospel must be liberated from dominant group interpretations. In the United States, the dominant group's oppression includes racism, economic exploitation, discrimination, and ethnocentrism. At the heart of these forms of oppression is a process of cultural assimilation. True liberation in this context, then, is the freedom to be autonomous and different, to live within the context of one's own culture, and to worship and serve Christ in one's own cultural context. In short, each cultural group must contextualize the gospel for itself.[11] From this understanding, calling for multiracial churches seems oppressive, supporting the older models of Anglo conformity or a white-dominated melting pot. From this perspective, the best way to bring about unity and reconciliation between groups is to recognize the right of each group to be Christian in their own, contextualized way. Apart from this, God becomes the God of the powerful, and in the process, we lose our ability to see the Divine's richness, depth, and breadth, and hear the Almighty's prophetic voice.

Cultural Preservation in a New Land

Like Hispanic congregations, Asian American churches have been important institutions in the community for as long as Asians have been immigrating to the United States.[12] Asian American congregations have helped sustain immigrants and their descendants as they have faced the harsh realities of life in the United States. Chinese American churches helped unify a community that was originally fraught with linguistic, socioeconomic, political, regional, and national-origin differences. Because of the enormous size and diversity of the Chinese diaspora, ethnic Chinese speak a number of dialects and languages. They also have many political allegiances, and these ethnic Chinese may hail from countries as varied as China, Taiwan, the Philippines, Vietnam, and Thailand. Similarly, Filipino American churches have received three waves of immigration spanning nearly ninety years. Their churches have brought together members who also exhibit linguistic, regional, and socioeconomic differences. Japanese American congregations have helped to preserve Japanese ethnic identity in the face of high rates of marriage outside their ethnic group.[13]

Asian American churches have even impacted the native countries that the immigrants left behind. For example, Korean American congregations played a crucial unifying role in the pre–World War II Korean American community's efforts to help fight for Korean independence from Japan.[14] Early Korean migrants to the United States were disproportionately Christian, largely because many of them had been recruited by missionaries from the United States. When Japan annexed Korea in 1910, these Koreans in the United States essentially became a "stranded people" with no country to call their own.[15] So they rallied together to fight for Korean independence, utilizing all their community resources. Historian Ronald Takaki notes, "The [Korean American] churches functioned as the religious arm of patriotic political organizations. . . . Koreans . . . gathered at church on Sundays to worship, socialize, and renew their commitment to the liberation of their homeland."[16] The fact that Syngman Rhee, the first president of the Republic of Korea in 1948, was an active member of Korean American churches during his time in the United States illustrated the historically close association of politics and religion within Korean American churches.[17]

Uniracial Asian American congregations have become such a prominent part of the religious landscape in the United States for several reasons. Many of them are the same as those cited in our discussions of Native American, African American, and Latino congregations. Asian Americans also seek a "spiritual home" in which they can worship in the style that is comfortable to them. There they can be free from racial prejudices that exist in the United States. As a result, Asian Americans gain important positions within their own churches—positions that would ordinarily be unattainable for immigrants in large non-Asian congregations. This newfound status is crucial to the identity of immigrants, especially males, who often experience downward occupational mobility when they immigrate.[18]

Furthermore, churches are open to all people, regardless of gender, age, or socioeconomic background. This stands in contrast to other types of ethnic or racial organizations such as alumni associations, professional associations, and informal social networks. In writing about the Korean American ethnic church, Won Moo Hurh and Kwang Chung Kim characterize it as a "microcosm" of both the informal and formal aspects of the Korean society that the immigrants left behind.[19] Illsoo Kim also sees the churches as "the substitute for ethnic neighborhoods" for Korean immigrants, who tend to be residentially assimilated.[20]

Through their Asian American churches, immigrant parents teach their children about their cultural heritage. Church members celebrate special Asian holidays as a group, thereby elevating the church to the status of an important center for ethnic heritage and community. In many communities, churches established Asian language schools in order to pass on their linguistic heritage to children born in the United States. Not only do Asian Americans reared in the United States learn about their ethnic heritage through the church, but there they also engage in regular face-to-face contact with fellow Asian Americans. This experience is especially valuable to those who are residentially assimilated and therefore do not encounter large numbers of Asian American peers in other contexts. Networks established through church membership can become important resources for the generations reared in the United States, not only in terms of providing mutual encouragement and support, but also in terms of linking potential romantic partners. Thus, the Asian American church has been the primary means of preserving ethnic/racial identity as well as cultural transmission.[21]

Although there have long been Christian communities in Asia, many immigrants from Asia choose to convert to Christianity after arriving in the United States. Religion for them does not involve maintaining their traditional beliefs, but it is the adoption of new beliefs that have long been associated with Western culture. Thus, the Asian immigrant member of an Asian American church enjoys the benefits of ethnic fellowship while simultaneously assimilating into United States society. Although their religious lives take place within the context of Asian American congregations, Asian American Christians may also be spared the suspicion and misconceptions that often accompany those who practice religions outside the Judeo-Christian fold. In essence, Asian American churches can encourage both assimilation and cultural preservation.

Holding on to Ethnicity

The vast majority of Asian American congregations are not only uniracial but uniethnic as well. In most Asian American churches, the overwhelming majority of members belong to the same ethnic group. There are a number of reasons for this ethnic segregation. First, most Asian American churches are *immigrant* congregations. Immigrants established them for the purpose of worshiping and having fellowship in their native tongues. The congregations usually create Sunday School programming for the generations born in the United States, but the ethnic church is most prominent among the first generation. The uniethnic character of the congregation is built into its original design. Furthermore, the uniethnic aspect of the church is arguably the most significant drawing factor for new members and visitors. When one asks members of ethnic congregations why they choose to attend their particular church, the answer is almost always, "Because I want to meet people who are like me [share my ethnic heritage]." Although they may eventually embrace Christianity, many Asian American churchgoers admit that their initial reason for attending a church was to meet coethnics. In a sense, any subsequent religious conversion stems from the original desire for ethnic fellowship.

Second, the large degree of ethnic separatism among Asian

American congregations is simply due to the enormous number of internal differences. The "Asian" racial category is a social construct in the United States that encompasses a wide range of cultures and histories. Although East Asian countries such as Korea, Japan, and China do share some cultural similarities based on Confucian ideals, each country has its own distinct culture, including language. The countries are also separated by centuries of hostility and competition, most notably Japanese colonization efforts in Asia. Thus, Asians who arrive in the United States do not think of themselves as "Asians," but rather as "Chinese," "Korean," "Filipino," and so on. The category of "Asian American" becomes even more problematic when one considers that it also includes those from the Indian subcontinent, whose cultures as well as physical appearance are quite different from those of East Asians. The uniethnic character of most Asian American congregations is largely a reflection of the great diversity that exists within the category. Whereas other groups with high numbers of immigrants—such as Latinos—may hail from different countries, they are technically still able to worship together in Spanish-speaking monolingual congregations. Asian Americans, on the other hand, can claim no unifying common language other than English.

Moving from Uniracial to Pan-Asian

Once the generation born in the United States comes of age, however, there is increasing evidence that Asian Americans become engaged in more racially and ethnically diverse congregations. Because second-generation Asian Americans are more proficient at English than at any other language, they no longer require ethnic segregation. Instead, they can choose to attend more ethnically and racially diverse congregations or recruit a more diverse membership into their pre-existing uniracial churches. Confronted with the challenge of promoting Christian ideals by shunning ethnic exclusiveness, these congregations are actively seeking a diverse membership. Whereas immigrant churches also incorporate ethnic identification into their names (e.g., First Korean United Methodist Church), the names of English-speaking Asian American churches reveal no ethnic or racial association. While these efforts to create more diversity in their churches are a start, many ministries remain overwhelmingly uniracial.

Recently, there has been a growing awareness of a pan-ethnic Asian American identity. In some cases, English-speaking uniethnic congregations sponsor joint events with congregations of other ethnicities, thereby fostering interethnic cooperation and understanding as Asian Americans. These pan-Asian networks are often developed at seminaries in the United States, where the future religious leaders of various uniethnic churches meet and befriend leaders of other races and ethnic groups. These leaders recognize that cooperation and fellowship with other churches can be a mutually beneficial endeavor that also serves to build up a stronger Asian American community.

In some cases, interethnic cooperation has led to the establishment of multiethnic Asian American congregations.[22] Although these churches may be classified as "uniracial" and therefore unimpressive to the outside observer, their congregations are made up of people of many different Asian American ethnic groups, and this is very notable. While English language ministries within ethnic Korean churches may have several Chinese American members and vice versa, congregations with at least 20 percent ethnic diversity are still very rare. Many of those that do exist tend to be on the West Coast, as the Asian American communities in that region have longer histories and are therefore more removed from their original ethnic cultures. The more generations a group has resided in the United States, the weaker the ethnic attachment may be; it is replaced by a stronger racial identification. Given their very high rate of marriage outside their ethnic group, Asian Americans who attend church may be more likely to join multiracial congregations over progressive generations in the United States.

The "White" Church

Many of the reasons that persons of color embrace uniracial congregations are found in their rejection by or reaction to white Christians. White racism in Christianity has been a primary reason for separate congregations. The rejection of Native Americans and African Americans by whites in the United States gave birth to racial segregation in the church. The paradigm of separation already existed when whites initially encountered Latinos by colonizing portions of Mexico and first knew Asians through immigration. Historically, whites often chose to be separate from persons of color because of perceived differences rooted in a sense of superiority in whiteness. When persons of color were included, it was usually in a subordinate status. Efforts to create some form of racial egalitarianism prior to World War II were of limited duration and sabotaged by white racism.

The present reality of separate white congregations in the United States is rarely justified using the harsh racist rhetoric of the past. In fact it is rarely considered abnormal or unbiblical to be an all-white congregation. It is a de facto segregation—a product of history or the makeup of one's neighborhood. As in the opening story in this chapter from Ken Fong's seminary class, we see that the professor believed his white congregation represented normal Christianity and Fong's congregation was a cultural curiosity. For many citizens of the United States, "white" Christianity is the norm and other racially specific congregations are "special" ministries. Many denominations have separate departments to serve the unique needs of culturally or racially specific congregations made up of persons of color. Yet we are unaware of any departments devoted to supporting white congregations as an explicitly stated mission. There are presently few rationales coming from the white community that are given for the existence of separate white congregations other than in the case of first-generation Europeans settling in the United States.

The Homogeneous Unit Principle

The primary exception comes from the church growth movement in the United States. Beginning in the 1970s, the writings of Donald McGavran and C. Peter Wagner have provided a major impetus for embracing the uniracial congregation as a model that they contend is socially relevant and biblically based. The central thrust in the church growth movement is evangelism. Many church growth experts believe that racial and cultural separation is a given in society. So they argue that rather than spending time trying to change this reality, one should use it to enhance efforts at evangelism. As Donald McGavran wrote, "People like to become Christians without crossing racial, linguistic, or class barriers. This principle is an undeniable fact. Human beings do build barriers around their own societies."[23]

McGavran's concept was called the homogeneous unit principle. C. Peter Wagner's book, *Our Kind of People,* used McGavran's premise as its central theme. The book was even promoted from this perspective. The back cover stated:

> Church growth beyond the melting pot—*Our Kind of People* attacks the Christian guilt complex arising from the civil rights movement and puts it to rest with a skillful mixture of scriptural precedent and human psychology. In doing so, Wagner transforms the statement that "11 a.m. on Sunday is the most segregated hour in America" from a millstone around Christian necks into a dynamic tool for assuring Christian growth.[24]

The church growth movement is primarily a white church phenomenon. Yet its basic concepts can apply in other racial settings as well: racial and cultural separation is a fact of life, so celebrate cultural difference and use it to evangelize people. Wagner writes that a "sign of a healthy, growing church is that its membership is composed of basically one kind of people."[25] He contends that his view was not influenced by racism when he declares:

> The homogeneous principle is just the opposite of racism. It is based on a high view of culture. It advocates the propriety of churches developing their Christian life-style in ways appropriate to the culture of their members. . . . we need to recognize that it is altogether possible for a church to develop basically within one homogeneous unit and still not be racist.[26]

According to Wagner, a congregation built on the premise of the homogeneous unit principle should never limit its membership based on race. He strongly states, "An important corollary of my hypothesis is that, while local congregations may in fact be basically homogeneous, in no case whatsoever should their doors be closed to those of other homogeneous units, either for worship or membership. This kind of exclusion, in my opinion, is clearly a form of racism and must be rejected on Christian ethical grounds."[27]

Both Wagner and McGavran suggest in their writings that congregations focused on overcoming racial separation waste energy better used for evangelizing non-Christians. Wagner wrote in the 1970s that most white churches attempting to become multiracial congregations were really using a white model with culturally diverse trappings. He wrote that "when integration of the local congregation is made a Christian virtue" that is the worst form of "assimilationist racism."[28] Wagner and McGavran do allow for a few exceptions, such as the development of what they call "conglomerate congregations." Wagner believes that this can only authentically occur when a pastor has a "missionary gift" that allows her or him to minister in a second culture. Since this gift is found in only 1 percent of Christians, according to Wagner's research, "the odds of success are so low" that he mentions it as an option "somewhat reluctantly."[29] Even when a congregation effectively develops a racially diverse constituency its opportunity for growth is tenuous. Wagner notes:

> If a given church decides to establish a philosophy of ministry around the principle of becoming a public showcase of socio-cultural integration, it can be done. After all, Christians are filled with the Spirit of Christ. In Christ there is no difference between Jew and Gentile or black and white. Bringing Christians from diverse cultures into a local fellowship will not be an easy job because it will require a degree of cultural circumcision on both sides, but with sufficient dedication, effort, and sacrifice, it can happen. However, when the task is completed, the resulting church will in all probability find itself rather limited as a base for effective evangelization in the future.[30]

From Donald McGavran's perspective, multiracial congregations truly occur only in places where integration has already happened:

> Only in true social melting pots is it a significant option. The old segments of society are in fact breaking down. Many mixed marriages are taking place. Children growing up together in school regard each other as essentially one people. There conglomerate congregations are both possible and desirable. There the best opportunity for growth may truly be that of bringing into one congregation converts of the new people being formed.[31]

In other words, only when society integrates should local congregations be multiracial. Therefore, according to Wagner and McGavran, multiracial congregations are only viable in a few circumstances, and even then rarely advisable.

Summary and Conclusion

At their broadest, the arguments for uniracial congregations among Latinos and Asian Americans are similar to those given for separate Native American and African American churches. Hispanic and Asian American congregations are places where their members can safely meet to fight the racism and oppression of the larger society. They are places where people can be accepted just as they are, where meaning is shared, where people are valued for their particularities, and where people do not have to curtail their "ethnic" ways to gain favor. Cultural practices and traditions can be celebrated, protected, and passed on to subsequent generations. Also leadership development occurs without the encumbrance of racism.[32] Thus, such congregations are places of refuge, an acceptable place within United States society for people to figuratively let their hair down.

Hispanic congregations are places where Latinos can develop spiritually and socially, free from the co-optive tendencies of the dominant Anglos. Here they can celebrate the symbols of their faith, sing in Spanish, and enjoy other traditions free from the larger culture's interference, which, at its best, seeks to curtail these beliefs and practices, and at its worse, seeks to obliterate them. True liberation must be culturally contextualized, and only culturally specific congregations can accomplish this. In Latino-specific congregations, a unique side of God is revealed. Hispanic cultures and religious practices have developed over a five-hundred-year period. If Latinos were to integrate into the dominant Anglo church in the United States, they could ultimately lose their way of understanding and worshiping God as well as their unique cultures. Such integration might also mean the continued subjugation of a people under the guise of an apolitical spirituality that seeks to be color blind and avoids responsibility for issues of social and economic justice. These costs may be too high, both for Latinos and for the larger culture.

The church growth proponents of the homogeneous unit principle argue that the best and most effective approach for developing growing vibrant churches is uniracial congregations. This is true for congregations of all races and cultures. In their view, white congregations that jump on the bandwagon of racial reconciliation risk sabotaging their efforts at evangelism. The priority of all Christian congregations is to "make disciples of all nations" (Matthew 28:19). This is achieved when each race and ethnic group evangelize within their own people group. When the evangelism task is complete, then racial reconciliation can be pursued.

As long as there is migration from Asia, there will always be Asian American congregations. Like Latinos, Asian Americans either need or desire to worship in their native tongues. However, the ethnic church among Asian Americans may be a transitional phenomenon because acculturation and structural assimilation dilute ethnic loyalties and identifications over time. Asian Americans leave their uniethnic churches in large numbers, even as early as the second generation. Therefore, individual congregations struggle to balance the demands of Christian universalism and the benefits of ethnic particularism. While newer arrivals will undoubtedly feel more at ease in ethnic-specific congregations, the generations born in the United States are moving toward a more multiethnic model (and possibly multiracial model). As they marry outside their ethnic group at fast rates, Asian Americans will inevitably look beyond their ethnic community for solidarity and meaning. In many ways, the Asian American church (as well as other ethnic or racial congregations) may be a barometer of public opinion regarding Asian Americans. If Asian Americans are increasingly accepted into the ranks of the larger society in the United States, they will feel less compelled to choose uniethnic/uniracial congregations. Should there be a wave of anti-Asian sentiment or exclusion, however, Asian Americans may retreat and organize themselves once again along racial and/or ethnic lines.

8 | ARGUING THE CASE FOR MULTIRACIAL CONGREGATIONS

Richard Twiss understands the ongoing dilemma surrounding racism and the church. He has often experienced it. He recounts one such incident: "So one afternoon I asked one of the pastoral leaders how I was supposed to relate to my Native culture as a Christian. I distinctly remember him opening the Bible he was carrying and reading from Galatians 3:28 (NIV) where Paul wrote, 'There is neither Jew nor Greek, slave nor free, male nor female, for you are all one in Christ Jesus.'" Twiss continues, "After reading the passage, this pastoral leader commented on how cultures should all blend together for us as Christians. He then concluded, 'So, Richard, don't worry about being Indian; *just be like us.*'"[1] After reflecting on the arguments for uniracial congregations in chapters six and seven, one may become convinced that separate congregations based on race and culture are the best option for the church—particularly for persons of color. As Richard Twiss's story illustrates, even much of what is articulated as biblical unity is actually an invitation to assimilate into white definitions of Christianity.

Yet we argue that when possible, congregations should be multiracial. We are calling for a movement that brings us closer to this goal. Our argument began as we described how Jesus preached and lived his vision of a house of prayer for all the nations. We showed how the congregations that emerged following the ministry of Jesus were presented in the Bible as established with the intention of including all people no matter what race or culture. The power of Christian faith was revealed as congregations bridged cultural and racial differences. These first-century church members were so unique that none of the prevailing religious designations fit. They no longer exclusively practiced Judaism and could not be categorized as emperor worshipers or pagans. There were no social organizations this inclusive. Their radical blending of people called for a new name. So they were labeled Christ followers—that is, Christians. If we claim to follow Jesus Christ and to have inherited the Gospel of the first-century church, we contend that our present-day congregations should exhibit the same vision for and characteristics of those first Christian communities of faith. Therefore, we even go so far as to say that a Christian, by biblical definition, is a follower of Jesus Christ whose way of life is racial reconciliation.

We find little disagreement with the assertion that first-century congregations were demographically diverse.[2] Yet after a long history of racial separation in the United States, is it really possible to embrace the biblical model for congregations? And is it even preferable in our racialized society? We cannot realistically turn back the clock to a time before racism. Although we have demonstrated that despite an extremely racist history in the United States, multiracial congregations are viable—and become even more so as we enter the demographically diverse twenty-first century—many find the arguments for uniracial congregations articulated in the previous two chapters compelling. Perhaps there is a place for both multiracial congregations and uniracial congregations in the United States. Certainly congregations populated predominantly by persons of color did not emerge as reactions to the concept of multiracial congregations but in response to white racism, or at least in response to particular needs not addressed by predominantly white congregations. Richard Allen, William Seymour, and many others attempted to work within multiracial settings before forming or resigning themselves to racially separate congregations (and in Allen's case a separate denomination).

So in this chapter we respond to those arguments presented in favor of uniracial congregations. We remain firm in our argument that when possible, congregations should be multiracial. In our responses, we often embrace what has been learned and developed in uniracial congregations, for these concepts are important for multiracial congregations as well. The arguments from chapters six and seven fall under these broad categories: (1) pragmatic reasons, (2) theological reasons, (3) cultural reasons, (4) activist reasons, and (5) sociological reasons.

Pragmatic Reasons

Many people believe that racial separation should not be viewed as a negative. It is just a fact of life. Given that premise, they argue that the most practical way to do ministry is from within the confines of racially and culturally specific groupings. Separation is easier. If people naturally want to stay with their own kind, then racially segregated churches provide the pragmatic solution. This is a central premise for many church growth proponents. Donald McGavran and C. Peter Wagner argued that most people do not want to cross the lines of race or culture to go to church. They assert that the most successful approach for developing growing, vibrant churches is the development of uniracial congregations. Their thesis suggests that this is true for congregations of all races and cultures, not just the white congregations that were their primary audience. Each racial and ethnic group should evangelize within their own group for the greatest effectiveness.

This argument is further expanded when one considers that many immigrants to the United States are not Christians. This means that ethnic congregations can be a major vehicle for evangelization and recruitment. It follows that many members of first-generation immigrant ethnic Christian congregations are converts. While religion is the ultimate focus of congregations, converts often admit that they initially attended a church out of a desire for ethnic fellowship. Once they began attending, they were introduced to Christian beliefs and slowly underwent religious conversion. Thus, the ethnic character of the congregation is a primary draw for new members and converts. Without uniracial congregations, these people might never have become Christians. Taking this element out of the church may hinder the ability of the Gospel to reach new people, particularly new arrivals to the United States.

Our Response

While racial separation may be sociologically comfortable, we do not accept it as ordained by God. According to the Bible, in the beginning God created one race, the human race (Genesis 1:26–27). Jesus and the first-century church believed they were commissioned to create congregations that more accurately reflected God's original intention for the human family. The day of Pentecost birthed a multicultural church that served as a re-creation of God's original intention. Racial separation in the United States is socially constructed. The church in the United States reflects a social reality rather than promoting a theological vision. Pastor Hozell C. Francis expresses some additional concerns in *Church Planting in the African American Context:*

> First, if new believers begin with their "own kind," will they not be inclined to remain with them and thereby perpetuate a segregated Christianity? Second, will not many see the homogeneous principle as an excuse for not reaching people, simply because of difference in race, religion, language, or the like? Many believers have regular contact with people who may have one or more distinctives. Yet they communicate about many matters such as politics, sports, or family concerns. Why not do the same in matters of religion? Third, homogeneity may give credence to those who hold a notion of superiority with respect to race, education, language, or other cultural identifiers. It may offer support to the segregationalist efforts in a number of these categories, especially at the popular level of racial superiority.[3]

Also, just because something is pragmatic does not mean that it is the right thing to do. It can be "pragmatic" for a church to avoid spending money on youth ministry or a homeless shelter because neither the youth nor the homeless are going to generate enough revenue to pay for these ministries. But churches support youth and homeless ministries because of their larger commitment to evangelism or social justice. Likewise we believe that churches should be committed to dealing with one of the most important moral issues of this day—racism—and must work toward producing racial reconciliation. To this end, even if it seems that multiracial churches are not pragmatic, churches should have important transcendent concerns that make the work toward racially integrated congregations valuable.

Due to the enormous challenges individuals face when immigrating to a new country—cultural change, language acquisition, economic hardship, and the like—it may not be possible to establish or maintain multiracial congregations in the case of first-generation immigrants. As long as there is migration from other countries to the United States there may be a need for ethnic-specific congregations. Even with this allowance, some congregations can provide ways to meet the particular needs of these groups while integrating immigrants into a multiracial community. We will offer some suggestions in this regard later in the chapter in our response to "sociological reasons." Another possible exception to the biblical call for multiracial congregations is language difference, which is particularly relevant for first-generation immigrants. As the technical possibilities for simultaneous translation become more affordable, this exception is less compelling. Simultaneous translation could make every Sunday a Pentecost experience with the preacher speaking in her or his language and the people in the pews hearing it in their own language. Even now some congregations have bilingual services because of their primary commitment to biblical unity. We noted in chapter five that Park Avenue United Methodist Church is such a congregation. Fenggang Yang says that even uniracial Chinese congregations often conduct worship services in as many as three languages simultaneously— English, Cantonese, and Mandarin—to overcome the linguistic barriers within the ethnic Chinese community.[4]

Also, the ethnic church may be a transitional phenomenon. We noted in chapter seven that many Asian Americans leave their uniethnic congregations as early as the second generation. While first-generation immigrants feel more at ease in ethnic-specific congregations, some among the second generation, born in the United States, are moving toward multiethnic and multiracial models. Also as interracial marriage occurs at increased rates, couples and families will look for congregations that can meet their needs for cultural and racial pluralism. We have argued that in the twenty-first century, multiracial congregations can be effective in evangelizing the highly diverse United States. Theologian Bruce Fong writes, "I believe that pursuing a strict homogeneous unit approach blinds us to how an incredibly diverse Christian fellowship that is united around Christ can stimulate the curiosity of unconvinced persons."[5] Building congregations around a homogeneous grouping is a sociological principle based on what is comfortable and marketable. Unity is the New Testament model of church growth based on the power of the Holy Spirit to reconcile people across socially constructed divides. First century congregations grew as a result of the coming together of Jews and Gentiles, not in spite of this phenomenon.

Theological Reasons

In chapters six and seven some theological reasons for separation were presented. One was that the church should be a place where individuals are affirmed as children of God. A person's dignity should be upheld and enhanced in his or her faith community. Racism in the church denies that God's image is imprinted on each human being. The pervasiveness of racism in the United States means that racially separate congregations for persons of color are important places to affirm their humanity. The origins of uniracial congregations among persons of color were often in this disavowal of the full humanity of persons who were not white. In racially separate congregations, human dignity and self-worth are nurtured and sustained.

We have also noted at several points that there is a long history of racism and brutality by whites toward persons of color in the United States. Native Americans have very little experience with white forms of Christianity that are not oppressive and demeaning. The African American church was born out of the tragic consequences of slavery. Asian Americans and Latinos have experienced racism in countless ways. Some African American and Native American theologians and social commentators claim that the white church in the United States is thoroughly oppressive and evil and suggest that white forms of Christianity may be beyond repair. While only a few "extreme" scholars and activists generally articulate these views, they possess great appeal and represent the feelings of some. Such mistrust of white Christians makes multiracial congregations that include whites difficult and undesirable for some.

Another point made was that the versions of Christian faith that emerge in racially separate contexts might not be compatible with white churches or with each other. For example, Native Americans focus on sacred places; the Virgin Mary of Guadalupe plays a significant role in Mexican Catholicism; and in many cases, African Americans are either more theologically conservative or more politically progressive than the various white forms of Christianity. The Christian experiences in communities of color are each unique and not easily duplicated within multiracial congregations.

Our Response

Congregations that do not attempt to affirm their members as children of God can hardly be described as Christian. Authentic multiracial congregations must be places where people feel spiritually uplifted and personally affirmed in a society where racism significantly impacts the self-esteem of individuals. Given the history of racism in the United States, it is easy to see why some persons of color may perceive that the Christianity of whites has no redeeming value. Multiracial congregations can serve as gathering spaces where whites and persons of color begin to see and relate to each other as human beings. White believers should not be defined only by the evil and tragic history of previous generations or the present-day privilege of accumulated benefits due to racism. Also persons of color should not be defined as "the other," someone so different or inferior as to require that relationships be maintained at a distance—token persons or cultural curiosities in the white man's church. Such stereotyping and dehumanizing of people—whether done by whites or persons of color—is exactly the type of racialized behavior we have to overcome in this society. Certainly such racial prejudice coming from persons of color has different meanings than when coming from whites. The goal of creating an authentic multiracial congregation will involve a process. We must be transparent in our own self-examination and full of grace toward others who are on the journey with us.

Obviously, multiracial congregations may not include whites. These congregations can be the coming together of African Americans and Asian Americans, or Latinos and Native Americans, or any combination of racial groups. In the United States racial separation also exhibits itself through racial lines drawn between groups of color. So multiracial congregations are also places where people of color cross the divide of race and learn to interact with one another amid cultural differences. Multiracial congregations are places to live out

God's call to unity. For future race relations to be healthy, there must be a mutual accountability to each other and no group can have a dominant position over another group.

The multitude of expressions of Christian faith that have developed during the era of racial separation in the United States will need to be synthesized in some way so as not to lose the distinctive contributions to our understanding of God. We all have much to gain from worshiping God in ways and styles developed in settings outside our own. Each represents how humans have reached out to the Almighty. We must restrain ourselves and not arrogantly behave as though our way of believing and worshiping is superior to other perspectives. This will not be easy. Nations have gone to war and people have ended relationships and lives over what are essentially theological belief systems. Developing a rich multicultural theology and way of worship must be at the top of the agenda of multiracial congregations.[6]

We are suggesting here the value of congregations integrating cultural perspectives that have emerged in racially separate contexts. We realize that doctrinal differences also exist. It may be possible for a white Catholic church to display a painting of Our Lady of Guadalupe and use this as a way of integrating Latino faith symbols. This could not happen in most Evangelical congregations due to doctrinal beliefs. We do believe that we need more unity across the five major doctrinal divisions in Christianity—Orthodoxy, Roman Catholicism, mainline Protestantism, Evangelicalism, and Pentecostalism. Our focus though is to call for a movement for multiracial congregations within these doctrinal traditions. Perhaps such a movement will encourage a move toward greater unity across the various Christian communions.

The combination of a theologically conservative and socially progressive perspective found among some African American Christians has gained favor among some white activists. Organizations such as the Christian Community Development Association and Evangelicals for Social Action tend to have a theologically conservative, politically progressive perspective. While these groups do not completely replicate the religious atmosphere of African Americans, their existence does create a social space where black Christians looking for allies can find some comfort. Multiracial congregations represent a wide range theologically and politically. Yet given the reality of the racism experienced by their members, for these congregations to be considered authentic they will need to address racism and therefore, become progressive at least on this issue.

Activist Reasons

A very important role for congregations in communities of color has been to encourage an activist faith in order to struggle against racism and injustice. This crystallized in various forms of liberation theology. Some congregations populated by persons of color have served as communities of resistance against racism in the United States. These congregations historically have been places where people of color can meet out of view of the dominant white society. Often social and political leaders of the resistance come from the religious community. Several examples from the African American community easily come to mind, such as Martin Luther King Jr. and Fannie Lou Hamer. Separate congregations have been essential places to fight white racism.

Our Response

We certainly applaud the significant advancements made because of the important contributions from congregations of color in the struggle against white systemic racism. In many cases, the uniracial congregation was the only place in society where persons of color had the relative freedom from white dominance to organize and plan strategies of resistance. Their faith also produced the vision and the perseverance to prevail. Even our ability to write this book and consider the possibility of multiracial congregations stands on the foundation laid by these congregations that demanded a more open society and a much more racially just Christianity in the United States.

Multiracial congregations must duplicate the role of these uniracial congregations by impacting society with an agenda for inclusion in mainstream life and a call for accountability in issues of racial injustice. The multiracial witness can further strengthen the possibility for reform in society. Moreover, it is not clear whether the best way for people of color to fight racial and social injustice is to maintain religious segregation. In fact, it is shortsighted to rely on racially segregated organizations. This means that people of color must effect social change by working against all dominant group members rather than by working with some whites who are sympathetic to their causes. This shortsightedness neglects the historical reality that there have always been whites who fought with people of color in the many movements for civil and human rights in the United States.

Research suggests that whites who attend church with people of color are more likely to have progressive racial attitudes than other whites.[7] Whether interaction with persons of color helps to change attitudes or more progressive whites tend to choose to worship with persons of color cannot yet be determined. But it is probable that interaction with persons of color may help persuade whites about the value of diverse perspectives. Because the support of at least some whites will be needed to correct institutional discrimination in society, people of color would do well to embrace possible opportunities to influence whites. Multiracial congregations offer such an opportunity. A major stumbling block, and we have found this to be true in our studies, will be the dominant group's perspective that faith and politics are unrelated. They will push this because they find it to be true in their experience. As we discuss in chapter ten, structures must be created that give equal voice to nondominant groups. Again we say authentic multiracial congregations address racism in society and within the church.

Cultural Reasons

Racially separate congregations provide a place to embrace and nurture culture. Cultures developed by people of color in the United States are distinct from those of whites and from each other. These unique features enrich the lives of persons of color and influence their faith traditions. Often the cultural style of whites inhibits the faith development of people of color. Worship styles in many settings are unique. Certainly the African American preacher has historically played a unique role in the life of the African American community. If multiracial congregations lead to assimilation, they sound the death knell of certain irreplaceable cultures and ultimately the loss of unique ways of understanding and worshiping God. These costs may be too high, both for persons of color and for the larger church.

Our Response

Cultures are always changing. Cultural changes almost always occur when there is the slightest interaction with another culture, but cultures will change even without such interaction. It is unrealistic to believe that we can preserve a pristine racial culture. Rather it seems reasonable to expect some change in every culture. Thus, the important question is not whether change can be prevented—it cannot; the question is whether change to one's culture is positive or negative. To this end, a multiracial congregation with egalitarian relationships between the races offers the best opportunity to learn about other cultures. It also encourages us to learn to accept the cultural changes that are best for our own culture while rejecting the potential changes that may be harmful.

Furthermore, in response to the strong fear of cultural assimilation, the Latino experience has much to offer regarding the hoped-for outcome of multiracial congregations. Essential to understanding Latino life and faith is the concept of *mestizaje,* the mixture of human groups. Within this very core of the argument for Hispanic churches lie the seeds of the argument for multiracial congregations. Latinos are living examples of the benefits of mixing human groups. The rich Latin cultures would not exist without such mixing. What new and rich ways of living and viewing the world wait to be created by the intertwining of a diversity of cultures! We owe it to ourselves and we owe it in obedience to God to find out.

Theologian Carlyle Fielding Stewart III argues that much the same process occurred in African American spirituality. He writes, "African American spirituality has coalesced the best of both worlds into a framework for human existence, and that its genius synthesizes certain aspects of Anglo and African cultures, thereby forming a unique African American identity."[8] We contend that many cultures in the United States are syntheses of the cultures with which they come in contact; this also evident in the culture of whites. Stewart defines the process for this occurrence among African Americans:

> It is my belief that the term "African" American signifies a confluence of the best of Africa and European-American experiences. . . . All too often the negative aspects of Anglo culture are accentuated in the black experience because of white racism. The genius of African American spirituality resides in its own elective affinities, the

manner in which it has subtly and thoroughly appropriated, integrated, transformed, and synthesized various aspects of African and
Anglo culture into a living hermeneutic of positive transformation
and human survival.[9]

The beauty and power of culture are realized—and this is so often
missed—when they are shared and lived with people raised in different
cultures. As animals need instinct to survive and thrive, humans need
culture. But because humans create culture, each individual culture is
limited. It perceives some things wrongly, or at least from a one-dimen-
sional perspective. For example, "God is love" is emphasized in some
cultures. True enough, God is love. But God is much more than that.
And the term "love" has a multitude of rich meanings. No single culture captures this richness. It is only revealed and made complete when
diverse perspectives and experiences are brought together (Ephesians
4:1–17). A commitment to being together with people of faith who
emphasize and speak to different experiences has a number of benefits:
it pushes us to understand others; we put ourselves in another's shoes;
and we are forced to get out of our own cocoon. In short, it asks us to
be other-centered, a true goal for a mature Christian.

If being in a multiracial congregation simply means people of
color have to conform to a dominant group's beliefs and practices,
then arguments for separation may well win the day. But if being a
true multiracial church means spiritual *mestizaje*, then we have people
and groups coming together to worship, learn, and care for one another.
This would include encouraging cultural development and working
side by side for liberation. If a true multicultural congregation is this,
and we argue that it must be, then power and hope can best be found
in our coming together.[10]

Over time, a new culture is developed, one that did not exist
before. People will move beyond simply representing their separate
groups. They will forge a new, common identity, even as they maintain their uniqueness. As we describe in more detail in chapter ten,
assimilation—to become one and the same—is not the goal.
Integration—to be united in our equally respected differences—is the
goal. The argument that we must get beyond incorporating people in
a superficial manner—sing a few songs from the culture, say a few
prayers in Spanish, get some people involved in the work of the

church—is a powerful one that sharpens the definition of what it means to be truly multiracial. This is not something to play at. It is serious business, involving the eternal lives of real people. Becoming a multiracial congregation is not an afterthought that we "tack on" to our normal way of doing church; it is a fundamental shift in understanding and practice.

Sociological Reasons

In order to survive in a white-dominated society in the United States where people of color have experienced the oppressive results of racism, Native Americans, African Americans, Latinos, and Asian Americans have developed parallel communities, often anchored by their congregations. Even if there were no oppressive dominant group structure, it is quite possible that racial and cultural groups would launch parallel communities for cultural survival. The uniracial church serves as a place of refuge and community development. Uniracial congregations provide a place of refuge from the daily grind of overt and covert racism. Racial and ethnic specific congregations are places where people are embraced for who they are, valued for their cultural particularities, free to communicate through shared experiences, and not pressured to change their "ethnic" ways so as to gain acceptance. These congregations celebrate, safeguard, and pass on to the next generation cultural practices and traditions. Uniracial congregations are places where leaders develop without the burden of racism and members develop spiritually and socially, emancipated from the co-optive tendencies of some whites.

Persons of color seek a spiritual "haven" to call their own. Especially as they experience the assimilation of themselves and their children into the mainstream culture of the United States. People of color need a space in which they can be part of the majority group and where they can practice Christianity in the way that is most beneficial for them. It is not unusual for middle-class people of color living in the suburbs to seek out uniracial congregations. They may attend integrated schools, work in multiracial environments, and live in integrated neighborhoods, but they may feel like whites surround them continually. The uniracial congregation allows Sunday to be the one day of the week when such individuals can find a refuge from white society.

Many uniracial congregations serve as community centers in their neighborhoods. The church serves many social functions, such as preserver of ethnic culture, cultural center of the community, and a place to foster business networks as well as social networks. In addition, immigrants who participate in church and serve in leadership positions within the church have better mental health than non-participating immigrants even though many of them have experienced downward occupational mobility in the United States.[11] Entrepreneurship in these uniracial congregations often produces faith-based community and economic development initiatives.

Finally, after hundreds of years of separate development it may be too late to change. Many uniracial congregations have long and treasured histories. They are anchors in their communities. The racially specific organizations within denominations and the historic African American denominations play an important role in society. One can argue that a move to multiracial congregations could disrupt the important function of parallel communities.

Our Response

Multiracial congregations will most likely also become parallel communities in a racist society. They will be places where people who desire to model the racially inclusive community called for in the New Testament find refuge from a racially polarizing society. Multiracial congregations certainly should be centers for community development that address the needs of their neighborhoods and places of refuge for people of color who are experiencing the daily assault of racism. Like uniracial congregations, multiracial congregations can also be centers of entrepreneurial activity through community and economic development. Membership in multiracial congregations can facilitate the establishment of interracial social networks and help people increase access to important information or job opportunities. Community development initiatives can be enhanced by the rich variety of cultural traditions and experiences brought to bear in the process.

One way to provide refuge is to develop what can be called a "Church within a Church" model. In this type of church, the overall membership is multiracial. However, there can be special fellowship groups within the larger congregation that exist to meet the specific needs of particular populations. For example, a growing number of Asian-language-based small groups are being established in large congregations. These Asian Americans are church members, but they still meet their fellowship needs through a small group devoted to their ethnic or racial group. This is comparable to a small group ministry devoted to single parents. In the case of Asian Americans born and raised in the United States, the special fellowship groups may use English, but they still address the different experiences that Asian Americans have in the United States. Through this "Church within a Church" model, members can benefit from membership in a multiracial congregation while still having the opportunity to have fellowship on a close level with coethnics.

The "Church within a Church" model could benefit first-generation immigrants. Language-specific worship services could be offered while at the same time the broader social networks of the entire congregation are available to meet the transition and networking needs of immigrant families. Another "Church within a Church" grouping could be around cultural preservation. This would serve each group's need to preserve culture and pass it on to the next generation, but it would also benefit the entire congregation as a source of education for living in a multicultural society. One can imagine the power of the interaction if the Norwegian group, the Ojibwe group, the Cambodian group, the Sudanese group, and the Honduran group gathered to exchange stories that emerge from their cultural group meetings. Such an assembly would demonstrate the essence of Christ's unity in the midst of diversity. The "Church within a Church" model could provide places for conversation around issues such as racial profiling, again offering support to persons experiencing this reality and later, education for persons unaware of its effect.

Another important need that multiracial congregations can address stems from the growing rate of racially mixed marriages and families. Some may argue that this is precisely the reason we need more ethnic congregations—to facilitate marriage among people of the same group and limit interracial unions. Ethnic congregations are not capable of stemming the tide. Those who understand the racist nature of historical antimiscegenation sentiments should be very hesitant to support the suppression of interracial marriages—even if such suppression is to preserve the cultures of people of color. Even those children who grow up in uniracial congregations can end up marrying outside their race. Therefore, recognizing the growing number of interracial couples, it is necessary to have congregations that can meet the needs of both spouses and their family, and to provide refuge in a society that has yet to fully embrace these arrangements. Such havens can be found only in a multiracial congregation.

Conclusion

Our premise remains that when possible, congregations should be multiracial. We have held high the standard of what it means to be an authentic multiracial congregation. We do not apologize for this. We do recognize that multiracial congregations are the result of a commitment to take a long and difficult journey toward authenticity. So we call for a movement toward more multiracial congregations. We grant the validity of three exceptions. First, in some locations, particularly certain rural areas, only one racial group resides. Obviously, a multiracial congregation is not possible. Yet even congregations in such settings must operate as New Testament congregations. They should be crossing any ethnic lines that exist: Germans and Italians, Vietnamese and Laotian, Trinidadian and Haitian, and the like. Also congregations that are in racially isolated areas should develop partnerships with congregations in other areas that are diverse and they should educate themselves as though next year their community will diversify. Many formerly racially homogeneous communities are now integrated. The Christian congregation should be the first group to welcome new neighbors. A second exception to our thesis is the lack of a common language. As we noted earlier, affordable technical possibilities for simultaneous translation may eliminate this exception in the future. The third exception allows for the unique circumstances of first-generation immigrant groups. The challenges of crossing cultures may be too great in the first generation of living in the United States. There may be a few unique situations we have missed that qualify as exceptions. We cannot anticipate every special circumstance in particular congregations. But these special cases are a small percentage of total churches.

The future of Christianity in the twenty-first century depends on practical, living examples of authentic reconciling faith. While multiracial congregations will never be perfect organizations, God's call to reconciliation through the life, death, resurrection, and abiding presence of Jesus Christ compels us to embrace the challenge of moving forward toward this goal. As we have contended in this chapter, to be authentic, multiracial congregations need to embrace the important functions provided in the context of uniracial congregations. Multiracial congregations must witness to their faith in Christ, affirm all people as fully human and created in the image of God, respect a wide range of culturally influenced theological perspectives, address racism in society and in the church, embrace a new *mestizaje* congregational culture, and provide a refuge to all who are battered by racism in society.

What are the next steps? We must equip ourselves for a movement toward the development of many more multiracial congregations. In chapter nine we discover the theology needed to sustain our efforts to develop multiracial congregations. In chapter ten, we further clarify the defining characteristics of authentic multiracial congregations. We also identify the challenges faced and offer some practical directives.

IV

DEVELOPING MULTIRACIAL CONGREGATIONS IN THE TWENTY-FIRST CENTURY

9 | THE TRUTH OF THE GOSPEL

During the late 1950s and early 1960s, Malcolm X proclaimed a message meant to empower African Americans by separating blacks from an unhealthy dependence on whites—economically, socially, psychologically, and spiritually. Although he was raised in a predominantly white community and attended schools where he was often the only African American child in the classroom, Malcolm X's parents instructed him in the tenets of Black Nationalism.[1] His religious faith, which he embraced as an adult, was based on a belief in the inherent evil of white people and the need to separate from them. Malcolm X referred to "the white race" as "a race of devils."[2] He preached, "The Scripture says that God will separate his (black) sheep from the (white) goats. . . .The goats are to be slaughtered. . . while the sheep are to be gathered into his pasture. . . . In like manner God has prepared a Doomsday for this sinful white world of colonizers, enslavers, oppressors, exploiters, lyncher. . . . White America is doomed!"[3]

Malcolm X's message sounded radically different in the last year of his life. Less than a month before he was assassinated at the age of thirty-nine in 1965, Malcolm X said in an interview, "I believe in recognizing every human being as a human being, neither white, black, brown nor red. When you are dealing with humanity as one family, there's no question of integration or intermarriage. It's just one human being marrying another human being, or one human being living around and with another human being."[4] A few days later he said in a press conference, "The worst form of a human being, I believe, is one who judges another human being by the color of his skin."[5]

Something happened to completely transform Malcolm X's worldview. When he returned from a pilgrimage to Mecca in 1964, he came back a changed person. He experienced a conversion when he embraced orthodox Islam in Mecca. Malcolm X no longer thought of whites as inherently evil. His critique of white racism remained sharp, but he embraced the humanity of whites. That change in thinking allowed room for Malcolm X to consider racial reconciliation as a possibility in the human experience. He further noted that the whites he met on his pilgrimage had an attitude that was untouched by racism. They did not think of themselves as whites in some superior fashion, but rather considered themselves simply to be human beings. When Malcolm X returned to the United States, he was convinced that if whites in the United States studied Islam maybe then racism could be addressed in significant ways.[6]

A similar story occurred over nineteen hundred years earlier. Saul of Tarsus (later known as the apostle Paul) was born into an oppressed ethnic minority in the Roman Empire. His family lived in the midst of a city where Greco-Roman culture prevailed. Although he was a citizen of Rome, Saul did not assimilate into the dominant culture. His perspectives and passions were rooted in the culture and religion of his family's country of origin—"a Hebrew born of Hebrews" (Philippians 3:6). His parents raised him as an observant Jew and he spoke fluent Aramaic, the language of the homes and streets of first-century Jews living in their conquered homeland. Saul was sent by his parents to Jerusalem to be educated under the tutelage of the leading Pharisee teacher Gamaliel (Acts 22:3). It seems that, while he was in Jerusalem, Saul fully embraced the viewpoint of religious separatists. Saul wrote that he was fervent in his education: "[I was] beyond many among my own people of the same age, for I was far more zealous for the traditions of my ancestors" (Galatians 1:14). When the first-century church emerged with its message of inclusion, Saul led the persecution: "I was violently persecuting the church of God and was trying to destroy it" (Galatians 1:13).[7]

Saul sounded radically different in the letters he later wrote to various congregations of this same church he had persecuted. Writing under his Greek name Paul, he declared, "There is no longer Jew or Greek, there is no longer slave or free, there is no longer male and female; for you are all one in Christ Jesus" (Galatians 3:28). In another letter he wrote, "For in the one Spirit we were all baptized into one body—Jews or Greeks, slaves or free—and we were all made to drink of one Spirit" (1 Corinthians 12:13).

Like the story of Malcolm X, something happened to Saul that completely transformed his worldview. While on the road to Damascus in Syria, where he planned to arrest followers of Jesus Christ, he was blinded by a light and heard a voice. The voice said, "Saul, Saul, why do you persecute me?" Saul recognized it as the voice of God and responded, "Who are you, Lord?" The voice replied, "I am Jesus, whom you are persecuting" (Acts 9:1–16). In the encounter and its aftermath, Saul realized that in order to be faithful to God he must adopt an inclusive perspective of humanity and proceed as a follower of Jesus Christ. This meant that he would minister to Gentiles as well as Jews. He excelled at his new calling.

A movement in Christianity toward more multiracial congregations in the United States will require a fundamental shift in belief systems and in organizational practices. Theologian Justo González writes, "The multicultural vision is sweet. But there is also a bitter side to it. There is the bitter side of having to declare that the vision of many peoples, many tribes, many nations, and many languages involves much more than bringing a bit of color and folklore into our traditional worship services. It involves radical changes in the way we understand ourselves, and in the way we run our business."[8] We explore what it means to embrace a theological worldview that can direct and sustain multiracial congregations. In chapter ten we discuss the necessary ingredients for organizing and implementing authentic multiracial congregations—how multiracial congregations should "run their business." Good theology leads to good practice. The late preacher of reconciliation, Samuel G. Hines, used to say, "Thinking reconciliation precedes doing reconciliation."[9] We must be anchored in a belief system that inspires and engenders racial unity, and keeps us from losing hope when difficulties assail us—and they will.

Worldview Change

Most of us need a worldview change to participate effectively in multiracial congregations. That might seem like a judgmental statement, but our racialized society in the United States has so shaped our thinking and ways of living that separation often feels normal and seems natural. As we have repeatedly stated and illustrated, Christianity came into being in the United States within a paradigm of racial separation, and theologies emerged to support this pattern. We must discover how to break out of this mold that has held us captive for too long, so we once again turn to the first-century church for Godly wisdom and fresh insights.

In order for Jesus' original disciples to minister to individuals outside their ethnic group, their view of the world had to be dramatically altered. The author of Acts described one such scenario (Acts 10:1–11:18). The apostle Peter was the acknowledged leader of the first-century Christian movement. One day while he was on the roof of his home praying, Peter went into a trance and saw a vision. In the vision he observed various food items that were not allowed as a part of his diet due to religious purity laws. A voice told him to eat of the food provided. Peter replied, "By no means, Lord; for I have never eaten anything that is profane or unclean" (10:14). Peter was repulsed by the suggestion that he eat something that was unclean. Then the voice said to Peter, "What God has made clean, you must not call profane" (10:15). This exchange occurred three times.

Peter was confused by the vision and could not comprehend its meaning. As he was reflecting on the strangeness of the heavenly encounter, Peter heard the Holy Spirit say to him that three men were looking for him and he should go with them. Shortly thereafter, three men arrived and escorted Peter to the home of a Roman centurion named Cornelius who lived in Caesarea. Peter's religious beliefs did not allow for such social interaction with Gentiles. Many Palestinian Jews also despised the Romans for their oppressive domination of the people of Israel. Peter may have been repelled by the thought of entering the house of a Roman Gentile living in Caesarea—a city named after the Roman emperor. It is possible that Peter struggled with strong feelings of bitterness and rage as he reached the home of this Roman military officer whose orders were to enforce the occupation of Peter's Jewish homeland. Perhaps it took a vision to get Peter to go and preach to Cornelius and his household, but he obeyed the word from the Spirit. And to Peter's surprise, according to his own retelling of the event, "And as I began to speak, the Holy Spirit fell upon them just as it had upon us at the beginning" (11:15).

Peter had traveled with Jesus for three years while Jesus taught about his vision of a house of prayer for all the nations. Peter was the keynote speaker on the day of Pentecost when the Holy Spirit came and people from various nations heard the Gospel in the local dialect of their native languages. Yet because he continued to interpret life through the lens of a racialized society, Peter needed a vision from God to walk through the door and enter the home of a Roman named Cornelius. In the middle of this Roman centurion's house Peter testified to a new worldview: "I truly understand that God shows no partiality, but in every nation anyone who fears him and does what is right is acceptable to him" (Acts 10:34–35).

Now the apostle Peter—the bishop of the church—had to return to Jerusalem and explain to the other church leaders that his thinking about God's vision for the racial makeup of the church had been transformed. So he recounted the story of his visit to the home of this Roman centurion in Caesarea. He concluded his remarks by saying, "And as I began to speak, the Holy Spirit fell upon them just it had upon us at the beginning. And I remembered the word of the Lord, how he had said: 'John baptized with water, but you will be baptized with the Holy Spirit.' If then God gave them the same gift he gave us when we believed in the Lord Jesus Christ, who was I that I could hinder God?" (Acts 11:15–17). The author of Acts recorded the reaction and response of the church leaders, "When they heard this, they were silenced. And they praised God, saying, 'Then God has given even the Gentiles the repentance that leads to life'" (11:18). The worldview of the early church was transformed by the three-way encounter between Peter, Cornelius, and the Holy Spirit.

According to the biblical narrative, a change in our theological worldview occurs when we encounter the Spirit of God and acquire a fresh view of God's intentions for our world. There was nothing in Peter's worldview that could conceive of a Gentile embracing Christian faith—which Peter understood to be an extension of his Judaism. In Peter's view, to be a Christian one must first be a Jew. (As we discussed in chapter two, Peter was not alone in this belief. Also, despite Peter's shift in perspective a few members of the early church did not adopt his worldview change.) Peter's Spirit-inspired vision was the first step in his transformation. The image of unclean food being declared clean caused Peter to struggle with his preconceived notions about how God had ordered life. Then when he saw firsthand that Cornelius and his entire household were experiencing God's power in the same way that he, Peter, and the disciples had experienced it on Pentecost, Peter had two choices: embrace a new worldview or reject God. So Peter reordered his thinking and way of living based on the revelatory vision and the experience of oneness with Romans at Cornelius's house. This shift by the leader of the church impacted the entire Christian movement.

A Theology of Oneness

The apostle Paul's conversion experience on the Damascus Road provides us with a greater understanding of the central message of this new Christian worldview that had been embraced by the first-century church—a theology that led to the establishment of multicultural, multiracial congregations wherever the believers traveled. We must remember that before Paul met Jesus Christ he was a staunch religious separatist. While Peter had accepted the separatist teachings of some religious groups of the day, Paul was part of the intelligentsia that shaped and promulgated this thinking, and eliminated those with counter viewpoints. This makes Paul's transformation all the more enlightening.

In 2 Corinthians 5:16–21, the apostle Paul described the impact of his encounter with Jesus Christ on his worldview.[10] Paul writes, "From now on, therefore, we regard no one from a human point of view, even though we once knew Christ from a human point of view, we know him no longer in that way. So if anyone is in Christ, there is a new creation: everything old has passed away, everything has become new!" (5:16–17). Paul uses theological language to describe how he was transformed by his experience of the grace of God on the Damascus Road. Jesus Christ saw beyond Paul's persona and behavior, as a persecutor of the church, to his essence as a human being created in the image of God. If God, through Jesus Christ, could reconcile with Paul, the declared enemy of the church, then Paul could reconcile with those he considered unworthy—Gentiles and Jewish Christians. As a "new creation" in Christ, Paul viewed Gentiles and Jewish Christians as his sisters and brothers in the faith. This was an amazing and dramatic departure from his previous view of humanity. The postconversion Paul viewed "the whole of life and humanity now through eyes touched by the risen Christ."[11]

The apostle Paul adopted a theology of oneness after his life-changing encounter with the risen Jesus Christ. This theology of oneness implied that in the beginning God created one race, the human race. Jesus came to restore God's original intention of the essential oneness of all humanity. Biblical scholar F. F. Bruce writes that Paul's understanding of oneness was rooted in a living relationship with Jesus Christ. Therefore, to be "in Christ" described

> an existence in which social, racial and other barriers within the human family were done away with. Among those barriers none was so important in Paul's eyes as that between Jew and Gentile. If before his conversion he looked upon it as one that had to be maintained at all costs, after his conversion he devoted himself to demolishing it doing in practice what had been done in principle by Christ on the cross.[12]

Paul's new worldview translated into a lifestyle of reconciliation and a practice of establishing congregations that bridged the divide between Jews and Gentiles.

One of Paul's clearest expressions of this theology of oneness is found in Galatians 3:28, "There is no longer Jew or Greek, there is no longer slave or free, there is no longer male and female; for you are all one in Christ Jesus." This statement came from the earliest days of the church.[13] A theology of oneness was not just Paul's particular slant on Christian faith, but his experience and teaching mirrored that of the earliest followers of the resurrected Jesus Christ. Scholars suggest that the Galatians 3:28 text was part of a baptismal formula used for welcoming new members into the church.[14] As biblical scholar Richard Longenecker states, "Early Christians saw it as particularly appropriate to give praise in their baptismal confession that through Christ the old racial schisms and cultural divisions had been healed."[15] Longenecker further declares:

When early Christians spoke of being "baptized into Christ" they also spoke of the old divisions between Jew and Gentile, slave and free, and male and female having come to an end. Certainly the proclamation of the elimination of divisions in these three areas should be seen first of all in terms of spiritual relations: that before God, whatever their differing situations, all people are accepted on the same basis of faith and together make up the one body of Christ. But these three couplets also cover in embryonic fashion all the essential relationships of humanity, and so need to be seen as having racial, cultural, and sexual implications as well. And that is, as I have argued elsewhere, how the earliest Christians saw them.[16]

The other passage of Scripture that reveals so much regarding the first-century church's theology of unity comes from the Letter to the Ephesians. There is some debate among scholars about whether Paul was the author or one of his associates wrote in his name after Paul's death; however, Ephesians captures the essence of Pauline thought and that of the first-century church concerning this theology of reconciliation and oneness. Regarding the relationship of Jews and Gentiles, the letter stated, "[Christ] has abolished the law with its commandments and ordinances, that he might create in himself one new humanity in place of the two, thus making peace, and might reconcile both groups to God in one body through the cross, thus putting to death that hostility through it" (Ephesians 2:15–16).

This Ephesians text dismisses the idea that evangelism (reconciliation with God) has priority over reconciliation between members of the human family. According to the passage, the two actions happen simultaneously.[17] More relevant to our discussion, the text declares that this reconciliation has already been accomplished through the death and resurrection of Jesus Christ. One reason the first-century church was so successful at establishing diverse congregations was that their theology informed them that God had already reconciled them across the line dividing Jews and Gentiles. All they had to do was *live* according to what Christ had already *done* on their behalf. When we gather together in multiracial congregations we are implementing what has already been realized through Christ's death on a cross.

Of course, living out this new understanding of faith and community was not easy for the first-century church. The difficulty was found primarily in the area of human relationships rather than in an inadequate theology. Paul regularly reminded the congregations with whom he corresponded that the power of the socially constructed divisions of their society had been eliminated through the death and resurrection of Jesus Christ. In Christ, Gentiles and Jews were one people. Today, our theology is often inadequate for the task of building unity. Our relational work is stifled without the solid foundational principle of oneness. A theology of relational unity through Jesus Christ leads to a restored sense of oneness in the Christian family. Biblical scholar James Earl Massey comments:

> The God-ordained relationship between Christian believers, of whatever previous backgrounds, is not just one of harmony but a oneness where neither group is dominant nor subservient anymore. The fence that once stood between them is now down. Because believers are reconciled to God, they are also related to one another. A new set of criteria applies now for human relations in the Church. In church life social distance must no longer be the order, and a sense of oneness and equality must prevail when previously-honored differences seek to intrude themselves.[18]

Believing that they were one in Christ encouraged those early believers to find relational common ground in their diverse faith communities. As we reclaim this belief in oneness we will rediscover an experience akin to the early Christian congregations.

In chapter eight we suggested that multiracial congregations should develop a hybrid culture—a *mestizaje* culture—that is a unique blend of all the cultures in the congregation (we will address this again in chapter ten). Of course this new culture is not meant to eliminate the cultures of individuals in the congregation. Rather it offers space for a new, shared existence. Perhaps this was what the author of Ephesians described when referring to Jews and Gentiles becoming "one new humanity" (2:15).

Paul did not promote a theology of oneness that encouraged the loss of one's own culture of origin, or the assimilation into another group's culture. Jewish Christians were not asked to become Gentiles. Nor were Gentile Christians asked to become Jews. Theologian William Campbell writes, Paul did not "discourage Jewish Christians from following a Jewish lifestyle after they had become Christians. . . . The two positions, i.e., Jewish Christians continuing to follow a

Jewish pattern of life, and Gentile Christians continuing to follow a Gentile pattern of life, are not mutually exclusive."[19] Historian Paula Fredriksen adds, "According to Paul, Gentiles in Christ should repudiate their traditional worship and commit exclusively to the God of Israel. . . . *And* they should not become Jews."[20] Jews could still be Jews. Greeks would remain Greeks. Ethiopians continued to embrace their culture. Yet, a new reality was born in Christ that denied "ultimate significance to ethnic distinctions."[21] Jews and Gentiles, from the continents of Africa, Asia, and Europe, were drawn to those early congregations because of a faith experience that elevated them above the fray of fractured relationships to a spiritual plane where they knew God and each other in fresh ways that brought healing.

Core Belief

We contend that more than a new theological worldview of oneness is required for congregations to sustain a multiracial membership over the long haul. This worldview must move to the deeper level of a core belief. Theologians Henry H. Mitchell and Nicholas C. Cooper-Lewter write that core beliefs "are the bedrock attitudes that govern all deliberate behavior and relationships and also all spontaneous responses to crises."[22] The new thinking acquired after the conversion to a new worldview needs to be cemented into one's belief system. Mitchell and Cooper-Lewter continue:

> Core beliefs are often mistaken for innate characteristics, because they are buried so deep. But they are not inherited or beyond the influences of training and spiritual discipline. They have been acquired through life experiences, worship, and cultural exposure, and they can be altered likewise. Core beliefs are not mere propositions to which assent is given. They are the ways one trusts or fails to trust. They are embraced intuitively and emotionally, with or without the ability to express them rationally. Core beliefs are perhaps most authentically expressed when uttered spontaneously in crisis situations.[23]

A core belief is a viewpoint that has become a nonnegotiable commitment and mind-set. It resides in the depths of our souls.

Perhaps it is easier to understand the notion of a core belief through an illustration. Martin Luther King Jr. was known for his commitment to the philosophy of nonviolence. Many in the civil rights movement of the 1950s and 1960s in the United States practiced nonviolent protest as a strategy for social change. Few were committed to it as a way of life. King's nonviolent ways were tested in September 1962 while he was giving the closing announcements at the annual convention of the Southern Christian Leadership Conference (SCLC).[24] The SCLC convention was the first integrated convention ever held in Birmingham, Alabama. As he was nearing the end of the convention's agenda, a white man walked onto the stage and punched King in the face with his fist. The strike to King's face "made a loud popping sound" as he struggled to remain upright. The audience sat silently in shock for a few seconds as the man continued to hit King. The people in the crowd regained their senses and pressed toward King. King biographer Taylor Branch recounts, "People recalled feeling physically jolted by the force of the violence—from both the attack on King and the flash of hatred through the auditorium."[25]

King's staff quickly arrived on stage to restrain the man. King asked that he not be arrested. Instead he and his staff talked with and prayed for the man, who was a white supremacist and member of the American Nazi Party. Branch describes the most poignant moment of the incident:

> After being knocked backward by one of the last blows, King turned to face [the man] while dropping his hands. It was the look on his face that many would not forget. Septima Clark, who nursed many private complaints about the strutting ways of the SCLC preachers and would not have been shocked to see the unloosed rage of an exalted leader, marveled instead at King's transcendent calm. King dropped his hands "like a newborn baby," she said, and from then on she never doubted that his nonviolence was more than the heat of his oratory or the result of slow calculation. It was the response of his quickest instincts.[26]

In that moment, Martin Luther King Jr. demonstrated to himself and those in the audience that nonviolence was a core belief.

In chapter two we described an encounter between the apostle Paul and the apostle Peter at the Antioch congregation (Galatians 2:11–14). While Peter was visiting the congregation in Antioch he stopped eating with Gentile members of the congregation because of pressure from some Jerusalem-based religious separatists. In a moment of crisis, Peter compromised his theological worldview, which had informed him of the oneness of all who were in Christ. This incident showed that for Peter, oneness had not become a core belief. He had accepted it as his doctrine, but it had not reached the depths of his soul as a nonnegotiable stance. As you recall, when Paul arrived in Antioch he immediately confronted Peter with his hypocritical actions. Unity in Christ was a core belief for Paul. It was firmly established in every thought he had and every action he took. Paul was outraged because Peter had violated a core belief that Paul had assumed to be essential to all the leaders in the church. When Paul challenged Peter and the others in Antioch who had followed Peter in separating from Gentiles, Paul declared "they were not acting consistently with the truth of the gospel" (2:14). The "truth of the gospel" to which Paul referred was God's power to unify Christians across the chasms of socially divided relationships—in this case, Jews and Gentiles.[27] When Peter withdrew from table fellowship with Gentiles, Paul interpreted that action as a denial of the reconciliation power that Jesus Christ enacted on the Cross.

Embracing a Core Belief of Oneness

A core belief is a worldview that has deepened to a nonnegotiable attitude and attribute. We believe that for multiracial congregations to sustain themselves across time, clergy and laity must embrace the theological worldview of oneness as a core belief. We briefly recommend a few ways to move ahead in this process. As we noted, the belief in oneness in the first-century church was proclaimed when people joined the church. When individuals were baptized into the church they were informed that in Christ there were no divisions based on race, class, or gender (Galatians 3:28). Every time there was a baptism, the congregants also reaffirmed this baptismal vow. Today, multiracial congregations—and all other congregations—should reinforce their belief in unity through preaching, teaching, Christian education, discipleship, catechism, new member classes, and baptismal services. No one should be able to miss the centrality of oneness in the Christian faith.

Not only must oneness be taught, it must also be experienced.

This is what transformed Peter's worldview and sustained Paul's core belief. One of the church's most powerful experiential tools is worship. The experience of multiracial, multicultural worship deepens one's soul commitment to reconciliation. Biblical scholar Donald Juel confirms this point when he writes that the baptismal formula of Galatians 3:28 presumes "not only the idea of a community formed from diverse members but of actual formation of such a community through the experience of worship."[28] Juel further notes that "many Christians who participate regularly in worship seldom experience anything that seems as culturally or socially potent" as what occurs in a congregation where people gather together from diverse cultures and races.[29] For many who do engage in worship experiences that unite people, the potency is so intoxicating (in a good way) that they feel something missing when they worship in uniracial settings.

In addition to the instruction about oneness and the experience of unity, we suggest that there is no substitute for fellowship. It is simply not enough to know all about unity and worship with people of different races on Sundays. Unless we develop *many* deep and intimate relationships with individuals outside our racial and cultural group, oneness will not become a part of our lifestyle.

Writing in the 1950s, at a time when interaction between the races was highly unusual, the late Benjamin Mays, president of Morehouse College, stated:

A person who does not believe in the segregation of the races but lives in a community where segregation is prescribed by law must find ways to have fellowship with those of other racial groups despite the law. He must act on his belief in Christian fellowship or he will cease to believe it. And the true Christian will always find ways to act. There are no known laws requiring churches to segregate races in their worship and membership. Here is an opportunity for the true Christian to act on his belief in Christian fellowship. A true Christian who believes in the fatherhood of God, the lordship of Jesus Christ, the brotherhood of man, and the dignity of every person and who believes that the church is God's house cannot deny membership to another Christian nor deny membership to one of the same faith. If Islam can admit all races to the mosque and if atheistic communism can embrace all races in its fellowship without segregation, certainly the Christian can do the same in his church, and it is wholly within his power to do so.[30]

In the 1950s, Mays said it was within the ability of Christians to find ways to fellowship across the racial divide. It should be even more so now. He was also correct in noting that belief and action are intertwined. With no action, belief dissipates. Developing oneness as a core belief requires ongoing action—and a profound fellowship with many people from outside our racial and cultural group.

We offer a final word about the idea of core beliefs. Courage is part and parcel of a stance that is nonnegotiable. If you refuse to accept the time-honored racial divisions in the United States as relevant to your life choices and behavior for long enough, you will face suffering of some sort. Some individuals, even family members, may reject you. Employers may eliminate your job or not hire you. You may be mocked publicly or ignored privately. People will misunderstand you and think you are crazy. This is because core beliefs emerge when we least expect to be confronted with a situation, and our response springs from that nonnegotiable truth of the Gospel. This aspect of core belief might get us in trouble.

The narrative in the Acts of the Apostles closes with the apostle Paul's arrest in Jerusalem and eventual voyage to Rome to stand trial (Acts 21:15ff). Paul was in Jerusalem to visit the church and deliver some financial support for their efforts. He was encouraged by the leaders in the Jerusalem congregation to visit the temple and undergo purification rites as a way of symbolizing his solidarity with Jewish Christians. Paul agreed and went. At the end of the process, Roman soldiers arrested Paul because his presence caused a disturbance. Many people assembled and Paul, not wanting to miss an opportunity to witness to his faith, asked if he might speak. The soldiers let him address the crowd. Paul proceeded to describe his conversion experience on the Damascus Road. When Paul started to tell them that God had also sent him to reach Gentiles, the crowd refused to listen anymore and chaos ensued. As biblical scholar Craig Keener writes, "Paul ended up in prison, first in Caesarea and then in Rome, because he refused to compromise an opportunity to proclaim the full implications of the gospel."[31] If Paul had just kept his mouth shut he could have gone on about his business. But his core belief, that the truth of the Gospel meant that both Jews and Gentiles were members of the family of God through Christ Jesus, compelled him to speak and accept the consequences of his actions.

Conclusion

Where was this theology of oneness when Malcolm X arrived on the scene? How could he have missed Christianity's radical notions of unity? As we noted at the beginning of this chapter, Malcolm X's transformation occurred through Islam and he recommended the study of Islam to address race relations in the United States. Malcolm X accompanied his parents to church as a child. Yet when he was searching for answers, the Christianity he encountered had nothing to offer him. As we implied in chapter three, the Christianity of the colonizer, the slave master, and the segregationist was not the same as that found in the first-century church. Christianity had been co-opted and corrupted by purveyors of white supremacy. This process was so effective that the apostle Paul—the former racial and religious separatist turned reconciler through an encounter with the resurrected Jesus Christ—was used by racists in the United States to support their belief that God ordained slavery and racial segregation. Our description of the church in the United States, detailed in chapter three, leads us to believe that much of the theology in the Christian church throughout the history of the United States has been defective and racist; it bears little resemblance to first-century biblical Christian faith. Malcolm X encountered an inauthentic Christianity.

We are calling for a fundamental reorientation of the Christian faith in the United States. There must be a transformation of the theology taught and lived in Christian congregations. A new theological worldview of oneness must be embraced and experienced. Then this oneness must gain the enduring power of a core belief. Only then can Christian congregations take their place as communities of healing and reconciliation in a world broken by racial discord and isolation. Believing that some congregations will adopt a theological worldview of oneness, we now discuss the characteristics of an authentic multiracial congregation.

10 | THE PROMISE AND THE CHALLENGES OF MULTIRACIAL CONGREGATIONS

Fort Bend County is a fast growing suburban area just south of Houston. In the late 1990s, after two and a half years of planning, the Houston Chinese Church started an offspring church in this fast growing and racially diverse area. With the aid of much prayer, planning, and 290 adults from the parent church, FBCC (Fort Bend Community Church in English, Fort Bend Chinese Church in Mandarin and Cantonese) was commissioned as a new church. At its first service, held in the rented church building of a white congregation, 452 adults and youth and 102 children attended. A year and a half later, FBCC moved into its own building. In just five years the church has grown to an average Sunday morning attendance of nine hundred adults and youth, and 250 children.

This nondenominational church is organized into three services—a Mandarin-language service, a Cantonese-language service, and an English-language service. The first two services are designed to attract immigrants from Taiwan, Hong Kong, and Mainland China. The English language service was designed for anyone preferring English, and tends to attract people who are younger than those found in the other two services. The Mandarin and the English services are attended by roughly the same number of people, with the Cantonese service being about half the size of the other two services. Adult Sunday School classes are taught in all three languages. Children and youth classes are taught largely in English.

The organization and growth of this church are impressive. Yet, given their mission to reach all peoples, the church leadership is not satisfied. Through prayer and study, they have concluded that God wants them to move beyond their specific ethnic and racial group. Currently the congregation is about 99 percent Chinese and Taiwanese. But they now have a vision to begin a multiracial ministry. The plan is for the Mandarin and Cantonese services to continue so that the church may reach non-English speaking recent immigrants. But in place of the English service, FBCC plans to start a multiracial service and a family-youth service, both in English. Members current-ly in the English service will be asked to choose from the two new services, or to attend a Chinese language service.

To this end, FBCC has organized a multiracial ministry planning committee. Led by their English-speaking Chinese pastor, Ed Lee, the committee is charged with taking the appropriate steps to begin a multiracial service and ministry.[1] Vital questions lie in front of them. What are the end goals? What does a successful multiracial ministry look like? What barriers will they face in reaching their goal of a suc-cessful multiracial ministry? What methods of implementation will help them reach their goals? In short, once a congregation has the pas-sion and commitment to become multiracial, how do they realize that hope?

The aim of this chapter is to draw on our three years of intensive research studying multiracial congregations across the country so that we can answer these key questions and provide a rough map for new church starts and for existing congregations that wish to become racially diverse. In our studies we compared multiracial congregations to uniracial congregations, attempting to determine how the former differed from the latter. We also followed selected churches as they moved from being uniracial to multiracial. Moreover, we interviewed nearly two hundred clergy and congregants to learn from them what barriers they faced and what methods of implementation they found useful. We asked people in multiracial congregations to give advice to those who wished to become more racially diverse. We bring our find-ings together here, highlighting key issues.[2]

Types of Multiracial Congregations

Given the salience of race in the United States—past and present—we acknowledge the truly impressive feat that is achieved when any congregation becomes multiracial. A stable multiracial congregation implies that a core group of leaders and members have taken steps to decrease the religious racial divide. It is equally impressive when uniracial congregations such as FBCC take the first bold steps to draw members of other races into their communities.

In the course of our fieldwork for the Multiracial Congregations Project, we encountered churches around the country that are demographically multiracial (no one racial group more than 80 percent of the congregation). Some had been so for years; others had just embarked on an effort to increase diversity in their ranks. These multiracial congregations had different degrees of stability in terms of membership and leadership. We also found that churches had different congregational cultures that reflected their denominational styles as well as their power structures. These variations made us realize that simply focusing on the goal of becoming multiracial in and of itself was not sufficient. We needed to elaborate on the ways in which members of different racial groups could relate to one another in one congregation.

During the course of our research we came across many different types of multiracial congregations. In some, we found that there is definitely one dominant racial group in terms of leadership or congregational culture. Members of the congregation who were not a part of the dominant racial group simply adapted to the existing congregational culture. In other congregations, we observed elements of several different cultures incorporated into the worship services, and we also noted a more racially integrated leadership. These congregations had arrived at their state only after struggling to respond to the voices of an increasingly diverse membership. In still other congregations, we noted that the relationship could not necessarily be characterized as racial integration; it was more a state of *coexistence*. The different racial groups may sit together in the pews, but the informal social networks within the congregations are racially separate. This type of congregation is still the result of a great deal of effort on the part of members and leaders, but the interactions among members of different racial groups in the church rarely move beyond exchanging pleasantries.

These observations led us to create the following three ideal-type categories to describe the overall congregational culture and the degree of racial integration: (1) assimilated multiracial congregation; (2) pluralist multiracial congregation; and (3) integrated multiracial congregation. Table 10-1 illustrates the characteristics of each type.

In the assimilated model, one racial group is obviously the dominant group within the congregation. This group's dominance is reflected in the worship services, activities, and leadership. Congregation members who do not belong to that dominant racial group simply "assimilate" into the existing culture. In other words, the way a congregation functions is not significantly changed by the presence of members from different racial groups. Although many assimilated multiracial congregations began as uniracial congregations and therefore still reflect the original racial culture, this is not always the

Table 10-1. Characteristics of Multiracial Congregation Models

	ASSIMILATED MULTIRACIAL CONGREGATION	PLURALIST MULTIRACIAL CONGREGATION	INTEGRATED MULTIRACIAL CONGREGATION
ORGANIZATIONAL CULTURE	Reflects one dominant racial culture	Contains separate and distinct elements of all racial cultures represented in the congregation	Maintains aspects of separate cultures and also creates a new culture from the cultures in the congregation
RACE OF LEADERSHIP (LAY OR CLERGY)	Dominant race	Representative of the different races in the congregation	Representative of the different races in the congregation
DEGREE OF SOCIAL INTERACTION ACROSS RACES	Can be high or low	Low	High

case. It is possible for a multiracial church that had been multiracial from the beginning to also be an assimilated multiracial congregation if there is one racial group whose power and racial culture is imposed on church culture.

A variety of explanations and justifications are used to support the maintenance of the status quo in assimilated congregations. In one fundamentalist Baptist congregation in the Midwest, we found that church culture was carefully preserved by the original white membership. Their reason for singing the same hymns and having the same elements in their worship services was their belief that those were the "true" hymns and elements called for by God. In the case of such congregations, openness to change is seen as a threat by worldly forces to pollute the purity of their church rituals. Even though a growing number of African American members may long to sing gospel songs from the African American tradition during the services, the element of music remains unchanged. This resistance to change is not seen as a "race issue"; rather, it is justified in theological terms.

Another church in our study was in the process of moving from a uniethnic Korean to pan-Asian and even multiracial membership. Although there were non-Korean members and leaders, the overall culture of the church was unmistakably Korean American. For example, fellowship events and dinners typically featured Korean cuisine, despite the large number of non-Koreans in attendance. Similarly, sermons featured numerous references to growing up as the children of Asian immigrants, despite a number of non-Asians in attendance. In this case, non-Korean/non-Asian members must essentially assimilate into the largely Korean American culture of this congregation. The Korean American members of this congregation are not necessarily trying to force assimilation upon the non-Korean members, but they still see their church as a "refuge" away from the dominant white society. Those non-Koreans who join the church are sympathetic to the Korean Americans' cultural needs and see the Korean-dominated church culture as an opportunity to learn more about other races. This church example highlights an important feature of assimilated multiracial congregations: the assimilation occurs into whatever the dominant racial culture of the church happens to be. In a predominantly white congregation, people of color may be the ones who assimilate. In a non-white congregation, like the one described above, however, it may be the white members who are assimilating into a non-white church culture. Thus, assimilation, as we use the term here, is not with respect to culture in the United States as a whole, but it is with respect to whatever happens to be the dominant culture of the church in question.

The second type of congregation that we found is the pluralist multiracial congregation. In this type of congregation, physical integration has occurred in the sense that members of different racial groups choose to gather in the same church and the same worship service. They are all members of the same congregation. Although this physical integration is notable, members do not move beyond coexistence to real integration of social networks. While official committees may be multiracial, the informal social networks still remain segregated by race. In some cases, there may even be an underlying sense of "us" and "them," which may or may not be accompanied by a certain degree of rivalry.

Unlike an assimilated congregation, a pluralist congregation often incorporates elements of the different racial cultures into the life of their congregation. For example, a Catholic congregation that we observed in the Midwest hung a mural of the Virgin of Guadalupe in the sanctuary. This was in deference to the tremendous significance that the Virgin held for the many Latino members. Similarly, the Masses often incorporated Spanish-language hymns, and fellowship events frequently featured ethnic Hispanic food. Nevertheless, when we interviewed members of this parish in their homes, we discovered that their church friendships and social circles were limited to those of their own race. In other words, the congregation's collective activities reflected elements of all cultures, yet the integration did not reach into the daily lives of its members. Congregants enjoyed a friendly smile or exchange with a diverse group of people on Sundays, but there was no significant attempt to foster friendships and relationships that might help members go beyond the coexistence level.

Whether a church can be considered assimilated or pluralist is partially determined by the degree to which elements of all racial cultures are reflected in church activities and in the amount of informal involvement that members have with those of other racial groups in the church. If there is a significant amount of social interaction across race on Sundays and during the week, but collective church-related activities reflect the culture of only one racial group, then the church is an assimilated congregation. In this case, there may be an obvious distinction between those members and leaders who truly have a sense of "ownership" of the church, in contrast to those who are de facto "guests." If collective activities reflect different cultures but there is little informal social interaction across races, the congregation is pluralist. In a pluralist congregation, members of the different racial groups all have a sense of ownership.

A third model—the integrated multiracial congregation—is to us the theological ideal, but it is also the rarest of the three. It is our belief that a truly multiracial congregation requires a *transformation* of congregational culture. It is no longer the old culture with certain accommodations made for members of different races, and it is no longer a mosaic with elements of separate and distinct cultures. Rather, the integrated multiracial congregation has developed a hybrid of the distinct cultures that have joined together in one church. Elements of different racial cultures are not incorporated to "appease" diverse constituencies; rather, the new hybrid culture is an expression of the congregation's unified collective identity. The relationships among members of different races in the congregation are strictly egalitarian. There is no sense of "us" and "them" according to race, but it is more "us" as a congregation and "them" outside our congregation. We are hard pressed to cite definitive examples of such congregations from our study, but some of the congregations that we discuss in chapter five have come quite close. We realize that this model holds multiracial congregations to a high standard. However, we believe that one of the most important ways in which multiracial congregations can impact the world is by reducing the racial divide. Unless congregations themselves exhibit egalitarian relationships and a new hybrid culture, they are limited in their power to promote equality and integration. While this goal may seem difficult in a worldly sense, we believe that the supernatural power of God can enable congregations to overcome racial barriers.

There is a fine line between assimilated and integrated congregations. One issue is the difficulty in determining the actual source of the original culture. For example, English-speaking Asian American congregations tend to sing choruses used for contemporary services in white churches instead of the hymns sung by traditional Asian congregations. This is an indication of the degree to which Asian Americans have already assimilated to white forms of Christianity. When a white person joins the congregation, is he or she assimilating to Asian American culture, when that culture itself has been influenced by white culture? To avoid confusion, it is necessary to note that an assimilated congregation is one in which members continue to behave as they would in the absence of a new racial group in the membership. In an integrated congregation, the members do things in a new way, truly integrating the diverse membership.

The integrated congregation is also distinguishable from the assimilated congregation in that no one racial culture is obviously dominant. Rather, integrated congregation members develop a new way of doing things that is particular to their own church. An integrated congregation does not necessarily require an equal representation of racial groups in the membership. Even if a church were 80 percent white and 20 percent Hispanic, it could still be an integrated congregation in its culture and operations.[3]

We have found it necessary to distinguish between different paths that multiracial congregations may follow in terms of their organizational culture and power structure. The path that the church follows has a tremendous impact on how members of different races relate to one another and to what extent the church overcomes the worldly and cultural differences among the membership. Critics of multiracial congregations might call such churches vehicles of assimilation, but that is not the goal. Authentic integration is the goal. Theologically, multiracial congregations should seek to integrate, not assimilate. In our opinion, a truly effective multiracial congregation not only reflects aspects of the cultures represented by congregation members, but it reflects a *new* and *unique* culture that transcends the worldly cultures. Such churches create a new *mestizaje* congregational culture by relying on the distinctiveness of its different cultures and peoples to create a unity far more complete than can be done otherwise. As a choir with sopranos, altos, tenors, and basses produces a richer sound than can any single voice range alone, so it is with an integrated multiracial congregation. The individual sections of the choir do not give up their uniqueness to create their music. Instead, they integrate their distinctive qualities into a cohesive new whole.[4]

Barriers to Integrated Multiracial Congregations

To become an integrated multiracial congregation, the members must consider the main barriers that congregations face. Even for a willing congregation, a fundamental barrier is that multiracial churches labor against sociologically natural leanings. A church that does not aim to become multiracial almost never does. Churches that aim to do so fail most of the time. Those that become multiracial often revert to being uniracial. As discussed in detail in *Divided by Faith*, even apart from racism, a number of sociological factors—such as the need for symbolic boundaries and social solidarity, similarity principles, and the status quo bias—constantly drive religious congregations to be racially homogeneous. These factors work similarly regardless of the racial group that predominates in the church.[5]

A key barrier to becoming a multiracial church is lack of leadership. Leaders will fail if they are not thoroughly convinced that being multiracial is God's design, if they are motivated instead by some politically correct or "in" concept—or guilt. Leaders must be willing to spend much time praying about the issues and to make the commitment this type of church demands. The necessary commitment involves head, heart, and history. By head we mean leaders are committed to learning all they can about multiracial ministry. By heart we mean leaders have a passion for becoming multiracial. And by history we mean that leaders already have a history of living integrated, multiracial lives. Leaders cannot lead a congregation in becoming multiracial if they, themselves, are living segregated lives.

A related barrier is the attempt to become multiracial solely with human power rather than with God's power. Human power doubts, waxes and wanes, and makes too many mistakes. Those with the vision and the hope to become multiracial should have the mind-set of the blind men in the Gospel of Matthew who ask Jesus for sight. They should remember both Jesus' question to the blind men: "Do you believe that I am able to do this?" and the men's reply: "Yes, Lord" (Matthew 9:28).

It is rare to meet individuals who think they are personally racially prejudiced. But as they attempted to develop multiracial congregations, clergy of the multiracial churches we interviewed noted that removing racial prejudice is an ongoing struggle within their congregations. This becomes a growing issue as other racial groups in the congregation increase in size. One major concern that arises is interracial dating between teens; in some churches we studied, people with children of or near dating age left the congregation to avoid this possibility. Another is what author Joseph Barndt calls cultural racism[6]—people seeing the cultural practices of the new group(s) as inferior or not belonging in the church, such as discouraging the introduction of new foods, opposing changes proposed or made in worship to meet the needs of new people, or discounting the ability of the nondominant group members to lead or communicate new revelations about God. Cultural racism is a powerful barrier, one nearly every multiracial church will have to face.

Related to this is the exercise of power. The importance of dominant group power as a barrier cannot be overstated. The exercise of power is not typically overt or mean-spirited but rather it is done in the name of cultural or theological purity. We saw the exercise of power act as a barrier to becoming fully multiracial repeatedly. At FBCC, the church discussed at the opening of the chapter, we noted that in English they are called Fort Bend Community Church, but in Chinese languages, they are called Fort Bend Chinese Church. To reflect their desire to be a place for all people, the leadership of FBCC wanted to change the Chinese language wording to replace "Chinese" with "Community." Many in this currently Chinese church were resistant to this change. In fact, at the time of this writing, enough were resistant that the change was not made. The pastors of this congregation intend to do more teaching on the need for this change, and then they will propose the name revision again. Another example of the use of power that we witnessed in some multiracial churches is that the dominant group held nearly all the positions of leadership within the congregation. Part of the reason for this is that those selecting leaders had clear guidelines for deciding which people were spiritually mature, but these guidelines were intertwined with cultural understandings of spiritual maturity. For instance, we studied a formerly all white congregation in which the definition of spiritual maturity came to include not getting overly zealous during worship. Such emotional displays of faith were interpreted to indicate a lack of personal control, and thus a lack of spiritual maturity. Because enthusiasm marked the preferred cultural style of worship of many of the African Americans and

Latinos in that congregation, it meant, de facto, that they could not be leaders.

This last example leads us directly to another major barrier. While intending to develop spiritual maturity in congregational members and to have unity in the body, many multiracial churches make the mistake of emphasizing unity and assimilation to the exclusion of diversity and the acknowledgment of uniqueness. A key reason that so many multiracial churches we studied were assimilated multiracial congregations was the majority group's belief that talking about uniqueness was divisive, unimportant, and ungodly. If congregational minority groups ever suggested that they needed time to meet as a cultural group, the dominant group in such churches often became upset, offended, and angry. Though such a mix of separate and corporate meetings and fellowship is perceived to be acceptable along gender and age lines, many people feel that to do the same along racial and ethnic lines simply reproduces the divisions found in the world outside the church building. We cite just such a case in our description of Park Avenue United Methodist Church in chapter five.

Because the first arrivals to multiracial congregations are often the most culturally assimilated of their group, such people can be the most vocal in resisting moves toward becoming integrated multiracial congregations. This is because they came to be in an assimilated church. Because these pioneers are often the racially different people majority group members know best, majority group members often poll these pioneers to see what minority group members think, and make erroneous conclusions based on this method.

This view is understandable, but it overlooks basic sociological issues affecting minority and majority group experiences within congregations. In our research, we found that all racial groups experience the benefits of multiracial congregations, but the costs are disproportionately born by the congregational minority groups. Take, for example, New Faith Church, an intentionally multiracial congregation in California.[7] During the time we studied it, this church of approximately 150 people was about 55 percent Filipino, 30 percent Anglo, 10 percent Latino, and 5 percent was African Americans, African immigrants, and other Asian ethnicities. The leadership was overwhelmingly Filipino and the cultural style of worship and social interactions was largely Filipino. In short, this church used an assimilationist approach. This approach had a profound impact on the experiences of the parishioners.

The most striking pattern in our in-depth interviews was the different ways in which Filipinos and non-Filipinos spoke about their experiences forming friendships and feeling a sense of belonging in the church. Specifically, Filipinos found it easy to establish close friendships in the church, but most non-Filipinos struggled with a lack of close ties within the congregation. Of the seventeen non-Filipinos interviewed, fourteen spoke of struggles and frustrations with relating to others in the church and of not feeling connected socially. In contrast, none of the Filipinos who were interviewed felt that they lacked close ties in the church. Additionally, the three non-Filipinos we interviewed who had left the church all mentioned a lack of belonging as their primary reason for leaving the church.

Most non-Filipinos felt they could not break into the "core" social group in the church, which in their view was composed of Filipinos:

> The Filipino relationship structure and ethic makes it hard for people outside of that to break in. . . . The founders of the church have a really tight group. . . . I have at different times been disillusioned by the difficulty fitting in. I'm an extrovert and get to know people easily, but I feel shut out (Kenyan female).

> For a long time I didn't have friends at church. I felt really out of place. I tried to understand the Filipino mentality and relate but I couldn't do it. I was trying to fit in. I even started to try to dress sort of like them and act like them, but I couldn't fit in (Anglo-American female).

> There isn't a sense of family or community there. It shouldn't have taken me this long to feel like I know people. I've been going for two years and just now I feel like I have friends at church. People say hi to you and are friendly, but there isn't enough interaction. It's not a family (Hispanic female).

In addition to feeling relationally excluded, non-Filipinos often felt left out of leadership and worship. Although she is completely committed to being in a multiracial church, this African American woman clearly expresses the exclusion she feels and what she does to deal with it:

> I get frustrated with the worship service. I have to prepare myself

before I go. I have to listen to Gospel music before I go in so I can get in a worshipping mindset. There's not any flexibility in the worship. You just have a set time for the songs and there's no room for the Spirit to work.

The Filipinos' views of the church stood in sharp contrast to those of non-Filipinos. When we asked the Filipino members if being in a multiracial congregation made anything more difficult, we received responses like these:

I don't think it makes things more difficult. There is a majority of Filipinos, but we don't treat it like a Filipino church. We're open to different ethnicities and cultures. A lot of people are attracted to it (Filipino male).

Everyone can see past skin color. It's not like Filipino churches where everyone's speaking the language, and if you don't speak it you feel out of it. We can learn from different people and can learn about different cultures (Filipino female).

Interviewer: So it doesn't make anything more difficult?

I don't think so. It makes everyone realize we have the same purpose, even though we've all been brought up differently (Filipino female).

I think it's awesome to see diversity, but we have one thing in common. We are unified. I don't think race is a problem. Everyone wants to learn from everybody. It's a testimony in itself. I don't think it makes anything more difficult. Since this is a young church, everyone is accepting. Older Filipinos are racist. With the young generation, the differences don't matter (Filipino male).

An important barrier, then, to becoming an integrated multiracial congregation is to assume that one's perception (be it the perception of a person or a group) is shared by everyone in the congregation. With Christian spirit, those in the majority group must reach out to others rather than requiring nonmajority people to do so. In this context we use the terms nonmajority and racial minorities to indicate the racial groups that are not the dominant group in the church, instead of the traditional definition of racial minorities in the United States as non-white. The majority group must be willing and even eager to listen to nonmajority people. Without this conscious approach, the consequences are typically a sense of frustration within the minority groups, the loss of opportunities to expand faith and community, a higher turnover rate of minority groups, difficulty in sustaining the multiracial character of the congregation, and either the forced assimilation of the minority group members that remain or the ability to attract only culturally assimilated minorities.

New Wine Needs New Wineskins

Recognizing the barriers to becoming integrated multiracial congregations is essential but not sufficient. What remains is a plan of implementation. In this final section, we provide practical advice on how to become part of an integrated multiracial congregation. For individuals, groups, and congregations with such a commitment, perhaps the most effective and efficient way for congregations to integrate is for people to leave their homogeneous congregation and become part of a different-race congregation, or for uniracial congregations to merge. However, in our experience, most people who desire a multiracial congregation want people to join their congregation. Part of the problem in developing multiracial congregations is that there are more people and congregations desiring others to join them than vice versa.

For this reason, many multiracial churches we studied became multiracial by reaching unchurched people or people new to the area. Once a church gains a reputation for being multiracial, it then can and often does attract people looking for mixed-race congregations. We do not have the space here to fully explore all of the practical advice we would like to give those integrating their own congregation (one of the co-authors is presently working on a book that will accomplish this task), but we want to provide the interested reader with some guidance about some of the main issues to address.[8]

Issues for Uniracial Churches to Address in Becoming Multiracial

WORSHIP

Worship style is often rooted in preferences nurtured by denominational or doctrinal tradition, ethnic or racial culture, and at times popular culture. Also generational issues merge in worship style preference, so race is one of many factors. Some people join or leave churches solely based on their like or dislike of the congregation's worship style. While it entails risk, an important issue for those in uniracial churches is their willingness to alter their worship style.[9]

The worship styles of multiracial churches tend to include the cultural elements of more than one racial group. The worship style of most integrated multiracial congregations tends to be a mixture of several different racial worship styles. For many, when they think of worship, they think music. But worship includes other aspects, such as the level of expressiveness accepted in a congregation (can "amen" be shouted?), the décor of the church (for example, the racial identity of the Christ figure in the artwork),[10] and sermon/homily styles (scholarly, emotive, or a combination).[11]

Worship style is an important way to symbolize to visitors acceptance of other races. An inclusive worship style communicates to visitors of different races that they, and their cultures, are respected. Such worship also has the potential to provide a more complete picture of God. In chapter five, the pastors of Park Avenue United Methodist Church called this "a sneak preview of heaven." Theologian Justo González believes that such worship represents God's vision—a heavenly house of prayer for all the nations living, breathing, meditating, singing, and shouting right here on earth. He writes, "Worship is a rehearsal and an act of proclamation. For both reasons, in order to rehearse and in order to proclaim, the church must make every effort to make certain that here and now, as there and then, 'every nation and tribe and people and language' be present and represented; that no one be excluded or diminished because of their tribe, or nation, or people, or language."[12]

It is vital to include elements of the worship styles of the racial and ethnic groups a ministry hopes to reach. For example, if African American Christians visit a predominantly white church that does not have any worship elements from their culture, then they may not be certain that the members of the church want African Americans in their congregation. If African Americans live in the neighborhood of that congregation, then it is critical to include elements of African American worship styles. We rarely, if ever, found a multiracial church that had large numbers of African Americans that did not have elements of African American worship styles.

RACIALLY DIVERSE LEADERSHIP

Most of the churches included in our study have racially diverse clergy and lay leadership, which reflects some of the racial makeup of the church members.[13] For example, if there is a large percentage of Latinos in a predominantly white congregation, then generally some of the leadership will be Hispanic—even if most of the leaders are white. Several of the church leaders we interviewed discussed how important it was for them to intentionally seek out members of different races for leadership positions. Multiracial leadership is important because members of different racial groups need to feel represented. This is especially important for people of color. We have noted that many persons of color fear that they will lose their culture if they attend a multiracial church. Having members of their race in positions of power helps to assuage this fear and increases the probability that they will have their contributions and concerns recognized. Racially diverse leadership is vital so that the perspectives of several racial groups can influence the major decisions of the church.

Finding racially diverse leadership means that uniracial congregations may have to change the way they typically find clergy and/or lay leaders. They may have to contact organizations and seminaries where there are many members of races different from their own. A color-blind approach is not viable since such an approach will likely produce only leaders who are members of the majority group. Our leadership philosophy sounds like affirmative action, and on that basis some may be inclined to reject it. One way to make this philosophy easier to accept is to think of racial identity as an additional asset for a given leadership position. If a congregation wants to reach a nearby Hmong population, then hiring a Hmong education minister will not only help to organize the church's educational ministry but will also give visiting Hmong a visual presence that makes the church more attractive to them. Being Hmong allows the minister to bring an additional asset to the ministry that a non-Hmong cannot bring. Multiracial churches, then, should intentionally use race as a factor to help them maintain, or build on, their racial diversity.

INTENTIONALITY

In their book, *Breaking Down Walls,* Raleigh Washington and Glenn Kehrein use the term "intentionality" when talking about bringing

Christians together across racial lines.[14] Churches that desire to become multiracial must prioritize becoming multiracial and retaining their racial diversity. Such churches will have to be explicit about their desire for a multiracial congregation. For example, FBCC, the church we discussed at the opening of the chapter, created a mission statement—"Embracing the many faces and races of our Community for Christ"—to institutionalize its commitment to being multiracial. We are not claiming that becoming multiracial should be the primary goal of the church, but it must be a goal, or perhaps better yet, a means to reach its larger goal. For instance, another church in our study, which made the move from being uniracial to multiracial, first created a mission statement that read "God's multiethnic bridge to Jesus Christ, who brings all people from unbelievers to missionaries." In this mission statement, being multiracial is a necessary means by which the congregation lived out its goal of reaching and maturing others.[15]

Intentionality is important because the social tendencies in the United States lean toward racial separation instead of integration. We have been taught subtle lessons about the importance of "staying with one's own kind." To overcome this propensity, it is important that the clergy and laity of the church are consistently in active conversation about how they can create and maintain their multiracial makeup. This sort of intentionality leads to innovations within the congregation such as programs that meet the specific needs of persons of color or efforts to develop the leadership roles of those not in the majority.[16]

Another important aspect of intentionality is the creation of structures in the church that allow people of different races to meet together and get to know one another across racial groups. We saw far too many multiracial churches that lacked real conversation between racial groups on the difficult and important topics of racism and racial alienation. If multiracial congregations are part of the answer to racism in the United States then such churches must intentionally create the honest dialogue that is so often missing within other integrated social institutions, like schools and workplaces.[17]

ADAPTABILITY

A multiracial congregation must be ready to adapt to new racial groups and cultures. While a uniracial church typically has a single racial culture to which it must adapt and in which it operates, a multiracial congregation brings to the mix individuals from several different cultures. In order to bring these cultures together, members of multiracial churches need to have flexibility and readiness to handle new problems. Sometimes this adaptation is easily predictable. For example, if a non-Hispanic congregation wants to reach a first-generation Hispanic population, then some of the programs must be in Spanish. Such a congregation would do well to invest in both persons with translation skills and the equipment that allows for translation into Spanish. On the other hand, sometimes the adaptation is not as easy to predict. Multiracial congregations are likely to generate interracial dating and marriages. It is not unusual for unexpected resentment to develop toward these relationships. Wise leaders prepare for such situations.[18] Whether the adaptation to the addition of new racial groups is easily anticipated or not, members of a multiracial congregation must be flexible enough to handle these changes.

Congregations should find ways to employ these concepts in ways that are consistent with their character and philosophy. We introduced these principles to give readers some ideas about how they can work toward developing a multiracial congregation. It is the task of church leaders to decide how to execute these concepts in keeping with the traditions, theology, and customs of their given congregation.

Starting Multiracial Churches

The concepts in this chapter were presented, for the most part, for congregations that are currently uniracial and want to become multiracial. There may also be new churches that originate with the intention of being multiracial. While the issues discussed in the previous section are useful for new congregations, two additional points are necessary. First, it is critical to try to start with a multiracial staff and congregation. One possibility for beginning with a multiracial congregation is to "borrow" members of another congregation within your denomination for a year or more. We have discovered congregations that encouraged their members to join a church startup to help create, from the beginning, a multiracial congregation. Having this multiracial atmosphere present from the origin of the church helps attract members of different races. Second, from the very beginning we believe that the new multiracial church should emphasize integration and not assimilation. New congregations have the opportunity to create the organizational norms that can be inclusive of several racial groups. They do not have to fight against a tradition that is already based within a given racial culture. We suggest that new church startups take advantage of that opportunity to make sure that new racial cultures are integrated into the church rather than merely expecting those cultures to adapt to the perspective of a single culture—thus forcing the members of other cultures to assimilate.

Conclusion

Congregations, when possible, should journey toward becoming integrated multiracial congregations. If they are willing to sacrifice and persevere, uniracial congregations, assimilated multiracial congregations, pluralist multiracial congregations, and new church startups can arrive at this destination. Creating authentic, reconciled, multiracial communities in the midst of divisions is hard, complex work. The barriers in a racialized society are many, and the degree of their entrenchment should never be underestimated. Courageous and visionary leadership among both clergy and laity is essential and a necessary ingredient for success. The journey requires a respect and appreciation for the cultures represented in the congregation in tandem with the willingness to travel into the unexplored territory of creating a new congregational culture.

Multiracial congregations require time, energy, and focus that could be used elsewhere. But neither the ease or difficulty of the task nor its simplicity or complexity are the issues on which to focus. We are called as Christians to live, work, serve, and be together, forging community that can occur only with God's help. Just imagine for a moment what would happen in communities across the United States—and in the nation as a whole—if multiracial congregations began emerging in cities, suburbs, and small towns. It is a compelling thought, a journey worth taking. Humbly doing so is our witness to the world.

EPILOGUE

THE MULTIRACIAL CONGREGATION AS AN ANSWER TO THE PROBLEM OF RACE

Theologian Eldin Villafañe describes a time when he heard the acclaimed Latino jazz musician Tito Puentes and his band. From his front row seat Villafañe fully experienced the excitement of the rhythms and the sounds of what has come to be known as Latin Jazz—"the fusion of Afro-Cuban, jazz, blues, and other music influences."[1] As Villafañe listened to this music that integrated elements of many cultural expressions, from assorted racial histories, he reflected on the church. This Latin Jazz experience enriched his insights regarding the role of the church in a racialized society. Regarding this metaphor of Latin Jazz, he writes:

> It seems to me to challenge the church to a biblical posture of a "racial Shalom" (peace—with its rich biblical meanings of healing, harmony, reconciliation, welfare, wholeness, and justice). It is a prophetic challenge to the church to be the "space" where the presence and contribution of all believers of all colors could be seen as "light" and could be savored as "salt" in a broken world. It is a prophetic challenge to the church to be a sign of the kingdom of God—a place where transformed relations and the presence of justice could be modeled.[2]

In the pages of this book we revisited the life and message of Jesus of Nazareth, who embodied a "racial Shalom" in his efforts to call the religion of his time and place to construct a house of prayer for all the nations. The congregations of the first-century church endeavored to create inclusive assemblies built on the foundation laid by the message and example of Jesus and empowered by the Holy Spirit. The first-century church did struggle internally with the ethnocentrism and the bigotry of society, but a theology of oneness enabled them to prevail in their efforts at developing inclusive congregations. When possible, the congregations of the first-century church were multiracial and their membership included people from across the many other lines that divided first-century society—economics, gender, culture, language, disease, and career choice. The New Testament model is a congregation united by its faith in Jesus Christ.

We also looked at the tragic history of Christian congregations and the color line in the United States. While there have been a few notable exceptions, most congregations have not been places of racial Shalom. There is a stark contrast between the first-century church and Christian congregations in the United States. The impact of racism on Christianity in the United States, from colonial times to the present, has produced a religion in which most congregations are uniracial. The racial division of congregations has become a defining characteristic of the Christian faith in the United States. We are deeply grieved by this fact. Congregations in the United States, in most cases, have failed to embrace the New Testament theology of oneness and practice of multiracial assemblies. Racism is a sin and a racially divided church does not reflect Jesus' vision of a house of prayer for all the nations.

Multiple cultural and racial versions of the Christian faith have emerged in the United States due to racism and as the result of pervasive racial separation. Therefore we presented many of the arguments that suggest racial separation as the best way to do church in the United States. We attempted to argue the case for racial separation as though we were true believers. We detailed the many valid points in these arguments. Yet, ultimately, our desire to embrace a faith rooted in the New Testament message and forms of congregating caused us to present counterpoints. In many cases we simply embraced the developments made in uniracial congregations as necessary for multiracial congregations.

Finally, we addressed the challenges and possibilities of multiracial congregations. We did not downplay the very real challenges facing those who seek to develop multiracial congregations. Yet we also celebrated the joys that come from embracing God's will. We pleaded for authentic multiracial congregations—not just the appearance of diversity without the substance of shared power, multicultural expressions of faith, and diverse social networks. Multiracial congregations must be inclusive of the cultural perspectives that inhabit their space. Yet they also endeavor to create a new culture emerging from their experience of oneness.

In 1959, African American theologian Howard Thurman summarized the challenge of developing multiracial congregations. While directed to the African American church in his day, in particular, it is an important word for our day; it applies to our own racial and cultural context. He wrote:

> The Negro church and the white church are under the same ethical imperative. They are both bound by the same commitment, and no extenuating circumstance can at the last be used as a permanent alibi for not obeying that imperative. The Negro church can no longer sit in judgment on the exclusiveness of the white church and at the same time be content to regard itself as immune to the same searching judgment. The great Negro denominations such as the National Baptist Conventions, the African Methodist Episcopal Church, and the African Methodist Episcopal Zion Church are under the same command of God to grapple with the issue of inclusiveness as it affects their local congregations and their national conclaves. . . . The Negro has a rich and redemptive heritage which must not be lost in this effort to become an integrated religious fellowship. How to conserve the essential idiom that has kept alive in the spirit of Negroes a courage and a vitality that has sustained that spirit in all of its vicissitudes, and at the same time to bring into its fellowship more and more of those who are not Negroes, until at last from both sides there is a common meeting place in which there will be no Negro church and no white church, but the church of God—that is the task we all must work to finish.[3]

A Movement for Multiracial Christianity

Now we must move forward with the task of reclaiming the vision of Jesus Christ and the New Testament model of inclusive congregations.

The world has rightly judged the church a failure in addressing the racial divide. Even so, we believe that multiracial congregations are God's plan for responding to racism. Given our history in the United States, such bold proclamations sound like empty words to many. So we must quietly, intentionally, persistently, and courageously begin to live our faith that God through Jesus Christ can reconcile us across these entrenched racial divides and that God has given each congregation, each individual, and each denomination the ministry of reconciliation. *We are calling for a movement in the church toward multiracial congregations!*

There is a role for each of us in a movement for multiracial congregations. We need more people willing to be prophets of multiracial Christianity. These are individuals who speak out for unity even in the face of unpleasant consequences. During the harsh days of apartheid in South Africa, social critic Njabulo Ndebele used his pen to voice unpopular truths about the evil of racism. The white supremacist government did not appreciate Ndebele's views, and he was forced into exile. Writer Graham Pechey, in the introduction to Ndebele's book *South African Literature and Culture: Rediscovery of the Ordinary*, called Ndebele "a prophet of the post-apartheid condition."[4] A movement for a new multiracial church needs prophets of the post-apartheid condition in the United States. We need people who not only speak truth to racism but who can envision a future church where racism is no longer a defining characteristic of our faith.

A movement for multiracial congregations needs theologians of multiracial Christianity. Seminaries and Christian colleges must become places where pastors and lay leaders are trained in a theology of oneness and equipped with skills to minister effectively in culturally diverse environments. Institutions of higher learning, as well as education programs at local congregations, must introduce what has been learned in various cultural settings. Most "Christian education" is Eurocentric in its content and presentation. The church needs to adopt what has been developed within the theological explorations occurring in the nonlinear cultural thinking of many Native Americans. Multiracial congregations must understand the various nuances of *mestizaje* as fleshed out by Latina and Latino theologians. Also, pastors and future pastors need to be prepared to launch new congregations that begin free from the deadly cancer of racism.

We need innovative congregations that are willing to take the lead in the church in modeling what it means to welcome persons from outside their racial constituency into their communal life. Congregations need to begin redesigning their mission statements, worship styles, and social practices in ways that reflect the New Testament call to be multiracial. Congregations must prepare to embrace the broad multicultural, international, and multilingual context of the United States in the twenty-first century. African American congregations must broaden their focus and welcome Hispanics and Asian Americans residing in their neighborhoods. White suburban congregations need to stop running away from communities of color and diversify their pastoral staffs and their congregational identities in order to welcome the many persons of color who live in the suburbs.

We need brave and courageous individuals who will be the activists in the movement for multiracial Christianity. Any Sunday, individuals can visit congregations made up of people of a race different from their own. These church visits can revive the spirit of those brave individuals who faced arrest in their attempts to integrate the segregated congregations of the southern United States during the civil rights movement. Such acts declare that God's church is called to be a house of prayer for people of all races. Visiting and even joining congregations composed of persons with experiences different from our own also will create awareness for those who have been raised in racially and cultural exclusive environments. This awareness can produce a worldview change.[5] The noted German theologian and vocal opponent to Hitler's Nazism Dietrich Bonhoeffer studied at Union Theological Seminary in New York City. On Sundays he would visit the Abyssinian Baptist Church in Harlem. Soon he was involved in the life of the congregation. When he returned to Germany, his sensitivity to anti-Semitism and the plight of Jews in Germany was heightened because he had lived his faith in an African American congregation in the United States.[6]

This book, *United by Faith*, is a plea for the church to be the church of Jesus Christ. We hope our efforts in studying multiracial congregations across the United States and in writing this book will spur the conscience of the church and the nation and produce a movement toward a more racially reconciled life together. This book is only a small part of that process. Others must contribute their thoughts.

And many more must take action. Whatever God's call is on your life, there are many ways for you to respond to this book's plea. While the book's primary focus has been race, a host of other "isms" plague the church. Find out what is dividing your church and your community and knock it down.

The spirit of the first-century church can return to congregations in the United States during the twenty-first century. There is no better time for such a visitation of the Spirit. The possibilities of this new millennium and a more demographically diverse society in the United States (and the world for that matter) make the twenty-first century *the century of multiracial congregations.*

"After this I looked, and there was a great multitude that no one could count, from every nation, from all tribes and peoples and languages, standing before the throne and before the Lamb . . ." (Revelation 7:9).

NOTES

Introduction: Divided or United by Faith?

1. Calculations made from *Statistical Abstract*, 2001, population tables and
   http://factfinder.census.gov/bf/_lang=en_vt_name=DEC_2000_SF1_U_QT3
   _geo_id=01000US.html, accessed August 2002.
2. http://www.census.gov/prod/2002pubs/01statab/pop.pdf, accessed August
   2002.
3. Emerson and Smith, *Divided by Faith*, chapters 1 and 7.
4. West, *Race Matters*.
5. Figures obtained from our own calculations using the 1998 National Congregations Study directed by Mark Chaves.
6. For more information on the research done by Emerson, Yancey, and Chai
   Kim through the "Multiracial Congregations and Their Peoples" project go to
   www.congregations.info.

1. A House of Prayer for All the Nations

1. Curtiss Paul DeYoung preached at the Christian Revival Center in Lenasia,
   South Africa, on July 11, 2000. What occurred after this visit is unknown. For
   the content of DeYoung's sermon, see Hines and DeYoung, *Beyond Rhetoric*,
   58–70.
2. Jeremias, *Jesus' Promise to the Nations*, 40.
3. Jeremias, *Jerusalem in the Time of Jesus*, 304–5.
4. Brown, *The Churches the Apostles Left Behind*, 131.
5. Barnett, *Jesus*, 104.

6. Horsley, *Galilee*, 238–45; Pazmiño, "Double Dutch," 138–39.
7. Barnett, *Jesus*, 48; Fredriksen, *Jesus of Nazareth*, 160.
8. Rousseau and Arav, *Jesus and His World*, 251; Fredriksen, *Jesus of Nazareth*, 160–61.
9. Barnett, *Jesus*, 105.
10. Theissen, *Sociology of Early Palestinian Christianity*, 64.
11. Borg, *Conflict, Holiness, and Politics*, 94–96.
12. Jeremias, *Jerusalem in the Time of Jesus*, 303–12.
13. Borg, *Jesus: A New Vision*, 101–2.
14. Nolan, *Jesus before Christianity*, 39.
15. Blount, "Apocalypse," 20. Other discussions of Jesus' outreach to Gentiles can be found in Massey, *Spiritual Disciplines*, 82–85; Myers, *Binding the Strong Man*, 186–231; and Witherington, *Gospel of Mark*, 173–84, 231–36.
16. Blount, "Apocalypse," 20–21.
17. Borg, *Conflict, Holiness, and Politics*, 97, 134.
18. Kee, *Who Are the People of God*, 190. Also see Jeremias, *Jesus' Promise to the Nations*, 44–45.
19. Biblical scholar Cain Hope Felder, in a speech titled, "Transforming the Texture and Urban Context of the Temple," given at the 2001 Congress on Urban Ministry, sponsored by the Seminary Consortium for Urban Pastoral Education, Chicago, Ill., March 28, 2001, noted that in the King James Version, Mark 11:18 reads, "Is it not written, My house shall be called of all nations the house of prayer?" Felder observed that this translation completely changed the meaning of the text. The King James Version's translation would not have given the religious leaders any reason to kill Jesus. This demonstrates that translators, like those working for King James in England in the 1600s (a time when England was involved in the colonization of other lands and the slave trade), can be biased by the politics of their social setting.
20. Blount, "Apocalypse," 16.

2. Congregations in the Early Church

1. Theissen, *Sociology of Early Palestinian Christianity*, 57.
2. Sonne, "Synagogue," 478–79.
3. Crowe, *From Jerusalem to Antioch*, 61.
4. Witherington, *Acts of the Apostles*, 250.
5. Ibid., 290, 293.
6. Barnett, *Jesus*, 360.
7. Brown, *The Community of the Beloved Apostle*, 37, 39, 55.
8. Theissen, *Sociology of Early Palestinian Christianity*, 17.
9. Barnett, *Jesus*, 363.
10. Theissen, *Sociology of Early Palestinian Christianity*, 58.
11. Stegemann and Stegemann, *Jesus Movement*, 251.
12. Rhoads, *Challenge of Diversity*, 2.
13. Longenecker, *Galatians*, 65; Horsley and Silberman, *Message and Kingdom*, 126; Barnett, *Jesus*, 263.
14. Horsley and Silberman, *Message and Kingdom*, 126; Barnett, *Jesus*, 264.
15. Witherington, *Acts of the Apostles*, 366–67; Longenecker, *Galatians*, 68.
16. Longenecker, *Galatians*, 69; Barnett, Jesus, 364.

17. Stark, *Rise of Christianity*, 161.
18. Crowe, *From Jerusalem to Antioch*, 79.
19. Ibid.
20. Stark, *Rise of Christianity*, 160–61.
21. Barnett, *Jesus*, 264.
22. For more detail on Manean see Keener, *IVP Bible*, 357–58.
23. Horsley and Silberman, *Message and Kingdom*, 142.
24. Stegemann and Stegemann, *Jesus Movement*, 268–71.
25. Stark, *Rise of Christianity*, 161.
26. Witherington, *Acts of the Apostles*, 371.
27. Elizondo, *Galilean Journey*, 106.
28. Witherington, *Acts of the Apostles*, 487.
29. Bruce, *Paul*, 228.
30. Horsley, *1 Corinthians*, 24.
31. Witherington, *Acts of the Apostles*, 538.
32. Ibid., 572.
33. Meeks, *First Urban Christians*, 168.
34. Keener, *IVP Bible*, 412.
35. Penna, *Paul the Apostle*, 52.
36. Horsley and Silberman, *Message and Kingdom*, 190.
37. Perkins, "Mark," 514.
38. Longenecker, *Galatians*, 75.
39. Bruce, *Paul*, 177–78.
40. Martyn, *Galatians*, 236.
41. Meeks, *First Urban Christians*, 161.
42. There are two primary views regarding the outcome of the Antioch crisis. We find the view presented by Longenecker and others the most persuasive. Longenecker writes in the *Word Biblical Commentary* that many "conclude that actually Paul lost and Peter triumphed at Antioch. . . . It may very well have been the case that at the time Paul wrote Galatians the Antioch church was siding more or less with Peter rather than Paul, and so Paul could only report what he said and the logic of his case. But from the high regard evidenced for Paul in Acts and the letters of Ignatius, it is difficult to believe that such continued to be true for long" (79–80). Achtemeier, *The Quest for Unity*, represents the other viewpoint. He writes, "Thus that elusive unity, for which Peter yearned and which Paul sought to achieve, which James attempted to preserve and which Luke labored to portray in his account of the early church—that unity in fact was not achieved. It was as much an ideal in relation to the earliest Christian communities as it remains an ideal in relation to the Christian churches of this day. That early unity existed, and continues to exist, only in the optimistic historical imagination of scholars who cannot bring themselves to believe that Paul really lost the dispute in Antioch, a loss with lasting results for the Christian church; or who cannot bring themselves to believe that Peter, after his right hand was offered to Paul in agreement with his apostolic mission to the Gentiles, could have betrayed Paul by siding with the emissaries from James, thus committing his prestige to a denial of the validity of Paul's theological position. Perhaps the present and the future of the church, and its goal of unity, would be better served by recognizing the situation for what it was, rather than hiding it beneath the patina of an overly optimistic historical imagination" (66).

43. There is a disagreement among scholars whether the events in Acts 15:1–35 and in Galatians 2:1–10 describe the same or a different meeting. We find the arguments for separate events the most persuasive. Examples of this perspective are found in Longenecker and Bruce. Longenecker writes, "Yet it is difficult to imagine why Peter and Barnabas ("even Barnabas") would have caved in under the pressure of Jewish Christians from Jerusalem if the decision and decrees of the Jerusalem Council had then been in existence. The situation at Syrian Antioch, it seems, could only have arisen where there were no clear guidelines to govern table fellowship between Jewish and Gentile Christians. While one could posit various reasons for Peter's action, only in the confusion of the pre-council period would such a pioneer in the Gentile mission as Barnabas have pulled back from full fellowship with Gentiles under Jewish Christian pressure" (*Word Biblical Commentary,* lxxxi–lxxxii).
44. Witherington, *Acts of the Apostles,* footnote 389, 454.
45. Bruce, *Paul,* 185.
46. Many scholars place the writing of the Gospel of Matthew in Antioch. This makes a good case for the enduring multicultural witness of the Antioch congregation. See Brown, *The Churches,* 129 and Gundry, *Matthew,* 7–8, 224.
47. Kee, *Who Are the People of God,* 226.
48. Theissen, *Sociology of Early Palestinian Christianity,* 111, 112.
49. Ibid., 115.

3. Congregations and the Color Line (1600–1940)

1. Lincoln, *Race, Religion,* 28–31; Horton and Horton, *In Hope of Liberty,* 131; Bennett, *Before the Mayflower,* 46; DeYoung, *Coming Together,* 76.
2. Lincoln, *Race, Religion,* 30–31.
3. Bennett, *Before the Mayflower,* 28–44; see also Usry and Keener, *Black Man's Religion,* 47.
4. Bennett, *Before the Mayflower,* 40; see also Collum, *Black and White Together,* 21.
5. Bennett, *Before the Mayflower,* 29; Usry and Keener, *Black Man's Religion,* 47.
6. Collum, *Black and White Together,* 17.
7. Kidwell, Noley, and Tinker, *Native American Theology,* 6–7; Noley, *First White Frost,* 24.
8. Kidwell, Noley, and Tinker, *Native American Theology,* 7.
9. Bennett, *Before the Mayflower,* 44–45; see also Takaki, *A Different Mirror,* 51–76.
10. Raboteau, *Slave Religion,* 96.
11. Ibid., 102.
12. Wilmore, *Last Things,* 70.
13. Scherer, *Slavery and the Churches,* 64.
14. Lincoln, *Race, Religion,* 48.
15. James, "Biracial Fellowship," 41; Sparks, "Religion in Amite County," 70.
16. James, "Biracial Fellowship," 44; Hatch, *Democratization of American Christianity,* 102; Harvey, *Redeeming the South,* 8.
17. Boles, "Introduction," 12.
18. Harvey, *Redeeming the South,* 8.
19. Hatch, *Democratization of American Christianity,* 102.
20. Ibid., 106.
21. Raboteau, *Slave Religion,* 134.

22. Ibid., 135.
23. Boles, "Introduction," 9.
24. James, "Biracial Fellowship," 49.
25. Sparks, "Religion in Amite County," 79.
26. Boles, "Introduction," 9.
27. Noley, *First White Frost,* 102.
28. Ibid., 106.
29. Harvey, *Redeeming the South,* 8-9.
30. Hatch, *Democratization of American Christianity,* 106.
31. Hall, "Black and White Christians," 97.
32. Raboteau, *Slave Religion,* 137; Scherer, *Slavery and the Churches,* 101; Hall, "Black and White Christians," 97.
33. Scherer, *Slavery and the Churches,* 101.
34. Hall, "Black and White Christians," 97.
35. Touchstone, "Planters and Slave Religion," 123.
36. Perry, *Breaking Down Barriers,* 16.
37. Raboteau, *Slave Religion,* 137.
38. Ibid., 181, 208.
39. Frazier, *Negro Church,* 23–25.
40. Raboteau, *Slave Religion,* 209–10.
41. Ochs, *Desegregating the Altar,* 13–14.
42. Ochs, *Desegregating the Altar,* 20; Miller, "Slaves and Southern Catholicism," 135.
43. Miller, "Slaves and Southern Catholicism," 135.
44. Ochs, *Desegregating the Altar,* 10–11.
45. Ibid., 2.
46. Ibid., 26–29.
47. Jordan, *White Man's Burden,* 139.
48. Raboteau, *Slave Religion,* 111; Scherer, *Slavery and the Churches,* 131–32.
49. Wood, *Arrogance of Faith,* 285–86.
50. Reimers, *White Protestantism,* 12.
51. Shattuck, *Episcopalians and Race,* 9.
52. Reimers, *White Protestantism,* 31–32; Shattuck, *Episcopalians and Race,* 8–9.
53. Reimers, *White Protestantism,* 58–60.
54. Ochs, *Desegregating the Altar,* 36.
55. Boles, "Introduction," 17.
56. Willis, "The Central Themes," 17.
57. Callen, "Overview Essay," 35.
58. Strong, *They Walked in the Spirit,* 26.
59. Ibid.
60. Brown, *When the Trumpet Sounded,* 156; see also Smith, *Quest for Holiness and Unity,* 165.
61. Smith, *Quest for Holiness and Unity,* 165.
62. Smith, *Quest for Holiness and Unity,* 163; Massey, *An Introduction,* 19.
63. Smith, *Quest for Holiness and Unity,* 166.
64. Smith, *Quest for Holiness and Unity,* 167; Massey, *An Introduction,* 22; Telfer, *Red and Yellow and Black and White and Brown,* 47–48.
65. Smith, *Quest for Holiness and Unity,* 168; Telfer, *Red and Yellow and Black and White and Brown,* 47–48.
66. Massey, "The National Association," 3–5.

67. Telfer, *Red and Yellow and Black and White and Brown*, 49.
68. Ochs, *Desegregating the Altar*, 2–3.
69. Ibid., 3–4.
70. Strong, *They Walked in the Spirit*, 37; Callen, "I Met the 'Evening Light Saints,'" 109; MacRobert, "The Black Roots of Pentecostalism," 302; Sanders, *Saints in Exile*, 27–28; Owens, "The Azusa Street Revival," 46. Callen notes, "Although the Azusa Street Revival was shepherded by an ordained minister of the Church of God, this reform movement that so significantly shaped Seymour has not readily owned this man and his significant ministry, primarily because of the 'tongues' issue" (110).
71. Synan, "The Pentecostal Century," 4.
72. Villafañe, *Liberating Spirit*, 89.
73. Strong, *They Walked in the Spirit*, 42.
74. Bartleman, *Azusa Street*, 54.
75. Synan, "The Pentecostal Century," 4–5.
76. Owens, "The Azusa Street Revival," 61–62; Wacker, *Heaven Below*, 43–44.
77. Wacker, *Heaven Below*, 227–31; Owens, "The Azusa Street Revival," 66; Sanders, *Saints in Exile*, 20; Synan, "The Holiness Pentecostal Churches," 101–5; Daniels, "African-American Pentecostalism," 277–78.
78. Deiros and Wilson, "Hispanic Pentecostalism," 302–3.
79. Villafañe, *Liberating Spirit*, 91–92.
80. Wyn Wade quoted in Patterson, *Rituals of Blood*, 217.
81. Patterson, *Rituals of Blood*, 202–18.
82. Scherer, *Slavery and the Churches*, 154–55, 156–57.
83. DuBois, "The Color Line and the Church," 169.

4. The Emergence of Multiracial Congregations (1940–2000)

1. Thurman, *With Head and Heart*, 132.
2. Thurman, *Footprints of a Dream*, 24.
3. Thurman, *Footprints of a Dream*, 24; see also Fluker, *They Looked for a City*, 16–18; Grier, "Howard Thurman," 50–51.
4. For the full story see Thurman, *Footprints of a Dream;* Thurman, *The First Footprints;* Thurman, *With Head and Heart*, 139–62; see also Fluker and Tumber, eds., *A Strange Freedom*, 220–24; Pollard, *Mysticism*, 69–90; Reimers, *White Protestantism*, 162–64.
5. Mays, "Introduction," xv.
6. Thurman, *With Head and Heart*, 140.
7. Reimers, *White Protestantism*, 163.
8. Thurman, *With Head and Heart*, 148.
9. Ibid.
10. Grier, "Howard Thurman," 61, 67.
11. Casford, "Fellowship Church."
12. Smith, *Howard Thurman*, 166.
13. Pollard, *Mysticism*, 24.
14. Reimers, *White Protestantism*, 159.
15. Ibid., 159–60.
16. Ibid., 160.
17. Ibid., 164–70.

18. Ibid., 167–68; Massey, *Aspects of My Pilgrimage,* 147–48, 167–68, 186.
19. Ibid., 165.
20. Webber, *God's Colony,* 71, 73.
21. Ochs, *Desegregating the Altar,* 423–40.
22. Ibid,, 426.
23. Ibid., 436.
24. Marsh, *God's Long Summer,* 127–41.
25. Ibid., 132.
26. Ibid., 128.
27. Ibid., 138.
28. Ibid., 139.
29. Shattuck, *Episcopalians and Race,* 135–60.
30. Ibid., 139–40.
31. Ibid., 155.
32. Ibid.
33. Ibid., 157.
34. Ibid.
35. www.glide.org, 18 February 2002; Williams, *I'm Alive!*
36. www.brooklyntabernacle.org, 18 February 2002; Cymbala, *Fresh Wind, Fresh Fire.*
37. www.hispowerportal.com/domain/hrc, 18 February 2002; Ahn, *Into the Fire.*
38. Synan, "Streams of Renewal," 351.
39. The advent of more multiracial congregations in the Church of God has not brought African Americans and whites closer to reconciling their national entities noted in chapter three. Many multiracial congregations that have African Americans in their membership relate to both the headquarters in Anderson, Indiana, and to the National Association of the Church of God in West Middlesex, Pennsylvania. This is particularly true when the pastor is an African American.
40. E-mail correspondence with the Reverend Daniel Harden, senior pastor of Kendall Church of God in Miami, Florida, on 4 March 2002.
41. Phone interview with the Reverend Gayle Salter, senior pastor of Eastside Church of God in Warren, Ohio, on 4 March 2002.
42. E-mail correspondence with the Reverend Ed Davila, senior pastor of River City Christian Outreach in San Antonio, Texas, on 3, 6 March 2002.
43. E-mail correspondence with the Reverend Paul Sheppard, senior pastor of Abundant Life Christian Fellowship in Menlo Park, California, on 2 March 2002; www.alcf.net, 1 March 2002.
44. The 1990s also produced a number of books on racial reconciliation. See Emerson and Smith, *Divided by Faith,* 51–68, for a discussion of this period and the notation of several publications. Also, co-authors of this book Curtiss Paul DeYoung and George Yancey contributed volumes on reconciliation. DeYoung wrote *Coming Together* and *Reconciliation* and, with Hines, *Beyond Rhetoric.* Yancey wrote *Beyond Black and White.*
45. Clancy, "A New Beginning."
46. Sack, "Shared Prayers, Mixed Blessings," 2–21.

5. A Closer Look at Four Multiracial Congregations

1. Unless noted, the material from this section comes from Hudnut-Beumler, *The Riverside Church;* the Riverside Church in the City of New York, *Fifty Years;* the

Riverside Church in the City of New York, 1997–1998; www.theriverside-churchny.org, 11 October 2001; and an interview with James Forbes on 30 January 2001 at the Riverside Church.

2. Hudnut-Beumler, *Riverside Church*, 6.
3. *The Christian Century*, quoted in Hudnut-Beumler, *Riverside Church*, 7.
4. Mays, *Seeking to be Christian*, 52.
5. Hudnut-Beumler, *Riverside Church*, 13.
6. Reimers, *White Protestantism*, 165.
7. For a discussion of this see Lincoln, *Black Church since Frazier*, 132–34, 179–90.
8. For a discussion of this see Villafañe, *Liberating Spirit*, 69–71.
9. http://www.theriversidechurchny.org, 11 October 2001.
10. The information on the Mosaic congregation came from interviews conducted by the Multiracial Congregations Project and a follow-up interview with an associate pastor of the congregation.
11. Suggested by research in Festinger, Riecken, and Schachter, *When Prophecy Fails*.
12. The information on St. Pius Catholic Church came from interviews conducted by the Multiracial Congregations Project, follow-up interviews with the pastor of St. Pius, and follow-up attendance at Mass.
13. Vanderholt, Martinez, and Gilman, *The Diocese of Beaumont*, 417.
14. Ibid., 243–45.
15. Ibid., 418.
16. Ibid., 244.
17. The material for this section comes from the following sources: interview with Mark Horst, 14 March 2002; Mellskog, "Embrace across the Races," 20–25; Drew, "A Church of Many Colors"; Pamela Huey, "Musical Melting Pot Stirs Diverse Congregation to Fill Church"; and several visits to worship services.
18. Huey, "Musical Melting Pot Stirs Diverse Congregation to Fill Church."
19. Drew, "A Church of Many Colors."
20. Interview with Horst.

6. Rejecting the White Man's Religion

1. Weaver, "From I-Hermeneutics to We-Hermeneutics," 1; Rausch and Schlepp, *Native American Voices*, 130–31.
2. DeLoria, *For This Land*, 146.
3. Weaver, "From I-Hermeneutics to We-Hermeneutics," 1–2; see also Takaki, *A Different Mirror*, 93–98.
4. Noley, *First White Frost*, 146.
5. Weaver, "From I-Hermeneutics to We-Hermeneutics," 2; Brown, *Bury My Heart*, 37–65.
6. Tinker, *Missionary Conquest*, 5.
7. Takaki, *A Different Mirror*, 88.
8. Rausch and Schlepp, *Native American Voices*, 134.
9. Twiss, *One Church Many Tribes*, 49.
10. Noley, *First White Frost*, 85.
11. Ibid., 21–24.
12. Noley, "The Interpreters," 52, 58.
13. Tinker, *Missionary Conquest*, 31.
14. Ibid., 40.

15. Ibid., 102.
16. Ibid., 117.
17. DeLoria, *For This Land*, 23–27.
18. Kidwell, Noley, and Tinker, *Native American Theology*, 10.
19. DeLoria, *For This Land*, 28.
20. For a full treatment of the uniqueness of Native American theology with a contrast to Euro-American perspectives see Kidwell, Noley, and Tinker, *Native Amer-ican Theology*. Also see DeYoung, *Coming Together*, 23–26, 73–76, 86–89.
21. Kidwell, Noley, and Tinker, *Native American Theology*, 12.
22. Tinker, "Reading the Bible as Native Americans," 174.
23. Twiss, *One Church Many Tribes*, 77, 28, 56.
24. Scherer, *Slavery and the Churches*, 92, 101; Johnson, Smith, and the WGBH Series Research Team, *Africans in America*, 91; Swartley, *Slavery, Sabbath, War, and Women*, 33.
25. Lincoln, *Race, Religion*, 269.
26. Mitchell, *Black Belief*, 15.
27. Frazier, *Negro Church*, 23.
28. Fauset, *Black Gods*, 5–7; Frazier, *Negro Church*, 6–9.
29. See DeYoung, *Coming Together*, 12–13.
30. Scherer, *Slavery and the Churches*, 89.
31. Bailey, *Shadow on the Church*, 220–28.
32. Woodson and Wesley, *Negro in Our History*, 226, documents that by 1836 the Methodist Church, which had first attacked slavery, disclaimed that position by stating that it did not have "any right, wish, or intention to interfere in the civil and political relation between master and slave, as it existed in the slaveholding states of the union."
33. Douglas, *Black Christ*, 3; see also Scherer, *Slavery and the Churches*, 149.
34. Lincoln and Mamiya, *Black Church*, 8.
35. Van Gelder, *Essence of the Church*, 72.
36. Washington, *Black Sects and Cults*, 102–3; Washington, *Black Religion*, 207, 209; Cone, *Spirituals and the Blues*, 16. Some of these same spirituals would later encourage twentieth-century civil rights activists.
37. Washington, *Black Sects and Cults*, 104; Washington, *Black Religion*, 32–34; Cone, *Black Theology and Black Power*, 94–103; Wilmore, *Black Religion and Black Radicalism*, 202–20; Lincoln and Mamiya, *Black Church*, 199–204; Lincoln, *Race, Religion*, 33–34; Genovese, *Roll Jordan Roll*, 232–55.
38. Mitchell, *Black Preaching* (Philadelphia: Lippincott, 1970), 65, quoted in Perry, *Breaking Down Barriers*, 71.
39. Morris, *Origin of the Civil Rights Movement*, 96–98.
40. Lincoln and Mamiya, *Black Church*, 10.
41. Yancey, unpublished paper "A Comparison of Religiosity between European-Americans, African-Americans, Hispanic-Americans and Asian-Americans."
42. Emerson, and Smith. *Divided by Faith*, 124, 125, 162–68.
43. Cone, *Black Theology*, 116–34.
44. Ibid., 135–52.
45. Billingsley, *Mighty Like a River*, xii.
46. Lincoln, *Black Church since Frazier*, 112–13.
47. Lincoln, *Race, Religion*, 53.

7. Separate but Equal

1. Fong, *Pursuing the Pearl*, 3–4.
2. Aquino, "Directions and Foundations of Hispanic/Latino Theology," 1:5–21; Bañuelas, "Introduction," 1–4; Elizondo, *Mestizaje*, chap. 1; Elizondo, *The Future Is Mestizo*, chap.1; Goizueta, "U.S. Hispanic Mestizaje and Theological Method," 4:21–30.
3. Figures for the United States taken from the 1999–2000 *Lilly Survey of American Attitudes and Social Networks*, Rice University, Department of Sociology.
4. Elizondo, "Our Lady of Guadalupe as Cultural Symbol," 120; Espín, "Tradition and Popular Religion," in *Frontiers of Hispanic Theology*, 62–87; Espín, "Popular Catholicism among Latinos," 308–59; Espín, "Popular Religion and an Epistemology (of Suffering)," 2:55–78.
5. Espín, "Tradition and Popular Religion," in *Mestizo Christianity*, 156.
6. Information gathered from http://www.sancta.org/intro.html, 12 October 2001. See also Elizondo, *Guadalupe* and DeYoung, *Coming Together*, 38–39.
7. Bañuelas, "U.S. Hispanic Theology," 75.
8. Elizondo, "*Mestizaje* as a Locus of Theological Reflection," 10.
9. Ibid., 9.
10. Aquino, "Directions and Foundations of Hispanic/Latino Theology," 1:5–21; Goizueta, "The History of Suffering as Locus Theologicus," 12:32–47.
11. Villafañe, *Liberating Spirit*, 103.
12. Our co-author Karen Chai Kim brings to this section her scholarship in the area of Asian American religion and the Asian American church. See Chai, "Competing for the Second Generation," 295–31; Chai, "Beyond 'Strictness' to Distinctiveness," 157–80.
13. Matsuoka, *Out of Silence*, 14–15.
14. Ibid.
15. Takaki, *Strangers from a Different Shore*, 278.
16. Ibid., 279.
17. Chan, *Asian Americans*, 99. Chan notes that Rhee started a church, along with a newspaper and community organization, as part of his plan to "create a power base for himself" in his political rivalry with Park Yong-man.
18. See Hurh and Kim, "Religious Participation of Korean Immigrants in the U.S.," 19–34.
19. Ibid.
20. Kim, "The Koreans," 233.
21. See Chai, "Protestant-Catholic-Buddhist."
22. One such church was included in the Multiracial Congregations Project.
23. McGavran, *Understanding Church Growth*, 163.
24. Wagner, *Our Kind of People*, back cover.
25. Wagner, *Your Church Can Grow*, 127.
26. Ibid., 132.
27. Wagner, *Our Kind of People*, 153.
28. Ibid., 146–47.
29. Wagner, *The Healthy Church*, 34–35.
30. Wagner, *Your Church Can Grow*, 137.
31. McGavran, *Understanding Church Growth*, 261.
32. Villafañe, *Liberating Spirit*, 106–7.

8. Arguing the Case for Multiracial Congregations

1. Twiss, *One Church Many Tribes*, 34.
2. For an argument that first-century congregations were homogeneous see Wagner, *Our Kind of People*, 109–36. On page 136, Wagner writes that the apostle Paul "taught that people need not cross racial, linguistic, or class barriers in order to become Christians. He was the first-century champion of the homogeneous unit principle." Counterarguments to Wagner are presented in Shenk, Exploring *Church Growth*, 171–303.
3. Francis, *Church Planting*, 102.
4. Yang, "Tenacious Unity in a Contentious Community," 333–61.
5. Fong, *Racial Equality in the Church*, 7–8.
6. For a multicultural hermeneutic on the Bible and theology see DeYoung, *Coming Together*, and González, *Out of Every Tribe and Nation*.
7. Yancey, "Racial Attitudes," 12:185–206; Yancey, "An Examination," 279–304.
8. Stewart, *Soul Survivors*, 4.
9. Ibid., 18.
10. Espín, "A Multicultural Church," 71. Espín suggests that a "cultural and religious *mestizaje*" is the best option for the future of the Catholic Church in North America.
11. See Hurh and Kim, "Religious Participation of Korean Immigrants in the U. S."

9. The Truth of the Gospel

1. For the story of Malcolm X's life see Malcolm X, *Autobiography*.
2. Malcolm X, *The End of White World Supremacy*, 64.
3. Ibid., 131.
4. Malcolm X, quoted in Pierre Berton, "Whatever Is Necessary," 186.
5. Malcolm X, *February* 1965, 67.
6. Malcolm X, *Autobiography*, 325–70.
7. For more autobiographical details concerning Paul, see Bruce, *Paul*, 41–44. For other references in Paul's letters to his role as persecutor of the church, see Acts 8:1–3; 9:1–2; 1 Corinthians 15:9; Philippians 3:6.
8. González, *For the Healing of the Nations*, 92.
9. Hines and DeYoung, *Beyond Rhetoric*, 2–6.
10. For a discussion of the relationship between 2 Corinthians 5:16–21 and Paul's conversion experience on the road to Damascus, see Massey, "Reconciliation," 205–7; Kim, "God Reconciled His Enemy to Himself," 107-13; Kim, *Paul and the New Perspective*, 214–38.
11. Massey, "Reconciliation," 206.
12. Bruce, *Paul*, 87–88.
13. Longenecker, *Galatians*, 151.
14. Longenecker, *Galatians*, 156–57; Campbell, *Paul's Gospel*, 106–10; Juel, "Multicultural Worship," 42–59.
15. Longenecker, *Galatians*, 157.
16. Ibid.
17. McKenzie, *All God's Children*, 130. McKenzie argues for the priority of reconciliation between Jews and Gentiles in the text when he notes, "Christ unites Jews and Gentiles in order to present the one new person to God for reconciliation."

18. Massey, "Reconciliation," 208.
19. Campbell, *Paul's Gospel*, 100.
20. Fredriksen, *Jesus of Nazareth*, 132.
21. Campbell, *Paul's Gospel*, 100.
22. Mitchell and Cooper-Lewter, *Soul Theology*, 3.
23. Ibid.
24. Branch, *Parting the Waters*, 653–56.
25. Ibid., 653, 654.
26. Ibid., 654.
27. Longenecker, *Galatians*, 76–77; Martyn, *Galatians*, 234–35, 240–45; Witherington, *Grace in Galatia*, 158–59.
28. Juel, "Multicultural Worship," 44.
29. Ibid.
30. Mays, *Seeking to Be Christian*, 77–78.
31. Keener, "The Gospel and Racial Reconciliation," 120.

10. The Promise and the Challenges of Multiracial Congregations

1. The information on FBCC came from its website, http://www.fbcchome.org, accessed 3 April 2002; interviews conducted by the Multiracial Congregations Project with the English pastor and Youth pastor, and internal reports prepared for the FBCC Church Council.
2. For readers desiring more depth of understanding regarding the issues addressed in this chapter, two books, at the time of this writing, are forthcoming by our co-authors. The first, *One Body, One Spirit*, written by George Yancey, is a practical book designed for religious leaders and laity. The issues discussed in the last section of this chapter are expanded with much more thorough examples and discussion in Yancey's book. For the larger question of the effects of integration on people and organizations involved, the models to be used, and the barriers that organizations face in trying to diversify, look for the book by Michael O. Emerson with Rodney Woo, *People of the Dream* (working title).
3. Pettigrew and Martin, "Shaping the Organizational Context," 43: 41–78. They argue that when a minority group reaches 20 percent, they have reached a critical mass and are large enough to be filtered throughout the entire organization in a nontoken manner.
4. For other ways to categorize different types of multiracial congregations see Peart, *Separate No More*, 129–42, and Pocock and Henriques, *Cultural Change and Your Church*, 133–42.
5. We do not have the space to discuss these sociological factors here; we recommend that interested readers see Emerson and Smith, *Divided by Faith*, 135–51.
6. Barndt, *Dismantling Racism*, 101–22.
7. All information on this congregation taken from Brad Christerson and Michael O. Emerson, October 2001, "The Costs of Diversity in Religious Organizations: An In-Depth Case Study," Paper presented at the annual meeting of the *Society for the Scientific Study of Religion*, Columbus, Ohio.
8. Yancey, *One Body, One Spirit*.
9. For more in-depth studies and practical suggestions on worship see Aghahowa, *Praising in Black and White*; Ammerman, *Congregation and Community*, 215–17; Black, *Culturally-Conscious Worship*; Black, *Worship Across Cultures*;

Blount and Tisdale, *Making Room at the Table;* Garlington, "The Eucharist and Racism"; Liebenow, *And Everyone Shall Praise;* and Maynard-Reid, *Diverse Worship.*

10. For a discussion on the impact of white images of Jesus Christ see DeYoung, *Coming Together,* 31–63.

11. For relevant books on preaching see Crawford, *The Hum;* Forbes, *The Holy Spirit and Preaching;* González and González, *Liberation Preaching;* Hines and DeYoung, *Beyond Rhetoric,* 108–24; Kim, *Preaching the Presence of God;* Lee, *Korean Preaching;* Lischer, *The Preacher King;* Massey, *The Burdensome Joy of Preaching;* Mitchell, *Black Preaching;* Moyd, *The Sacred Art;* Nieman and Rogers, *Preaching to Every Pew;* Rose, *Sharing the Word;* Smith, *Preaching Justice;* Smith, *Social Crisis Preaching;* and Thomas, *They Like to Never Quit Praisin' God.*

12. González, *For the Healing of the Nations,* 110.

13. For resources on leadership see Davis and White, *Racial Transition in the Church,* 14–47; DeYoung, *Reconciliation,* 135–42; Foster, *Embracing Diversity;* Law, *The Wolf Shall Dwell with the Lamb;* Massey, "Developing a Visionary Church," 27–41; Ortiz, *One New People,* 107–17; and Peart, *Separate No More,* 143–63.

14. Washington and Kehrein, *Breaking Down Walls,* 127–28.

15. For more background in developing an understanding of the mission of multiracial congregations see Cenkner, *The Multicultural Church;* Foster and Brelsford, *We Are the Church Together;* Ortiz, *One New People;* Peart, *Separate No More;* and Rhodes, *Where the Nations Meet.*

16. For resources on discipleship and education initiatives in multiracial congregations see Breckenridge and Breckenridge, *What Color Is Your God?;* Foster and Brelsford, 130–54; Jones, *Transforming Discipleship;* Pazmiño, *Latin American Journey;* Wilkerson, *Multicultural Religious Education.*

17. For more insights on facilitating dialogue see DeYoung, *Coming Together,* 175–77; Law, *The Bush Was Blazing;* Law, *The Wolf,* 79–88; and Massey, *Spiritual Disciplines,* 69–87.

18. One valuable resource that can help leaders is Yancey and Yancey, eds., *Just Don't Marry One.*

Epilogue: The Multiracial Congregation as an Answer to the Problem of Race

1. Villafañe, *Seek the Peace of the City,* 57.
2. Ibid., 57–58.
3. Thurman, *Footprints of a Dream,* 156–57.
4. Pechy, Introduction, 1.
5. Co-author Curtiss DeYoung had such an experience. See Emerson and Smith, *Divided by Faith,* 60–62.
6. See Young, *No Difference in the Fare.*

BIBLIOGRAPHY

Achtemeier, Paul J. *The Quest for Unity in the New Testament Church: A Study in Paul and Acts*. Philadelphia, Pa.: Fortress Press, 1987.

Aghahowa, Brenda Eatman. *Praising in Black and White: Unity and Diversity in Christian Worship*. Cleveland, Ohio: United Church Press, 1996.

Ahn, Ché. *Into the Fire: How You Can Enter Renewal and Catch God's Fire*. Ventura, Calif.: Renew Books, 1998.

Ammerman, Nancy Tatom. *Congregation and Community*. New Brunswick, N.J.: Rutgers University Press, 1997.

Aquino, María Pilar. "Directions and Foundations of Hispanic/Latino Theology: Toward a Mestiza Theology of Liberation." *Journal of Hispanic/Latino Theology* 1(1993): 5–21.

Bailey, David T. *Shadow on the Church: Southwestern Evangelical Religion and the Issue of Slavery 1783–1860*. Ithaca, N.Y.: Cornell University Press, 1985.

Bañuelas, Arturo J. "Introduction." In *Mestizo Christianity: Theology from the Latino Perspective*, ed. Arturo J. Bañuelas, 1–4. Maryknoll, N.Y.: Orbis Books, 1995.

———. "U.S. Hispanic Theology: An Initial Assessment." In *Mestizo Christianity: Theology from the Latino Perspective*, ed. Arturo J. Bañuelas, 53–82. Maryknoll, N.Y.: Orbis Books, 1995.

Barndt, Joseph. *Dismantling Racism: The Continuing Challenge to White America*. Minneapolis, Minn.: Augsburg Press, 1991.

Barnett, Paul. *Jesus and the Rise of Early Christianity: A History of New Testament Times*. Downers Grove, Ill.: InterVarsity Press, 1999.

Bartleman, Frank. *Azusa Street: The Roots of Modern-day Pentecost*. 1925. Reprint. South Plainfield, N.J.: Bridge Publishing, 1980.

Bennett, Lerone, Jr. *Before the Mayflower: A History of Black America*, 6th. rev. ed. New York: Penguin Books, 1962, 1993.

Berton, Pierre. "Whatever Is Necessary: The Last Television Interview." In *Malcolm X as They Knew Him*, ed. David Gallen, 179–87. New York: Carroll & Graf Publishers, 1992.

Billingsley, Andrew. *Mighty Like a River: The Black Church and Social Reform*. New York: Oxford University Press, 1999.

Black, Kathy. *Culturally-Conscious Worship*. St. Louis, Mo.: Chalice Press, 2000.

———. *Worship across Cultures: A Handbook*. Nashville, Tenn.: Abingdon Press, 1998.

Blount, Brian K. "The Apocalypse of Worship: A House of Prayer for *ALL* the Nations." *In Making Room at the Table: An Invitation to Multicultural Worship*, ed. Brian K. Blount and Leonora Tubbs Tisdale, 16–29. Louisville, Ky.: Westminster John Knox Press, 2001.

Blount, Brian K., and Leonora Tubbs Tisdale. *Making Room at the Table: An Invitation to Multicultural Worship*. Louisville, Ky: Westminster John Knox Press, 2001.

Boles, John B. "Introduction." *In Masters & Slaves in the House of the Lord: Race and Religion in the American South, 1740–1870*, ed. John B. Boles, 1–18. Lexington: University Press of Kentucky, 1988.

Borg, Marcus J. *Conflict, Holiness and Politics in the Teachings of Jesus*. 1984. New ed. Harrisburg, Pa.: Trinity Press International, 1998.

———. *Jesus: A New Vision—Spirit, Culture, and the Life of Discipleship*. San Francisco, Calif.: Harper & Row, 1987.

Branch, Taylor. *Parting the Waters: America in the King Years 1954–63*. New York: Simon and Schuster, 1988.

Breckenridge, James, and Lillian Breckenridge. *What Color Is Your God?: Multicultural Education in the Church*. Grand Rapids, Mich.: Baker Books, 1995.

Brown, Charles Ewing. *When the Trumpet Sounded: A History of the Church of God Reformation Movement*. Anderson, Ind.: Warner Press, 1951.

Brown, Dee. *Bury My Heart at Wounded Knee*. 1970. Reprint, New York: Washington Square Press, 1981.

Brown, Raymond E. *The Community of the Beloved Disciple: The Life, Loves, and Hates of an Individual Church in New Testament Times*. New York: Paulist Press, 1979.

———. *The Churches the Apostles Left Behind*. New York: Paulist Press, 1984.

Bruce, F. F. *Paul: Apostle of the Heart Set Free*. Grand Rapids, Mich.: William B. Eerdmans, 1977.

Callen, Barry L. "Overview Essay: A Developmental Profile of the Church of God Movement." In *Following the Light: Teachings, Testimonies, Trials and Triumphs of the Church of God Movement, Anderson*, comp. and ed. Barry L. Callen, 18–55. Anderson, Ind.: Warner Press, 2000.

———. "I Met the 'Evening Light Saints.'" In *Following the Light: Teachings, Testimonies, Trials and Triumphs of the Church of God Movement, Anderson*, comp. and ed. Barry L. Callen, 109–11. Anderson, Ind.: Warner Press, 2000.

Campbell, William S. *Paul's Gospel in an Intercultural Context: Jew and Gentile in the Letter to the Romans*. Frankfurt am Main, Germany: Peter Lang, 1992.

Casford, Jack. "Fellowship Church." *Russian Hill Neighbors*. Fall 1997. Available: http://www.rhn.org/histfell.htm, 13 February 2002.

Cenkner, William, ed. *The Multicultural Church: A New Landscape in U.S. Theologies*. New York: Paulist Press, 1996.

Chai, Karen J. "Competing for the Second Generation: English-Language Ministry at a Korean Protestant Church." In *Gatherings in Diaspora: Religious Communities and the New Immigration*, ed. R. Stephen Warner and Judith G. Wittner, 295–331. Philadelphia, Pa.: Temple University Press, 1998.

———. "Protestant-Catholic-Buddhist: Korean Americans and Religious Adaptation in Greater Boston." Ph.D. diss., Harvard University, 2000.

———. "Beyond 'Strictness' to Distinctiveness: Generational Transition in Korean Protestant Churches." In *Korean Americans and Their Religions: Pilgrims and Missionaries from a Different Shore*, ed. Ho Youn Kwon, Kwang Chung Kim, and R. Stephen Warner, 157–80. University Park: Pennsylvania State University Press, 2001.

Chan, Sucheng. *Asian Americans: An Interpretive History*. Boston, Mass.: Twayne Publishers, 1991.

Chaves, Mark. National Congregations Study. Data File and Codebook. Tucson: University of Arizona, Department of Sociology, 1998.

Clancy, Frank. "A New Beginning: What Happens When Two Small Churches— One White, One Black—Become One?" *USA Weekend*, 10–12 September 1999.

Collum, Danny Duncan. *Black and White Together: The Search for Common Ground*. Maryknoll, N.Y.: Orbis Books, 1996.

Cone, James H. *Black Theology and Black Power*. New York: Seabury Press, 1969.

———. *The Spirituals and the Blues*. Westport, Conn.: Greenwood Press, 1972.

Crawford, Evans. *The Hum: Call and Response in African American Preaching*. With Thomas H. Troeger. Nashville, Tenn.: Abingdon Press, 1995.

Crowe, Jerome. *From Jerusalem to Antioch: The Gospel across Cultures*. Collegeville, Minn.: The Liturgical Press, 1997.

Cymbala, Jim. *Fresh Wind, Fresh Fire: What Happens When God's Spirit Invades the Heart of His People*. With Dean Merrill. Grand Rapids, Mich.: Zondervan, 1997.

Daniels, David, III. "African-American Pentecostalism in the 20th Century." In *The Century of the Holy Spirit: 100 Years of Pentecostal and Charismatic Renewal*, ed. Vinson Synan, 265–91. Nashville, Tenn.: Thomas Nelson Publishers, 2001.

Davis, James H., and Woodie W. White. *Racial Transition in the Church*. Nashville, Tenn.: Abingdon Press, 1980.

DeLoria, Vine, Jr. *For This Land: Writings on Religion in America*, ed. James Treat. New York: Routledge, 1999.

DeYoung, Curtiss Paul. *Coming Together: The Bible's Message in an Age of Diversity*. Valley Forge, Pa.: Judson Press, 1995.

———. *Reconciliation: Our Greatest Challenge—Our Only Hope*. Valley Forge, Pa.: Judson Press, 1997.

Deiros, Pablo A., and Everett A. Wilson. "Hispanic Pentecostalism in the Americas." In *The Century of the Holy Spirit: 100 Years of Pentecostal and Charismatic Renewal*, ed. Vinson Synan, 293–323. Nashville, Tenn.: Thomas Nelson, 2001.

Douglas, Kelly Brown. *The Black Christ*. Maryknoll, N.Y.: Orbis Books, 1994.

Drew, Duchesne Paul. "A Church of Many Colors." *Star Tribune*, 17 February 2002.

DuBois, W. E. B. "The Color Line and the Church." In *DuBois on Religion*, ed. Phil Zuckerman, 169–71. Walnut Creek, Calif.: AltaMira Press, 2000.

Elizondo, Virgil P. "Our Lady of Guadalupe as Cultural Symbol: The Power of the Powerless." In *Liturgy and Cultural Religious Traditions*, ed. Herman Schmidt and David Power. London, England: *Concilium*, 1977.

———. *Mestizaje: The Dialectic of Birth and Gospel*. San Antonio, Tex.: MACC, 1978.

————. *Galilean Journey: The Mexican-American Promise.* Maryknoll, N.Y.: Orbis Books, 1983.

————. *The Future Is Mestizo: Life Where Cultures Meet.* New York: Meyer-Stone, 1988.

————. "*Mestizaje* as a Locus of Theological Reflection." In *Mestizo Christianity: Theology from the Latino Perspective,* ed. Arturo J. Bañuelas, 5–27. Maryknoll, N.Y.: Orbis Books, 1995.

————. *Guadalupe: Mother of the New Creation.* Maryknoll, N.Y.: Orbis Books, 1997.

Emerson, Michael O., and Christian Smith. *Divided by Faith: Evangelicals and the Problem of Race in America.* New York: Oxford University Press, 2000.

Espín, Orlando. "Tradition and Popular Religion: An Understanding of the *Sensus Fidelium.*" In *Frontiers of Hispanic Theology in the United States,* ed. Allan F. Deck, 62–87. Maryknoll, N.Y.: Orbis Books, 1992.

————. "Popular Catholicism among Latinos." In *Hispanic Catholic Culture in the United States: Issues and Concerns,* ed. Jay Dolan and Allan Figueroa Deck, 308–59. South Bend, Ind.: Notre Dame University Press, 1994.

————. "Popular Religion and an Epistemology (of Suffering)." *Journal of Hispanic/Latino Theology* 2 (1994): 55–78.

————. "Tradition and Popular Religion: An Understanding of the Sensus Fidelium." In *Mestizo Christianity: Theology from the Latino Perspective,* ed. Arturo J. Bañuelas, 146–74. Maryknoll, N.Y.: Orbis Books, 1995.

————. "A Multicultural Church: Theological Reflections from Below." In *The Multicultural Church: A New Landscape in U.S. Theologies,* ed. William Cenkner, 54–71. New York: Paulist Press, 1996.

Fauset, Arthur H. *Black Gods of the Metropolis.* Philadelphia: University of Pennsylvania Press, 1944.

Festinger, Leon, Henry W. Riecken, and Stanley Schachter. *When Prophecy Fails.* Minneapolis: University of Minnesota Press, 1956.

Fluker, Walter E. *They Looked for a City: A Comparative Analysis of the Ideal of Community in the Thought of Howard Thurman and Martin Luther King, Jr.* Lanham, Md.: University Press of America, 1989.

Fluker, Walter E., and Catherine Tumber, eds. *A Strange Freedom: The Best of Howard Thurman on Religious Experience and Public Life.* Boston: Beacon Press, 1998.

Fong, Bruce W. *Racial Equality in the Church: A Critique of the Homogeneous Unit Principle in Light of a Practical Theology Perspective.* Lanham, Md.: University Press of America, 1996.

Fong, Ken Uyeda. *Pursuing the Pearl: A Comprehensive Resource for Multi-Asian Ministry.* Valley Forge, Pa.: Judson Press, 1999.

Forbes, James. *The Holy Spirit and Preaching.* Nashville, Tenn.: Abingdon Press, 1989.

Foster, Charles R. *Embracing Diversity: Leadership in Multicultural Congregations.* Washington, D.C.: The Alban Institute, 1997.

Foster, Charles R., and Theodore Brelsford. *We Are the Church Together: Cultural Diversity in Congregational Life.* Valley Forge, Pa.: Trinity Press International, 1996.

Francis, Hozell C. *Church Planting in the African-American Context.* Grand Rapids, Mich.: Zondervan, 1999.

Frazier, E. Franklin. *The Negro Church in America.* 1963. Reprint. New York: Schocken Books, 1974.

Fredriksen, Paula. *Jesus of Nazareth: King of the Jews.* New York: Vintage Books, 1999.

Garlington, Tee. "The Eucharist and Racism." In *Ending Racism in the Church,* ed. Susan E. Davies and Sister Paul Teresa Hennessee, 74–80. Cleveland, Ohio: United Church Press, 1998.

Genovese, Eugene. *Roll Jordan Roll: The World the Slaves Made.* New York: Pantheon, 1974.

Goizueta, Roberto S. "U.S. Hispanic Mestizaje and Theological Method." *Concilium* 4 (1989): 21–30.

———. "The History of Suffering as Locus Theologicus: Implications for U.S. Hispanic Theology." *Voices from the Third World: Journal of the Ecumenical Association of Third World Theologians* 12 (1989): 32–47.

González, Catherine G., and Justo L. González. *Liberation Preaching: The Pulpit and the Oppressed.* Nashville, Tenn.: Abingdon Press, 1980.

González, Justo L. *Out of Every Tribe and Nation: Christian Theology at the Ethnic Roundtable.* Nashville, Tenn.: Abingdon Press, 1992.

———. *For the Healing of the Nations: The Book of Revelation in an Age of Cultural Conflict.* Maryknoll, N.Y.: Orbis Books, 1999.

Grier, Barnett John Wesley. "Howard Thurman: An Examination and Analysis of Thurman's Idea of Community and the Viability of the Fellowship Church." D.Min. diss., School of Theology at Claremont, 1983.

Gundry, Robert H. *Matthew: A Commentary on His Handbook for a Mixed Church under Persecution.* 2nd ed. Grand Rapids, Mich.: William B. Eerdmans, 1994.

Hall, Robert L. "Black and White Christians in Florida, 1822–1861." In *Masters and Slaves in the House of the Lord: Race and Religion in the American South, 1740–1870,* ed. John B. Boles, 81–98. Lexington: The University Press of Kentucky, 1988.

Harvey, Paul. *Redeeming the South: Religious Cultures and Racial Identities among Southern Baptists 1865–1925.* Chapel Hill: The University of North Carolina Press, 1997.

Hatch, Nathan O. *The Democratization of American Christianity.* New Haven, Conn.: Yale University Press, 1989.

Hines, Samuel George, and Curtiss Paul DeYoung. *Beyond Rhetoric: Reconciliation as a Way of Life.* Valley Forge, Pa.: Judson Press, 2000.

Horsley, Richard A. *Galilee: History, Politics, People.* Valley Forge, Pa.: Trinity Press International, 1995.

———. *Abingdon New Testament Commentaries: 1 Corinthians.* Nashville, Tenn.: Abingdon Press, 1998.

Horsley, Richard A., and Neil Asher Silberman. *The Message and the Kingdom: How Jesus and Paul Ignited a Revolution and Transformed the Ancient World.* New York: Grosset/Putnam, 1997.

Horton, James Oliver, and Lois E. Horton. *In Hope of Liberty: Culture, Community and Protest among Northern Free Blacks, 1700–1860.* New York: Oxford University Press, 1997.

Hudnut-Beumler, James. *The Riverside Church in the City of New York: A Brief History of Its Founding, Leadership and Finances.* New York: The Riverside Church, 1990.

Huey, Pamela. "Musical Melting Pot Stirs Congregation to Fill Church." *Saint Paul Pioneer Press,* 13 November 1994.

Hurh, Won Moo, and Kwang Chung Kim. "Religious Participation of Korean Immigrants in the U.S." *Journal for the Scientific Study of Religion* 29 (March 1990): 19–34.

Hutcherson, Ken. *Here Comes the Bride*. Sisters, Ore.: Multnomah Books, 1998.

James, Larry M. "Biracial Fellowship in Antebellum Baptist Churches." In *Masters and Slaves In the House of the Lord: Race and Religion in the American South, 1740–1870*, ed. John B. Boles, 37–57. Lexington: The University Press of Kentucky, 1988.

Jeremias, Joachim. *Jesus' Promise to the Nations*. 1958. Reprint. Philadelphia: Fortress Press, 1982.

———. *Jerusalem in the Time of Jesus*. Philadelphia: Fortress Press, 1969.

Johnson, Charles, Patricia Smith, and the WGBH Series Research Team. *Africans in America: America's Journey through Slavery*. New York: Harcourt Brace, 1998.

Jones, Stephen D. *Transforming Discipleship in the Inclusive Church*. Valley Forge, Pa.: Judson Press, 1984.

Jordan, Winthrop D. *The White Man's Burden: Historical Origins of Racism in the United States*. New York: Oxford University Press, 1974.

Juel, Donald H. "Multicultural Worship: A Pauline Perspective." In *Making Room at the Table: An Invitation to Multicultural Worship*, ed. Brian K. Blount and Leonora Tubbs Tisdale, 42–59. Louisville, Ky.: Westminster John Knox Press, 2001.

Kee, Howard Clark. *Who Are the People of God: Early Christian Models of Community*. New Haven, Conn.: Yale University Press, 1995.

Keener, Craig S. *The IVP Bible Background Commentary, New Testament*. Downers Grove, Ill.: InterVarsity Press, 1993.

———. "The Gospel and Racial Reconciliation." In *The Gospel in Black and White: Theological Resources for Racial Reconciliation*, ed. Dennis L. Okholm, 117–30. Downers Grove, Ill.: InterVarsity Press, 1997.

Kidwell, Clara Sue, Homer Noley, and George E. "Tink" Tinker. *A Native American Theology*. Maryknoll, N.Y.: Orbis Books, 2001.

Kim, Eunjoo Mary. *Preaching the Presence of God: A Homiletic from an Asian American Perspective*. Valley Forge, Pa.: Judson Press, 1999.

Kim, Illsoo. "The Koreans: Small Business in an Urban Frontier." In *New Immigrants in New York*, ed. Nancy Foner. New York: Columbia University Press, 1987.

Kim, Seyoon. "God Reconciled His Enemy to Himself: The Origin of Paul's Concept of Reconciliation." In *The Road from Damascus: The Impact of Paul's Conversion on His Life, Thought, and Ministry*, ed. Richard N. Longenecker, 102–24. Grand Rapids, Mich.: William B. Eerdmans, 1997.

———. *Paul and the New Perspective: Second Thoughts on the Origin of Paul's Gospel*. Grand Rapids, Mich.: William B. Eerdmans, 2002.

Law, Eric H. F. *The Wolf Shall Dwell with the Lamb: A Spirituality for Leadership in a Multicultural Community*. St. Louis, Mo.: Chalice Press, 1993.

———. *The Bush Was Blazing but Not Consumed: Developing a Multicultural Community through Dialogue and Liturgy*. St. Louis, Mo.: Chalice Press, 1996.

Lee, Jung Young. *Korean Preaching: An Interpretation*. Nashville, Tenn.: Abingdon Press, 1997.

Liebenow, R. Mark. *And Everyone Shall Praise: Resources for Multicultural Worship*. Cleveland, Ohio: United Church Press, 1999.

Lincoln, C. Eric. *The Black Church since Frazier*. New York: Schocken Books, 1974.

———. *Race, Religion, and the Continuing American Dilemma*, rev. ed. New York: Hill and Wang, 1999.

Lincoln, C. Eric, and Lawrence H. Mamiya. *The Black Church in the American Experience*. Durham, N.C.: Duke University Press, 1990.

Lischer, Richard. *The Preacher King: Martin Luther King Jr. and the Word That Moved America.* New York: Oxford University Press, 1995.

Longenecker, Richard N. *Word Biblical Commentary, Volume 41, Galatians.* Dallas, Tex.: Word Books, 1990.

———, ed. *The Road from Damascus: The Impact of Paul's Conversion on His Life, Thought, and Ministry.* Grand Rapids, Mich.: William B. Eerdmans, 1997.

MacRobert, Iain. "The Black Roots of Pentecostalism." In *African-American Religion: Interpretive Essays in History and Culture*, ed. Timothy E. Fulop and Albert J. Raboteau, 295–309. New York: Routledge, 1997.

Marsh, Charles. *God's Long Summer: Stories of Faith and Civil Rights.* Princeton, N.J.: Princeton University Press, 1997.

Martyn, J. Louis. *The Anchor Bible, Galatians, Volume 33A.* New York: Doubleday, 1997.

Massey, James Earl. *An Introduction to the Negro Churches in the Church of God Reformation Movement.* New York: Shining Light Survey Press, 1957.

———. *Spiritual Disciplines: Growth through the Practice of Prayer, Fasting, Dialogue, and Worship.* Grand Rapids, Mich.: Francis Asbury Press, 1985.

———. "The National Association: A Positive Force." In *National Association of the Church of God: Diamond Jubilee*, ed. Wilfred Jordan and Richard Willowby, 3–5. Anderson, Ind.: Warner Press, 1991.

———. *The Burdensome Joy of Preaching.* Nashville, Tenn.: Abingdon Press, 1998.

———. "Developing a Visionary Church That Has Integrity: The Cornerstone of Our Dream for the New Century." In *Leading with Vision*, comp. Dale Galloway, 27–41. Kansas City, Mo.: Beacon Hill Press of Kansas City, 1999.

———. "Reconciliation: Two Biblical Studies." In *A Mighty Long Journey: Reflections on Racial Reconciliation*, ed. Timothy George and Robert Smith, Jr., 199–222. Nashville, Tenn.: Broadman and Holman, 2000.

———. *Aspects of My Pilgrimage: An Autobiography.* Anderson, Ind.: Anderson University Press, 2002.

Matsouka, Fumitaka. *Out of Silence: Emerging Themes in Asian American Churches.* Cleveland, Ohio: United Church Press, 1995.

Maynard-Reid, Pedrito U. *Diverse Worship: African-American, Caribbean and Hispanic Perspectives.* Downers Grove, Ill.: InterVarsity Press, 2000.

Mays, Benjamin E. *Seeking to Be Christian in Race Relations.* New York: Friendship Press, 1957.

———. "Introduction." In *God and Human Freedom: A Festschrift in Honor of Howard Thurman*, ed. Henry James Young, xiii–xix. Richmond, Ind.: Friends United Press, 1983.

McGavran, Donald A. *Understanding Church Growth*, 3rd. ed. Revised and edited by C. Peter Wagner. Grand Rapids, Mich.: William B. Eerdmans, 1990.

McKenzie, Stephen L. *All God's Children: A Biblical Critique of Racism.* Louisville, Ky.: Westminster John Knox Press, 1997.

Meeks, Wayne A. *The First Urban Christians: The Social World of the Apostle Paul.* New Haven, Conn.: Yale University Press, 1983.

Mellskog, Pam. "Embrace across the Races." *Vital Ministry* 1, no. 3 (January/February 1998): 20–25.

Miller, Randall M. "Slaves and Southern Catholicism." In *Masters and Slaves in the House of the Lord: Race and Religion in the American South, 1740–1870*, ed. John B. Boles, 127–52. Lexington: University Press of Kentucky, 1988.

Mitchell, Henry H. *Black Belief.* New York: Harper & Row, 1975.
———. *Black Preaching: The Recovery of a Powerful Art.* Nashville, Tenn.: Abingdon Press, 1990.
Mitchell, Henry H., and Nicholas C. Cooper-Lewter. *Soul Theology: The Heart of American Black Culture.* San Francisco, Calif.: Harper & Row, 1986.
Morris, Aldon. *The Origin of the Civil Rights Movement: Black Communities Organizing for Change.* New York: Free Press, 1984.
Moyd, Olin B. *The Sacred Art: Preaching and Theology in the African American Tradition.* Valley Forge, Pa.: Judson Press, 1995.
Myers, Ched. *Binding the Strong Man: A Political Reading of Mark's Story of Jesus.* Maryknoll, N.Y.: Orbis Books, 1988.
Nieman, James R., and Thomas G. Rogers. *Preaching to Every Pew: Cross-Cultural Strategies.* Minneapolis, Minn.: Fortress Press, 2001.
Nolan, Albert. *Jesus before Christianity.* 1976. Reprint. Maryknoll, N.Y.: Orbis Books, 1978.
Noley, Homer. *First White Frost: Native Americans and United Methodism.* Nashville, Tenn.: Abingdon Press, 1991.
———. "The Interpreters." In *Native American Religious Identity: Unforgotten Gods,* ed. Jace Weaver, 48–60. Maryknoll, N.Y.: Orbis Books, 1998.
Ochs, Stephen J. *Desegregating the Altar: The Josephites and the Struggle for Black Priests, 1871–1960.* Baton Rouge: Louisiana State University Press, 1990.
Ortiz, Manuel. *One New People: Models for Developing a Multiethnic Church.* Downers Grove, Ill.: InterVarsity Press, 1996.
Owens, Robert. "The Azusa Street Revival: The Pentecostal Movement Begins in America." In *The Century of the Holy Spirit: 100 Years of Pentecostal and Charismatic Renewal,* ed. Vinson Synan, 39–68. Nashville, Tenn.: Thomas Nelson, 2001.
Patterson, Orlando. *Rituals of Blood: Consequences of Slavery in Two American Centuries.* Washington, D.C.: Civitas/Counterpoint, 1998.
Pazmiño, Roberto W. "Double Dutch: Reflections of an Hispanic North-American on Multicultural Religious Education." In *Voces: Voices from the Hispanic Church,* ed. Justo L. González, 137–45. Nashville, Tenn.: Abingdon Press, 1992.
———. *Latin American Journey: Insights for Christian Education in North America.* Cleveland, Ohio: United Church Press, 1994.
Peart, Norman Anthony. *Separate No More: Understanding and Developing Racial Reconciliation in Your Congregation.* Grand Rapids, Mich.: Baker Books, 2000.
Pechy, Graham. Introduction to *South African Literature and Culture: Rediscovery of the Ordinary,* by Njabulo S. Ndebele. Manchester, England: Manchester University Press, 1994.
Penna, Romano. *Paul the Apostle: Jew and Greek Alike.* Collegeville, Minn.: The Liturgical Press, 1996.
Perkins, Pheme. "Mark." In *The New Interpreter's Bible,* conv. ed. Leander E. Keck, 507–733. Nashville, Tenn.: Abingdon Press, 1995.
Perry, Dwight. *Breaking Down Barriers: A Black Evangelical Explains the Black Church.* Grand Rapids, Mich.: Baker Books, 1998.
Pettigrew, Thomas F., and Joanne Martin. "Shaping the Organizational Context for Black American Inclusion." *Journal of Social Issues* 43 (1987): 41–78.
Pocock, Michael, and Joseph Henriques. *Cultural Change and Your Church: Helping Your Church Thrive in a Diverse Society.* Grand Rapids, Mich.: Baker Books, 2002.

Pollard, Alton B., III. *Mysticism and Social Change: The Social Witness of Howard Thurman*. New York: Peter Lang, 1992.

Raboteau, Albert J. *Slave Religion: The "Invisible Institution" in the Antebellum South*. New York: Oxford University Press, 1978.

Rausch, David A., and Blair Schlepp. *Native American Voices*. Grand Rapids, Mich.: Baker Books, 1994.

Reimers, David M. *White Protestantism and the Negro*. New York: Oxford University Press, 1965.

Rhoads, David. *The Challenge of Diversity: The Witness of Paul and the Gospels*. Minneapolis, Minn.: Fortress Press, 1996.

Rhodes, Stephen A. *Where the Nations Meet: The Church in a Multicultural World*. Downers Grove, Ill.: InterVarsity Press, 1998.

Riverside Church in the City of New York. *Fifty Years: A Time to Celebrate*. New York: Riverside Church, 1981.

————. *1997–1998: Year in Review*. New York: Riverside Church, 1998.

Rose, Lucy Atkinson. *Sharing the Word: Preaching in the Roundtable Church*. Louisville, Ky.: Westminster John Knox Press, 1997.

Rousseau, John J., and Rami Arav. *Jesus and His World: An Archaeological and Cultural Dictionary*. Minneapolis, Minn.: Fortress Press, 1995.

Sack, Kevin. "Shared Prayers, Mixed Blessings." In *How Race Is Lived in America: Pulling Together, Pulling Apart*, ed. correspondents of the *New York Times*, 2–21. New York: Times Books, 2001.

Sanders, Cheryl J. *Saints in Exile: The Holiness-Pentecostal Experience in African American Religion and Culture*. New York: Oxford University Press, 1996.

Scherer, Lester B. *Slavery and the Churches in Early America 1619–1819*. Grand Rapids, Mich.: William B. Eerdmans, 1975.

Shattuck, Gardner H., Jr. *Episcopalians and Race: Civil War to Civil Rights*. Lexington: The University Press of Kentucky, 2000.

Shenk, Wilbert R., ed. *Exploring Church Growth*. Grand Rapids, Mich.: William B. Eerdmans, 1983.

Smith, Christine Marie, ed. *Preaching Justice: Ethnic and Cultural Perspectives*. Cleveland, Ohio: United Church Press, 1998.

Smith, Kelly Miller. *Social Crisis Preaching*. Macon, Ga.: Mercer University Press, 1984.

Smith, Jr., Luther E. *Howard Thurman: The Mystic as Prophet*. Richmond, Ind.: Friends United Press, 1991.

Smith, John W. V. *The Quest for Holiness and Unity: A Centennial History of the Church of God (Anderson, Indiana)*. Anderson, Ind.: Warner Press, 1980.

Sonne, Isaiah. "Synagogue." In *The Interpreter's Dictionary of the Bible: An Illustrated Encyclopedia, R-Z*, ed. George Arthur Buttrick, 476–91. Nashville, Tenn.: Abingdon Press, 1962.

Sparks, Randy J. "Religion in Amite County, Mississippi, 1800–1861." In *Masters and Slaves in the House of the Lord: Race and Religion in the American South, 1740–1870*, ed. John B. Boles, 58–80. Lexington: The University Press of Kentucky, 1988.

Stark, Rodney. *The Rise of Christianity: A Sociologist Reconsiders History*. Princeton, N.J.: Princeton University Press, 1996.

Stegemann, Ekkehard W., and Wolfgang Stegemann. *The Jesus Movement: A Social History of Its First Century*. Minneapolis, Minn.: Fortress Press, 1999.

Stewart, Carlyle Fielding, III. *Soul Survivors: An African American Spirituality.* Louisville, Ky.: Westminster John Knox Press, 1997.

Strong, Douglas M. *They Walked in the Spirit: Personal Faith and Social Action in America.* Louisville, Ky.: Westminster John Knox Press, 1997.

Swartley, Willard M. *Slavery, Sabbath, War, and Women: Case Issues in Biblical Interpretation.* Scottsdale, Pa.: Herald Press, 1983.

Synan, Vinson. "The Pentecostal Century: An Overview." In *The Century of the Holy Spirit: 100 Years of Pentecostal and Charismatic Renewal,* ed. Vinson Synan, 1–13. Nashville, Tenn.: Thomas Nelson, 2001.

———. "The Holiness Pentecostal Churches." In *The Century of the Holy Spirit: 100 Years of Pentecostal and Charismatic Renewal,* ed. Vinson Synan, 97–122. Nashville, Tenn.: Thomas Nelson, 2001.

———. "Streams of Renewal at the End of the Century." In *The Century of the Holy Spirit: 100 Years of Pentecostal and Charismatic Renewal,* ed. Vinson Synan, 349-80. Nashville, Tenn.: Thomas Nelson, 2001.

Takaki, Ronald. *Strangers from a Different Shore: A History of Asian Americans.* Boston: Little, Brown, 1989.

———. *A Different Mirror: A History of Multicultural America.* Boston: Back Bay Books—Little, Brown, 1993.

Telfer, David A. *Red and Yellow and Black and White and Brown: Ministry and Evangelism in Ethnic Communities.* Anderson, Ind.: Warner Press, 1981.

Theissen, Gerd. *Sociology of Early Palestinian Christianity.* Philadelphia, Pa.: Fortress Press, 1978.

Thomas, Frank A. *They Like to Never Quit Praisin' God: The Role of Celebration in Preaching.* Cleveland, Ohio: United Church Press, 1997.

Thurman, Howard. *Footprints of a Dream: The Story of the Church for the Fellowship of All Peoples.* New York: Harper & Brothers, 1959.

———, ed. *The First Footprints: The Dawn of the Idea of the Church for the Fellowship of All Peoples—Letters between Alfred Fisk and Howard Thurman, 1943–1944.* San Francisco, Calif.: Printed by Lawton and Alfred Kennedy, 1975.

———. *With Head and Heart: The Autobiography of Howard Thurman.* New York: Harcourt Brace Jovanovich, 1979.

Tinker, George E. *Missionary Conquest: The Gospel and Native American Cultural Genocide.* Minneapolis, Minn.: Fortress Press, 1993.

———. "Reading the Bible as Native Americans." In *The New Interpreter's Bible, Volume 1,* conv. ed. Leander Keck, 174-80. Nashville, Tenn.: Abingdon Press, 1994.

Touchstone, Blake. "Planters and Slave Religion in the Deep South." In *Masters and Slaves in the House of the Lord: Race and Religion in the American South, 1740–1870,* ed. John B. Boles, 99–126. Lexington: University Press of Kentucky, 1988.

Twiss, Richard. *One Church Many Tribes: Following Jesus the Way God Made You.* Ventura, Calif.: Regal, 2000.

Usry, Glenn, and Craig S. Keener. *Black Man's Religion: Can Christianity Be Afrocentric?* Downers Grove, Ill.: InterVarsity Press, 1996.

Van Gelder, Craig. *The Essence of the Church: A Community Created by the Spirit.* Grand Rapids, Mich.: Baker Books, 2000.

Vanderholt, James F., Carolyn B. Martinez, and Karen A. Gilman. *The Diocese of Beaumont: The Catholic Story of Southeast Texas.* Beaumont, Tex.: Diocese of Beaumont, 1991.

Villafañe, Eldin. *The Liberating Spirit: Toward an Hispanic American Pentecostal Social Ethic*. Lanham, Md.: University Press of America, 1992.

———. *Seek the Peace of the City: Reflections on Urban Ministry*. Grand Rapids, Mich.: William B. Eerdmans, 1995.

Wacker, Grant. *Heaven Below: Early Pentecostals and American Culture*. Cambridge, Mass.: Harvard University Press, 2001.

Wagner, C. Peter. *Our Kind of People: The Ethical Dimensions of Church Growth in America*. Atlanta, Ga.: John Knox Press, 1979

———. *Your Church Can Grow: Seven Vital Signs of a Healthy Church*, rev. ed. Ventura, Calif.: Regal Books, 1984.

———. *The Healthy Church: Avoiding and Curing the 9 Diseases That Can Afflict Any Church*. Ventura, Calif.: Regal Books, 1996.

Washington, Joseph R. *Black Religion: The Negro and Christianity in the United States*. Boston: Beacon Press, 1964.

———. *Black Sects and Cults*. Garden City, N.Y.: Doubleday, 1972.

Washington, Raleigh, and Glen Kehrein. *Breaking Down Walls: A Model for Reconciliation in an Age of Strife*. Chicago, Ill.: Moody Press, 1993.

Weaver, Jace. "From I-Hermeneutics to We-Hermeneutics." In *Native American Religious Identity: Unforgotten Gods*, ed. Jace Weaver, 1–25. Maryknoll, N.Y.: Orbis Books, 1998.

Webber, George W. *God's Colony in Man's World: Christian Love in Action*. Nashville, Tenn.: Abingdon Press, 1960.

West, Cornel. *Race Matters*. Boston: Beacon Press, 1993.

Wilkerson, Barbara, ed. *Multicultural Religious Education*. Birmingham, Ala.: Religious Education Press, 1997.

Williams, Cecil. *I'm Alive! An Autobiography*. San Francisco, Calif.: Harper & Row, 1980.

Willis, David W. "The Central Themes of American Religious History: Pluralism, Puritanism, and the Encounter of Black and White." In *African-American Religion: Interpretive Essays in History and Culture*, ed. Timothy E. Fulop and Albert J. Raboteau, 7–20. New York: Routledge, 1997.

Wilmore, Gayraud S. *Last Things First*. Philadelphia, Pa.: Westminster Press, 1982.

———. *Black Religion and Black Radicalism: An Interpretation of the Religious History of Afro-American People*, 2nd. ed. Maryknoll, N.Y.: Orbis Books, 1983.

Witherington, Ben, III. *The Acts of the Apostles: A Socio-Rhetorical Commentary*. Grand Rapids, Mich.: William B. Eerdmans, 1998.

———. *Grace in Galatia: A Commentary on St. Paul's Letter to the Galatians*. Grand Rapids, Mich.: William B. Eerdmans, 1998.

———. *The Gospel of Mark: A Socio-Rhetorical Commentary*. Grand Rapids, Mich.: William B. Eerdmans, 2001.

Wood, Forrest G. *Arrogance of Faith: Christianity and Race in America*. New York: Random House, 1990.

Woodson, Carter G., and Charles Wesley. *The Negro in Our History*, 11th ed. Washington, D.C.: Associated Publishers, 1966.

X, Malcolm. *The Autobiography of Malcolm X*. As told to Alex Haley. 1965. Reprint. New York: Ballantine Books, 1973.

———. *The End of White World Supremacy: Four Speeches*, ed. Benjamin Karim. New York: Arcade Publishing, 1971.

———. *February 1965: The Final Speeches*, ed. Steve Clark. New York: Pathfinder, 1992.

Yancey, George. *Beyond Black and White: Reflections on Racial Reconciliation*. Grand Rapids, Mich.: Baker Books, 1996.

———. "An Examination of Effects of Residential and Church Integration upon Racial Attitudes of Whites." *Sociological Perspectives* 42, no. 2 (1999): 279–304.

———. "Racial Attitudes: Difference in Racial Attitudes of People Attending Multiracial and Uniracial Congregations." *Research in the Social Scientific Study of Religion* 12 (2001): 185–206.

———. *One Body, One Spirit: Principles of Successful Multiracial Churches*. Downers Grove, Ill.: InterVarsity Press, 2003.

Yancey, George, and Sherelyn Yancey, eds. *Just Don't Marry One: Interracial Dating, Marriage, and Parenting*. Valley Forge, Pa.: Judson Press, 2002.

Yang, Fenggang. "Tenacious Unity in a Contentious Community: Cultural and Religious Dynamics in a Chinese Christian Church." In *Gatherings in Diaspora: Religious Communities and the New Immigration*, ed. R. Stephen Warner and Judith G. Wittner, 333-61. Philadelphia, Pa.: Temple University Press, 1998.

———. *Chinese Christians in America: Conversion, Assimilation, and Adhesive Identities*. University Park, Pa.: Pennsylvania State University Press, 1999.

Young, Josiah Ulysses, III. *No Difference in the Fare: Dietrich Bonhoeffer and the Problem of Racism*. Grand Rapids, Mich.: William B. Eerdmans, 1998.

INDEX

civil rights activism, 68–70, 80, 109
Civil War, 52
Clark, Septima, 157
class divisions, 47
clergy
    African Americans as, 47, 50, 56,
        57, 61, 67–68, 108
    multiracial pastoral teams, 92,
        94–95, 179
    as owners of enslaved Africans, 45,
        50
    pastoral visitation, 72
    on slavery, 46
    in white supremacist organizations,
        60
Coalition of Hispanic Christian
    Leadership, 80
coexistence in multiracial congrega-
    tions, 164, 167
colleges, Christian, 184
Colonial America, 43–45, 46–48
community centers, churches as, 141
composition of congregations, 12, 164
compromise, 81–82
Cone, James, 110
conglomerate congregations, 125
congregations
    assimilated multiracial, 165–67,
        165, 168, 169, 172–72
    integrated multiracial, 165, 165,
        168–69, 172, 174
    pluralist multiracial, 165, 165,
        167–68
Congress of Racial Equality (CORE),
    109
Conroy, Francis X., 89, 90
Cooper-Lewter, Nicholas C., 156
core beliefs, 156–60
courage, 160, 180, 185
creativity, 84
crime, fears of, 2
Crowe, Jerome, 23
Crucified Christ symbol, 115
Culotta, Salvador, 89
culture
    See also music
    churches as cultural centers, 141
    context of early church, 22–23, 26
    cultural awareness, 180

cultural preservation, 104–5,
    118–20, 155, 171
leadership of congregation, 177
in The Mosaic Church, 84, 85
music and African American her-
    itage, 108
oppression in white culture, 111
organizational culture, 165
in Riverside Church, 82
segregated religious communities,
    113, 126, 137–40
worship styles, 175
Cymbala, Carol, 71
Cymbala, Jim, 71, 73

dating, interracial. See marriage and
    dating, interracial
Davila, Ed, 72–73
De León, Victor, 57
decor of church, 176
definition of multiracial congrega-
    tions, 3, 76, 198n 3
DeLoria, Vine, 100, 104, 111
denominations, 52–53, 106, 162
    See also specific denominations
DeYoung, Curtiss Paul, 4, 10,
    187n 1, 193n 44, 199n 5
Diego, Juan, 115
Diocese of Beaumont: The Catholic
    Story of Southeast Texas
    (Vanderholt, Martinez, Gilman),
    87
disciples of Jesus, 15–18, 21–22, 24,
    150
discrimination, 117
DiStefano, John, 89
Divided by Faith: Evangelical Religion
    and the Problem of Race in
    America (Emerson and Smith),
    3, 170
Douglas, Kelly Brown, 107
DuBois, W. E. B., 61
Dwight, Perry, 49

early church. See first-century church
East Harlem Protestant Parish, New
    York City, 66–67
Eastside Church of God, Warren,
    Ohio, 72

Printed in the United States
32083LVS00002B/31-33

9 780195 152159